1 MONTH OF
FREE
READING

at

www.ForgottenBooks.com

By purchasing this book you are eligible for one month membership to ForgottenBooks.com, giving you unlimited access to our entire collection of over 1,000,000 titles via our web site and mobile apps.

To claim your free month visit: www.forgottenbooks.com/free20442

ISBN 978-1-5284-4898-7
PIBN 10020442

SPORT IN MANY LANDS.

BY

H. A. L.

"THE OLD SHEKARRY"

AUTHOR OF "THE HUNTING GROUNDS OF THE OLD WORLD," "THE FOREST AND THE FIELD,"
ETC., ETC.

IN TWO VOLUMES.—VOL. I.

WITH 164 ILLUSTRATIONS.

"I cannot rest from travel, I will drink life to the lees."

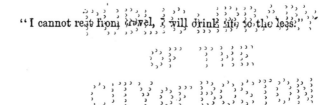

LONDON:
CHAPMAN AND HALL, 193, PICCADILLY.
1877.

LONDON:

BRADBURY, AGNEW, & CO., PRINTERS, WHITEFRIARS.

TO

WILLIAM INGRAM, Esq., M.P.,

THE FOLLOWING PAGES ARE

Dedicated

AS A MARK OF ESTEEM

BY HIS FRIEND

"THE OLD SHEKARRY."

CONTENTS.

CHAPTER I.

DEER STALKING AND DRIVING.

CHAPTER II.

CHAMOIS AND IBEX STALKING.

CHAPTER III.

WILD-FOWL SHOOTING.

CHAPTER IV.

HOG-HUNTING IN INDIA.

CHAPTER V.

BEAR-HUNTING.

CHAPTER VI.

TIGER, PANTHER, AND LEOPARD HUNTING.

CHAPTER VII.

ELEPHANT HUNTING IN INDIA.

CHAPTER VIII.

BISON AND BUFFALO HUNTING.

CHAPTER IX.

SOUVENIRS OF SPORT IN INDIA.

CHAPTER X.

THE GAME OF *THE* HIMALAYA.

CHAPTER XI.

SPORT IN *THE* DOON.

CHAPTER XII.

SPORT IN THE HIMALAYA AND THIBET.

CHAPTER XIII.

UNLOOKED-FOR RENCONTRES.

LIST OF ILLUSTRATIONS.

—◆—

MEMOIR OF MAJOR LEVESON.

THE author of "Sport in Many Lands," Henry Astbury Leveson, was born on the 18th of June, 1828, and died at Brighton on the 7th of September, 1875. Few men have led such an adventurous career. When stirring events were occuring in any quarter of the globe, he was ever among the first to volunteer to take part in them. On many occasions his wish was gratified. The records of more than one of England's big and little wars would not be complete without a grateful mention of the dashing and useful services of Major Leveson.

At the age of seventeen, young Leveson obtained a commission in the East India Company's service, and sailed for Madras. It was in India, at that time a still more romantic and alluring country to an adventurous disposition than it is now, that he developed his hunting tastes, and acquired much of his experience in wild sport. During this early period of his career he became renowned as a tiger slayer, a "pig sticker," and a successful hunter of many kinds of large and savage game. He spent some time at Hyderabad, and in the traditions of the Deccan Hunt his name and his fame are still remembered.

After passing nine years in India he found himself in England at the outbreak of the Crimean War. He at once volunteered to serve in the coming campaign. He was

appointed to a post on the Turkish staff, and immediately
proceeded to the seat of war in the Danubian provinces.
During the advance of the Turkish troops upon Bucharest he
did good service as a light cavalry officer, by effectively harass-
ing the rear of the retreating Russians.   From Bucharest
Major Leveson returned to Constantinople, whence he started
afresh for Anatolia to assist in the military survey of the
country between Kars and Alexandropol.   For his accuracy
and promptitude in this duty he received the thanks of General
Guyon (Korshid Pasha).   Shortly afterwards he was appointed
by Lord Raglan to the general staff of the Turkish division,
under orders to proceed from Varna to the Crimea.   Major
Leveson was the only English officer thus employed.

Upon landing at Old Fort he superintended the disem-
barkation of the division, and was subsequently engaged in the
affair at Boulganac.   He also took part in the battle of the
Alma, storming the hill with the centre division of the French
troops.   A ball passed through his fez, but he came out of the
action unhurt.   A little later he commanded a brigade of the
Turkish army in the countermarch to the south side of Sebastopol,
and eventually assisted in the occupation of Balaclava.   On
October 8th, 1854, he was in command of a Turkish brigade,
attached to the French force under General Sol and General
Monet, when ground was first broken in front of Sebastopol.
Shortly afterwards he superintended the construction by the
Turkish troops of a series of earthworks and batteries between
the village of Kadekoi and the camp of General Bosquet's division.   Major Leveson received the thanks and warm approbation
of the French commander-in-chief, for the rapidity and skill
with which this work was performed.

On the 5th of November he was present at the battle of

Inkerman. The Turkish division to which he belonged, was not engaged in this action; but, unable to remain passive while hard fighting was going on, he attached himself to the 63rd Regiment, and with it was hotly engaged throughout the day. Major Leveson's horse was shot under him, and he himself received a severe blow on the hip from a fragment of shell. He succeeded, however, in retaking from the enemy a French brass gun and two powder waggons, which the Russians had previously captured. Throughout the campaign he was in the habit of sending home a succession of graphic letters, describing its progress. Two days after Inkerman, he wrote:—

"We fought a desperate battle on the 5th, and gained a dear bought victory. I am, thank God, all right, although my horse had one of his legs shattered, and I received a severe contusion on the hip from the fragment of a shell. It is, however, merely a severe bruise, and I shall be all right in a day or two. An old friend of mine, Lieut.-Colonel S— of the 63rd Regiment, was killed at my side. I was with his corps, my division not being engaged. I was one of the first up, and I retook a French brass gun and two carriages for ammunition which the Russians had taken from the French. . . . . . The Russian dead seemed to me at least four to one of ours, and they had time to carry off lots of their wounded. They have received very large reinforcements, and their army is something between eighty and a hundred thousand strong; rather formidable, is it not? To oppose this force we have but fourteen thousand English·troops and about thirty thousand French. We have some Turks, but they are not worth much, and as yet have done nothing but eat and rob. . . . . . This victory has cost us the eighth of our number and many more would ruin us. . . . . . They say that we are to receive a reinforcement of

thirty thousand French troops.   I hope they will arrive soon, as
our numbers are getting beautifully small, and ' a dale aisier to
muster,' as an Irish corporal was heard to say as his company
told off only twenty-three men out of eighty that went into
action.   We began (or rather the Russians did) the fight at
five o'clock in the morning, and it lasted for twelve hours, for
it was near five when firing ceased.   The officers had more
than their share of killed and wounded ; they lost an unduly
large proportion.   The French behaved well, but, somehow, the
brunt of the battle always falls upon the English, and we pay
the piper.   There will be many a house of mourning when the
Gazette is published, but at present we hardly know all our
loss, and that of the Russians can never be exactly known.
They lie in hundreds unburied yet, and, indeed, many of their
wounded are on the field still, for we have not had time to
remove them.   They are a barbarous lot and deserve little or
no pity.   Their wounded men frequently fired on our soldiers
while the latter were giving them to drink, and they kill all our
wounded when they get the chance.   I saw one of our men
take a fearful revenge on some of them.   One out of a heap of
wounded Russians fired a shot at one of our soldiers when his
back was turned.   He came back, and not finding the culprit,
he bayoneted all the wounded he found near.   I had the
pleasure of settling a few of their officers, for after my horse
was struck I took a sergeant's rifle and went with the skir-
mishers of the 30th.   We were following the Russians, who
were in full retreat, when I noticed their officers turning round
and trying to make their men stand.   Finding this was the
case, I kept my rifle for them only and cut two of them over, as
well as a bugler who was trying to sound a call.   I took his
bugle and will send it to my uncle as a trophy if I get a

chance. This was the only way I could find out the officers, who dress like the men. I did not feel my hurt much until night, but I am now very stiff, which will wear off in time. I must now turn in, or rather on, for I have had but the ground and my blanket for a bed since I set foot in Russia. I am quite used to it now, and sleep as well as I did on that horrid machine that took up half the room in M. The proverb is true that ' use is second nature,' for now mother earth serves me for a bed, a table, a chair, a writing desk, and a pillow; for I always pile up a heap to go under my head, though I prefer sand, when I can get it, as being more comfortable, and I manage to write a letter without tearing up quires now."

Major Leveson was present during the whole of the siege of Sebastopol. He was engaged in several sorties and volunteered for both assaults. He also served with the Turkish artillery at the battle of the Tchernaya. In 1855 he was sent to Eupatoria, to report upon the fortifications there, and in October of the same year he accompanied the Turkish troops into Anatolia, and on the expedition under Omar Pasha to relieve Kars.

In November he distinguished himself in the affair on the Ingur river, and was subsequently dispatched to survey the country between Suchum-Kaleh and Kutais. For his able maps and plans of this district, which were sent to the British government, he received the thanks of Lord Stratford de Redcliffe and of Lord Clarendon. At the close of the campaign he was recommended by Sir William Codrington, Commanding-in-chief in the Crimea, to the Secretary at War for future reward.

For his services during the campaign he received the Turkish war medal and three clasps, as well as the British medal and clasp for Sebastopol.   He was also recommended for the Legion of Honour.

Major Leveson, whose opinions were as independent as his character was resolute, was a keen critic of the inaction and mismanagement that were displayed in high places at the commencement of the campaign.   His view of the circumstances, formed at the moment and on the spot, is of course in many points open to correction by the light of subsequent fuller knowledge of the different facts.   It is, however, worth while to give it here, if only to show that he was not a mere fighting soldier of fortune, but that he thought out the problems of war for himself and was capable of striking with his head as well as with his hand.   In March 1855 he wrote as follows :—

"Disgusted as we all are here with the manner things have been going on of late, I intend in my present letter to try and point out in a cursory manner what I consider are the glaring faults that have justly aroused the indignation of the public at home, and the present visible discontent in the allied army.

"It was one of Napoleon's great maxims, (and a more true. one never was uttered) that 'Better *one* bad general than *two* good ones.'—In my humble opinion the army from the beginning has been labouring under the great disadvantage of having two leaders, and although it must be said that the utmost good will has appeared to exist between them, yet events have hitherto shown, that each (perhaps imperceptibly to himself) has been pulling his own way; indeed it could not be otherwise, for as well might one body have two minds.

"In fact, it appears to me that the allied armies are like two partners in a game of whist, each playing his own game, and trying to win with his own hand against Russia with a dummy (Austria). Let us hope, in spite of the disadvantage we are labouring under, that we hold in our two hands trumps enough to win the odd trick (Sevastopol). Now for a review of what I take to be the fatal errors that have been made since the beginning of the campaign.

" After the experience we ought to have had of the fatal un- healthiness of Varna from the fearful mortality of the Russian army in 1828, was it expedient in us to send our fine fellows there to perish miserably by disease, as several thousands did ; when, had it been determined to aid the Turkish army under Omar Pasha, a single division sent at once to the field of action or Schumla would have been much more efficient than our whole army inactive, encamped on those pestilential shores. How much better would it have been if, instead of this ' seemingly unnecessary ' step, the combined army had been landed at once on the shore of the Crimea without wasting as we did the precious time at Gallipoli and Varna. Then, the enemy unprepared, had not had time to strengthen Sevastopol, and it must have fallen an easy prize to our arms ; our brave fellows would have been saved from the pestilence of Varna, and the heavy loss we have sustained up to this time from the enemy and the fearful exposure to the climate. This was a fatal error ; but it was not the only time that *unnecessary delay* allowed our prize to escape when almost within reach, for again, after our having landed in the Crimea, and having conquered the enemy at the battle of the Alma, why was not advantage taken of the victory ? Why did we remain until the third day on the field ? The troops of the enemy were in perfect *déroute* and had we followed them we might have entered the town with them—fatal delay. It is said that the French

general wanted to pursue them at once ; but no—Lord R. would
not take advantage of the victory, he must remain three days
to bury the dead with the whole army, although a couple of
battalions aided by the fleet could have done it, and also embarked the wounded, in a much shorter time.   Why were we
obliged to lose the advantages we had gained, by delaying, to
bury the Russian dead, when the Cossacks could have done
it ?

"Having arrived before Sevastopol and the siege having been
determined on, why was the place not properly invested according to the commonest rules of war ; was it necessary to extend
our lines to Balaclava, when the Bay of Kamiesch would have
answered our purpose as well ? for had we not taken up such
an extended position, we had troops enough to invest the
approaches of the place ; and the garrison of the fortress, then
not numerous, and undefended by their present works, could not
have held out for any length of time ; while the army outside,
dispirited by recent defeat, was not in a state to do us much
harm.   At that time a successful *coup de main* might have
been attempted without much fear of the result.   The Russians
had not proved such formidable foes that the victors of the
Alma need have dreaded the result of a general assault,
aided by the fleet.   But no, delay again was the cause of our
misfortune ; we allowed the enemy to collect his scattered
army, to gather reinforcements, to throw up outworks and
batteries on the land side, which was before undefended, and
when our batteries opened fire on the 17th Oct., we found we
could not hold our own.

"Then followed the Balaclava affair ; and I may mention a
few points that there appeared to me to have been wrong :—

"1st. The redoubts occupied by the Turks were useless.

"2nd. Had it been intended that the ground should have been occupied, there should have been simple epaulements, armed with field batteries, which could have been withdrawn when the place was untenable, instead of heavy pieces of position.

"3rdly. Was it advisable to trust our British guns with a few raw Turkish conscripts of a month's service (though many of fifty years of age), alone in an unsupported position, without any of our officers or men to look after them? Had we had the same number of our own indomitable Highlanders, or as many devil-may-care Zouaves in the room of those undisciplined Turkish peasants in the unsupported redoubts, would they not also have been sacrificed to no purpose, the enemy having ample means and overpowering numbers? · Poor wretched Turks, their officer mounted his horse and ran away first, and they followed; but what could be expected from them when even their government would not punish the cowardly scoundrel who showed them such an example. With regard to the results that followed, and the glorious bravery of the British cavalry in that unadvised and hopeless charge, I shall leave them to an abler pen to describe and explain.

"The day after Balaclava we repaid the Russians a portion of the debt we owed them, and Sir De Lacy Evans gave them a lesson they are not likely to forget.

"The Battle of Inkerman followed, and to the stern bulldog courage of our British infantry did we owe not only our victory, but our very existence in the Crimea. This alone has not failed; we are not indebted to the superior generalship of our chief, Heaven knows!—In all the exposure to the rigour of the Russian winter, in the arduous duties of this unexampled campaign, with sickness, famine, and death stalking through our camp, their invincible courage alone has kept them up, and it is

grievous to think that the greater part of their sufferings might
have been avoided, or, at any rate, greatly alleviated, had we
only had a chief with more energy and forethought.

".Since the battle, what have we done ? The French daily
grumble louder and lounder at our want of action, and with
good cause too. Is Lord Raglan waiting until some peace is
patched up, that our batteries are not ready. Why is it that we
are not ready to open fire as soon as our ally ? England has
not stinted us with the means, but it is mismanagement that
has been our scourge, and has almost proved the ruin of the ex
pedition. The future has a brighter aspect. The troops are in
good health and spirits, though much discontented with the
delay. The weather still continues fine, and the works are
getting on. We ought to be ready to open fire from all our
line of attack on Tuesday next, the 2nd of April, though I
am not very sanguine as to the result, as the enemy have a
fearful number of guns now mounted. Omar Pasha and his
Turks are to come here very shortly, and we may expect to
begin the fun in earnest then, as his divisions can take up a
part of our line of defence, and leave our troops to aid the
assault. The railroad is getting on famously, and it is certainly
very creditable to the managers and engineers. It will be completed up to Lord R.'s head-quarters in the course of a few
days, and is already in use as far as it goes.

" We are bombarding the city rather heavily just now, and,
indeed, the firing has been rather heavy for the last few
days."

While Major Leveson was serving with the Turkish
contingent, the following testimony to his ability and zeal
was sent by the Turkish Commander-in-chief to the British
Ambassador.

"TO LORD STRATFORD DE REDCLIFFE.

"MY LORD,

"I have the honour to bring to your notice, Major H. A. Leveson of the Indian Army, who has served with the Ottoman forces since their first landing in the Crimea, and who has on all and every occasion exhibited great zeal and ability in the performance of his duties, and in maintaining the discipline of the division to which he is attached. He was present at the battle of Inkerman, where he was the first to retake a French 12 lb. brass howitzer, which had been taken by the enemy on all its horses being killed. I consider him to be an active, intelligent, and meritorious officer, and of great experience, derived from former Indian campaigns, and have thought fit to advise your Lordship of this, as it was through your instrumentality that his services were rendered available to the Ottoman Government, and placed at the disposal of H. H. the Seraskier, to whom I have written, recommending that they should be employed on a more extensive scale, as I am convinced that he will do credit to whatever situation he may be placed in.

"I am, my Lord,

"&c. &c.

(Signed.)   "OSMAN PASHA.

"Commanding-in-Chief Ottoman Troops."

It is interesting just now to observe that though Major Leveson, in his correspondence, spoke in favourable terms of some of the Turkish generals, he was by no means enamoured of the Ottoman service. In a letter dated Sept., 1854, he says, —"From what I have seen of the Turkish service, I do not like it, and shall quit it as soon as the campaign is over. I believe, as a body, they are the most detestable race of people under the sun, and I think that their kingdom will soon pass away into other hands." And speaking of the Battle of Balaclava, he says that the Turks, who held the redoubts on that occasion, " all behaved in an infamous manner and bolted without hardly firing a shot, leaving the guns to the Bears. The Lieutenant-Colonel in command was the first to run. He mounted his horse on the approach of the Russians, and told his men to save themselves as they best could." Major Leveson, however, was fully aware of the many merits of the Turkish private soldiers, for in another letter he remarks—"I know that the men are good soldiers if properly led, and that they will follow me, as they have ten times more confidence in us (English officers), than in their own officers."

In 1856, Major Leveson returned to England. During the next three or four years he made several sporting excursions to different parts of the world, some of the incidents of which are related in these volumes, and others in his previous works.

In 1860 the Italian revolution took place, and Major Leveson lost no time in joining Garibaldi. In June of that year he sailed from Genoa for Messina, and, in September, entered Naples with the victorious Garibaldian forces. The campaign was so brief and bloodless that he had little chance of distinguishing himself. Garibaldi, however, showed that he appreciated Major Leveson's energetic character, and, on more than one occasion, gave him proofs of friendship.

When the short Italian campaign was over, Major Leveson again returned home.

For the next year or two he occupied himself with sport, and with writing and publishing one of his works. In 1863, he was appointed Colonial Secretary at Lagos, on the west coast of Africa. While he held this appointment, an African chief, at the head of a large armed force, committed serious aggressions upon the British territories around Lagos. There were no troops in the colony, and Major Leveson, on account of his previous military experience, was ordered by the Governor to raise a small native corps. Major Leveson threw himself into this work with characteristic energy. In one short week he levied, armed, drilled, and roughly disciplined a modest force of Houssas. With forty men of this rapid and raw levy, armed only with old flint firelocks, he defeated and dispersed a hostile body of natives, fifteen hundred strong, and armed with European cannons and muskets. To induce his new-fledged soldiers to do their duty, their leader was obliged to dangerously expose himself. Just as he had assured his little, but to the colony, important victory, he was struck by an iron bullet, which entered his head just below the right ear, shattered his lower jaw, and remained embedded in the bone. The medical resources of the colony were unequal to the extraction of the ball; the wound refused to heal, and the continuous agony and want of sleep from which he suffered, severely affected his previously robust health. On the 8th of February, 1864, therefore, he was invalided home. The skill of the greatest European surgeons of the day was, however, powerless to relieve him. Sir W. Fergusson, Nélaton, and other eminent operators, attempted to trace and take out the bullet, but always in vain. To the last day of Major Leveson's life the unhealed wound remained a constant source of trouble and suffering to him, which he bore to the end with untiring patience and fortitude. As some compensation, a grant of £500 was voted to him by the colony, and a similar sum by Parliament. His weakened state, however (his iron constitution, for the time, was at last shattered) caused Major Leveson to lose his valuable appointment.

He lost it through gallantly doing his duty, and the British government never conferred another upon him.

Two or three years later, Major Leveson, who always stoutly held that difficulties were only made to be overcome, and much of whose career is a proof that in his case the belief was not an extravagant one, volunteered to attempt, single-handed, a negotiation with Theodore of Abyssinia, for the release of Consul Cameron and the other English captives detained at Magdala. But it was determined to send out an armed force under Sir Robert Napier, to condignly punish the Abyssinian sovereign, and Major Leveson's rather startling proposal fell through. He, however, accompanied the expedition, and remained with it throughout the campaign ; the last military expedition in which he took any part.

From this brief sketch of Major Leveson's military career, it will be seen that he was an experienced and resolute officer. It will, however, be rather as an intrepid and successful sportsman, than as a soldier, that he will be remembered.

His military services would have been a chief, as well as a meritorious, feature in the career of another man. But in Major Leveson's case, brave, energetic, and dashing as were his services under arms, the fame of the soldier was overshadowed by that of the hunter.

Many another bold *sabreur*, long since forgotten, has doubtless acquitted himself in the field as gallantly as the subject of this brief Memoir, but it will be long before the prowess of a hunter will again become such a household word among sportsmen as was, and still is, that of " the Old Shekarry."

In the intervals of his other occupations he found time to range nearly the whole world in quest of sport. On the Bavarian and Italian alps, by the marshes of many a French river, in German forests; over the hot plains of the Deccan, amid the mountain ranges of the Himalayas, in the Wynaad, the Nirmuhl, and other teeming jungles, on the Bhowani, the Cauvery, and many another Indian river, to far Thibet; through the deserts of Asia Minor, up the passes of the Caucasus; in various districts of savage Africa; and across that wide sweep of western prairie, the endless ante-chamber of the Rocky Mountains, Major Leveson wandered for months at a time in search of wild and savage game of all kinds. His excursions were as successful as they were adventurous. With rifle, spear, and hunting-knife, he killed in these different hunting grounds more game, and of a more varied description, than has probably ever fallen to the bag of any other sportsman.

On one occasion he accompanied Jules Gérard, the famous French lion-killer, on a most interesting hunting trip in Algeria. M. Gérard was a sincere admirer of Major Leveson's achievements; and sought his permission to translate one of his books, "The Hunting Grounds of the Old World," into French. It was readily given, and in 1862 a French translation of that work was published in Paris, with the following preface from M. Gérard's pen :—

"Mon ami, le Major Leveson, surnommé le vieux Chasseur, m'ayant autorisé à faire connaître en France les belles chasses qu'il a faites dans l'Inde, je me suis empressé de profiter de cette grâcieuse autorisation. J'espère que, même en dehors du monde du sport, ces récits intéresserout le lecteur.

"JULES GÉRARD."

" 1862."

Possessing an iron frame, nerves that never betrayed him, and the gift of an unerring aim, Major Leveson was fortunate enough to add to these qualities a fluent and graphic pen. His contributions to various periodical publications under the *nom de plume* of H. A. L., or "the Old Shekarry," describing his sporting excursions in all parts of the world, are well known. They teemed with daring adventures and hairbreadth escapes but they were invariably written with an unconscious *naïveté*, and a straightforward absence of egotism, that showed that their writer was unaware that the perils he was depicting were such as few, even of the world's picked men, would have cared to face.

Besides his contributions to periodical literature, he wrote "The Hunting Grounds of the Old World," "The Forest and the Field," "The Camp Fire," and "Wrinkles; or Hints to Sportsmen and Travellers upon Dress, Equipment, Armament, and Camp Life." This last little book has become a standard work of its kind, and is generally considered invaluable to sportsmen. He also published "England rendered Impregnable," a work full of novel but clever and by no means extravagant suggestions. The *Times*, in speaking of one of his works, observed, "A sincere devotion to his art elevates Major Leveson into a kind of troubadour of hunting crusades; gives eloquence to his pictures of forest scenery; and no mean grace to the improvised songs with which he was wont to beguile the evening after a day's sport." And the *Saturday Review* paid him a just compliment by remarking :—" 'The old Shekarry' is essentially a sportsman, and not a butcher of game. His object has been not to slaughter for the sake of slaughtering, but, save in the case of animals hostile to man, such as tigers and rogue elephants, to kill as much as was necessary for the supply of himself and his followers, and no more."

Some, perhaps, may ask, *cui bono* such earnest and continuous pursuit of mere sport? What fitting end can be gained by such life-long devotion to the killing of wild animals? It may be replied that Major Leveson, though gifted, as his writings show, with an observant mind and no small share of imaginative enthusiasm, was essentially a man of action. When circumstances were favourable he proved that this craving for physical excitement was capable of a wider scope than could be found in what must be acknowledged to be the pastime of sport. In the Crimea, in the Principalities, in Italy under Garibaldi, at Lagos, in Abyssinia, he showed that the more earnest, the more important the purpose of the stirring action of the moment, the higher rose his energy, his courage, and his enterprise; and if, when the world was at rest, and battle fortunately absent from its stage, he followed the dictates of a daring nature, and sought in the boldest and most adventurous forms of sport the outlet which war no longer afforded him, it would be hard to blame him.

It is not given to all men to be perpetually satisfied with the monotonous routine of business, or with the empty and effeminate amusements of fashion. After all, wider and more full of the fresh generous air of life than the red-tape existence of the careful official, or the petty and frivolous pursuits of the Park lounger, is the adventurous career of a fearless wanderer like "the Old Shekarry." It is such as he who by the influence of their deeds, and the emulation excited by their example, have endowed the nation with that tone of manly vigour, that moral ozone, which has contributed so much to the prestige and reputation of England.

An epitome of his career would not be complete without mentioning that when this country was disquieted by the long silence of Livingstone, Major Leveson characteristically volunteered his services to Earl Granville, as chief of a search expedition. Lord Granville referred him with a strong recommendation to the Royal Geographical Society. But the reputation of the " Old Shekarry " was, perhaps, a little too dashing for the mild sages who then ruled at Burlington House, and the search was vainly entrusted to other and far less experienced hands.

After his return from Abyssinia he never enjoyed really sound health again. The wound in his head was perpetually breaking out afresh, and the constant hæmorrhage from it did much to weaken a frame, that, once of iron, was now suffering from the effects of the repeated hardships to which it had been exposed. From these effects alone, possibly, he would have recovered. Had he never, perhaps too gallantly taken the field at Lagos, he might have been alive and vigorous at this day. But the African bullet at last did its work. All through 1875 Major Leveson was gradually sinking, and, after much pain borne with his accustomed resolution, he died in the autumn, prematurely worn out by wounds and exposure, at the comparatively early age of forty-seven.

H. F.

SPORT IN MANY LANDS.

CHAPTER I.

DEER STALKING AND DRIVING.

RED DEER.

LONG before the Norman Conquest, the Saxon Thanes had their chases and deer-parks, and in those days wild red deer were common all over Merrie England, and stag-hunting was not only the great recreation of our early kings and nobles in time of peace, but also a national pastime in which the people were indulged on high days and holidays. During the Civil Wars, and more especially whilst the Roundheads were in power, the parks and deer-preserves of England were more or less devastated by the people, and in many places red deer, which were common in the land, became extinct through wanton destruction, so that in the present day, out of the three hundred parks in England, only about thirty contain red deer, and they are in a semi-domesticated state. The exhilarating sport of following the stag with horse and hound has for centuries been a pastime dear to the English people, but the chase of the wild red deer seems to be gradually dying out from amongst us, for even in the New Forest, in Hampshire, the royal red deer is found no more, and it is years since Her Majesty's Buckhounds, with Davis on his grand old grey, Hermit, at their head, was wont for a time to forsake the hunting cart, and to come down each spring and show the world what stag-hunting really was, when a thousand horsemen were sometimes to be counted at the meet of the Royal Hounds, and the gathering attracted here the *élite* of the hunting world from all parts of the King-

A ROYAL HEAD.

dom. Since those days, the red deer have been shot down, and the sylvan glades of Exmoor know them no more.

The stag, or red deer (*Cervus elaphus*), is of a tawny brown colour, deepening to black along the ridge of the back during the summer months, but as the hair grows long during the autumn, it assumes a greyish hue, which again changes to a reddish brown as the long winter coat falls off.

The stag produces a new head of horns every year, and his age is indicated by them. The first year he has only a horny

STAG'S HEAD WHEN THE HORNS ARE SHED.

excrescence covered with a thin skin; during the second year the horns come out, and are straight and single; the third year they have two antlers, the fourth three, the fifth four, and the sixth five. At six years old, when the fifth head has grown, he is said to possess a full head, and now becomes "a royal stag." A fully developed horn has a *brow, bay,* and *tray* antler, and two points also at the top. The first three are termed the *rights,* the two points the *crockets,* the horn itself the *beam,* the width between the tips the *span,* and the rough part at the junction with the skull the *pearls.* During the first year a stag is called a *calf,* the second a *knobber,* the third a *brock,* the fourth a *staggard,* the fifth a *stag,* and the sixth a *hart.* The female is called the first year a *calf,* the second a *hearse,* and the third a *hind.*

The horns of the stag are cylindrical, having the branches, more or less in number, according to the age of the animal, pretty regularly distributed both to the right and left. When a stag is ten years old, the antlers flatten out, and become more or less palmated, throwing out points resembling fingers. When these are arranged in a circular shape, the stag is said to carry a *round head.* The horns are shed annually in the spring, first becoming loose, and then dropping off entire; but not always simultaneously, for there is sometimes a short interval between the shedding of one and of the other antler. This gradual loosening of the old horns is produced by the progressive internal growth of the new horns, which forces them out of their sockets, so that at last, the tops of the new horns becoming slightly prominent, the old ones fall by their own weight. A good-sized pair of horns weighs about 12lbs. On the horns being shed, an excrescence, containing a considerable quantity of blood, and covered with brown down, appears for a day or two, and from this the new antlers protrude, gradually assuming their natural shape, according to the age of the animal. The horns attain their full growth and solidity in about three months, up to which time they are covered with a skin, as shown in the engraving, which promotes their growth by facilitating the conveyance of nutriment to them; but when the horns have reached maturity, the animal clears them of this skin by rubbing them against the branches of trees.

Soon after the new horns are grown, the period of pairing

begins, and the stags leave the recesses of the forest in search of the hinds. At these periods they become remarkably fierce and restless, flying from place to place and uttering a deep guttural bellowing, their note of defiance to each other. The females, whom they call with a loud

STAG'S HEAD SHOWING THE YOUNG HORNS.

tremulous voice, at first avoid them, but are at last overtaken. Should two stags approach the same hind, a combat *à outrance* immediately takes place. If nearly equal in strength, they threaten, paw the ground, set up terrible cries, and rush impetuously one against the other, fighting on their feet and knees, and giving and parrying blows with great agility and consummate skill. This combat never terminates but in the death or flight of one of the rivals, and the conqueror remains master of the seraglio until driven away by another more powerful competitor, who assumes the possession of all his privileges. Sometimes the younger stags run cunning, and seek the hinds whilst the old ones are fighting, but this is rarely the case, as the hinds prefer the old stags. Stags are very inconstant, having often several females at a time, but when a stag has but one hind, his attachment to her does not continue above a few days, then he leaves her and goes in quest of another, with whom he remains a still shorter period, and in this manner he passes on from one to another, scarcely eating, sleeping, or resting for two or three weeks, the extent of the rutting season, when, having worn himself out and become enfeebled and thin, he retires from the herd to recuperate and restore his exhausted strength; but he rarely recovers his former robust condition until the following spring. The roaring or bellowing of the stag becomes stronger, louder, and more tremulous as he increases in age, and in the early part of the rutting season it may be constantly heard the whole night long.

The hind does not begin to breed until three years old, and then goes about eight months with young. The usual season of parturition is May or the beginning of June, when she generally brings forth one fawn — very rarely two — the body of which is covered with white spots on a yellow ground. At six months old the young change their appearance, and the rudiments of antlers appear. The calf never quits the dam during the whole summer, and the hinds are very assiduous to conceal their young in the most obscure retreats, as the stag is their avowed enemy, and would kill them if he came across them. The hind's young do not desert their mother when they cease to suck, but continue to attend her as

THE CHALLENGE.

long as she lives; and as they—*i.e.* the females among them—in their turn bear each of them offspring, the old hind is often accompanied by several successive generations, who continue to remain together and form a herd, headed by some patriarchal old stag.

The dimensions of the red deer are as follows :—Height at shoulder, 3 feet 11¼ inches; girth at shoulder, 4 feet 7 inches; height from top of head to fore foot, 5 feet 6 inches; length of antler, 2 feet 6 inches; from top of antler to ground, 7 feet 10 inches; gross weight, 308lbs. The age of the red deer is about forty years, but some old writers say that he lives to be three times that of man; and that "there is strong evidence for believing that this popular belief has some foundation in fact, as many very old men have known particular deer all their life-time, and have had the same knowledge handed down to them from their fathers, and even their grandfathers."

The favourite food of red deer is grass, leaves, fruit, and buds, but in the winter, when none of these can be got, they are compelled to eat moss, heath, lichens, and the bark of young trees.

In England, in consequence of the cultivated state of the country, red deer are almost unknown in their wild natural condition, except a few on the moors and forests which border on Cornwall and Devonshire; but in Ireland, on the Mountains of Kerry, they are still in the normal state, whilst in the highlands of Scotland they abound in vast numbers, some of the herds counting as many as two thousand head. The large tracts of land in Scotland on which red deer are preserved, which are called "forests," are not, as might be supposed by the uninitiated, densely wooded lands, but consist of mountainous districts covered with heather, and intersected with deep glens and corries, morasses, and patches of pasture land. Some of the largest of these forests belong to the Marquis of

VICTORY.

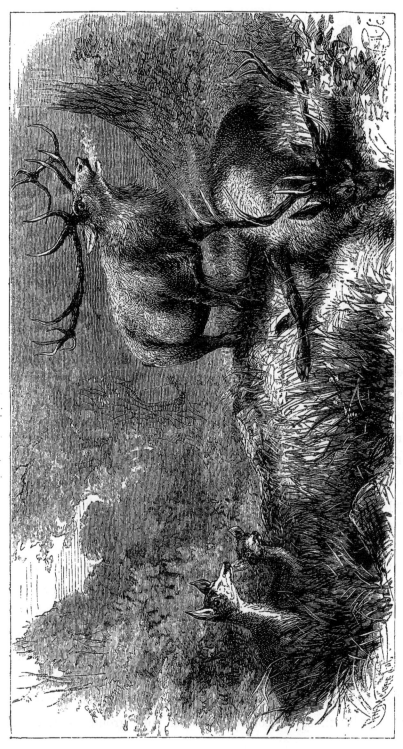

VICTORY.

Huntly, the Dukes of Sutherland, Athol, Leeds, Richmond, Portland, the Earl of Dalhousie, the Marquis of Bute, Lord Breadalbane, and Lord Fife. Besides these, there are the deer forests of Balmoral and Invercauld, as well as others on the western isles. These forests comprise many hundred thousand acres of land devoted almost exclusively to deer, as no sheep are ever permitted to intrude, and even grouse are not always protected, as their presence often interferes with deer-stalking. In Scotland deer are killed either by driving or stalking.

Deer-stalking is an art not to be learnt in a day, as it requires a considerable knowledge of woodcraft, besides coolness, perseverance, great endurance, prodigious powers of exertion, combined with the gifts of a steady hand and a quick eye.

The deer-stalker should not only be able to run like an antelope, but he should possess the bottom of an Arab horse, to enable him to keep the game in view; he should be able to creep like a leopard, and to run with his back bent almost double, and at a pinch to wriggle himself along the ground, *ventre à terre*, like an eel. He should be able to wade or swim torrents, to keep his footing on slippery, water-worn stones, remembering, if he does fall, to keep his rifle dry, whatever becomes of himself. He should never go *rashly* to work, keeping always *cool, wary,* and *steady,* never allowing any untoward circumstances to interfere with his equanimity and self-possession.

Before commencing operations, he should carefully survey his line of route, marking any cover that inequalities in the ground, or bushes, rocks, &c., might give. I need not add that temperance and moderation go a long way to keep *the hand in* and the nerves steady. When I first began deer-stalking, my mentor endeavoured to instil the following general rules in my mind, and several years' subsequent experience has proved to me that his theory is correct. Be on your ground betimes in the morning; consult the clouds, and keep well to the leeward, even if you have to make a circuit of miles; be silent as the grave; when you step on stones or dry leaves, &c., tread as lightly as a ghost; keep under cover; exercise extreme judgment in approaching your game, which is a happy mixture of wary caution combined with prompt decision and boldness of

STAGS IN WINTER.

execution. Memo.—All this is useless if you do not use straight powder.

There is no animal more shy or solitary by nature than the stag. He takes alarm from every living thing in the forest; the slightest sound, be it only the fall of a leaf or the scratching of a grouse, will scare and set him off in a moment. Except in certain embarrassed situations, *they always run up wind,* their great security lying in their extreme keenness of scent, for they can smell a taint in the air at an almost incredible distance.

When a hart is disabled and run down by dogs, and he feels that he cannot escape by speed, he will choose the best position he can, and defend himself to the last extremity with his antlers. Powerful dogs may pull down a full-grown stag when running and breathless, but not a *cold hart* (one that has not been wounded), for when he stands at bay, he takes such a sweep with his antlers that he could exterminate a whole pack, should they attack in front only.

Deer, like many other animals, seem to foresee every change of weather, for they leave the hills and descend into the plains whenever any rough weather is about to take place.

The system of following deer in the middle of the day, when they naturally rest after feeding all night, is not beneficial to a forest. It is much more difficult to get near the best stags when they have taken up a position of rest than it is at dawn, when they are straggling back from their night's banquet; and they are more easily alarmed by frightened grouse and ptarmigan during the day. Their position is, moreover, guarded by straggling hinds and small stags, and for one shot you will get at midday you will get three at dawn, and with less disturbance of your stock of deer on the ground. Some people, who dislike going out before dawn, call the early shot a poaching system; but for filling a larder with venison, and keeping your deer quiet, the shot at dawn and in the evening is the best. During the day the deer should be undisturbed if the stock is to be kept on the ground, and they should be hunted by deer hounds as little as possible.

The following are some of the terms generally used in deer-stalking. The deer's haunt is called his lair; where he lies, his harbour; where he rolls, his soiling-pool; where he breaks through a fence, his rack; if he goes to water, he takes soil; if

DEER STALKING IN SCOTLAND.

he heads back, he is blanched; if he lies down in water, he is said to be sinking himself.

Any sportsman well versed in woodcraft can distinguish the slots of the stag from those of the hind, as the foot of the stag is better formed, and the impressions of his feet are rounder and further removed from each other. Again, he steps more regularly, and brings the hind foot into the impression made by the fore foot. The hind takes shorter steps than the stag, and her hind feet do not strike the track of the fore feet regularly, the stride being generally shorter and spread out wider. It requires some experience, however, to distinguish the trail of a young stag from that of a hind. Stags of six or seven years have their fore feet much larger than their hind feet, and as they grow old, the sides of their hoofs become worn and rounded off.

There are certain signs by which a sportsman well versed in woodcraft can tell the nature of his quarry by the slot. Thus, although there is apparently very little difference in the formation of the hoof of a stag and that of a hind, the slot or imprint which one animal leaves behind it on the ground is very unlike that left by the other. The chief difference is, that the stag in walking presses the two divisions of the cloven hoof together, which the hind does not; and whilst the impression left by the stag's hoof is sharp and well marked, that of the hind is blurred and indistinct. The peculiar manner in which a stag treads on the ground, presses the points of the hoof forward into the soft earth, and causes a long *narrow ridge* to rise all along the centre of the slot. The hind, which treads with the divisions of the cloven hoof comparatively wide apart, leaves a much *broader* division. Again, the slot of a stag is less pointed and more obtuse in its curvature than that of a hind, and a stag in walking points his hoofs outwards, which a hind does not. The length of the stride, too, is an important consideration, as the stag takes a much longer step than the hind, and from the length of the step an experienced deer-stalker is enabled to dis-. tinguish the age of the stag. Thus, a stag that covers 18 inches in his step, will carry ten points on his head, whilst a hart of fourteen will step about 20 inches. There are other distinctions by which the trail of a stag may be distinguished from that of a hind, he bites the blades of grass clean off; she pulls and breaks it. Nor must another very distinctive peculiarity be omitted. The fecomets of a stag are always united in a mass like a bunch of grapes, whilst those of the hind fall separately as with sheep. Their state will also tell, how long it was since the animal passed along the trail.

DEER-DRIVING IN AUSTRIA.

" The gay green wood! 'Tis a lovely world,
  With beauty that's all its own;
  And pleasant it is in the summer time
  To roam through that world alone."

AUSTRIA is essentially a land of sportsmen, as each of the nationalities that compose the Empire have a certain innate speciality, or *forte* peculiar to the race. Thus the Hungarians are world-renowned horsemen, and as bold cross-country riders may be seen following the Pardubitz stag-hounds as in a Pytchley field; the Bohemians are celebrated for their skill in the art of venery, and their knowledge of woodcraft; and the Tyrolese are famed marksmen and mountaineers. Naturally such a

AUSTRIAN JAGER.

combination produces numberless ardent votaries of St. Hubert, and as the land abounds in all kinds of game, which for centuries has been rigidly preserved by the lords of the soil, there are few countries in Europe that offer such inducements for sportsmen.

In the latter part of September, my friend Elliot and I were staying at the Hotel Noelbeck, Salzburg, to recuperate, after a pretty severe tramp in the Tyrol, when we were invited by an eminent physician, one of our Vienna acquaintances, to join him and another sportsman at a grand battue that was to take place near Engelhardtzell, on the Danube ; and two days afterwards three of us found ourselves comfortably located at the Hirsch, where we were joined by the *Jäger-meister,* under whose direction the drive was to take place. As one or two of the Arch-dukes were expected to be present on this occasion, besides a great gathering of noble sportsmen from Vienna, we did not anticipate getting much sport ourselves, as the big-wigs would naturally be posted in the places where the game was most likely to break; but it was a fine chance of seeing a battue conducted on a large scale, and as luck would have it, the arrangements were made so that all the guests got a fair chance of sport. Early in the morning of the eventful day, there was a great assembling and marshalling of the company, each of the guests appearing in *jäger* attire of some kind or another, which generally consisted of a loose grey Tyrolese coat and trousers garnished with green binding and large buck-horn buttons, Hessian, or long Russia leather boots, and green "Tegern see" hat ornamented with either eagle's plumes or the tail feathers of a black cock. Most of the sportsmen had very short double-barrelled small-bore rifles, with short stocks most artistically carved and ornamented, and fitted with all kinds of elaborate back-sights and hair-triggers ; consequently our long-barrelled Purdey's and Westley-Richards' rifles, grey wide-awakes, Norfolk jackets, and breeches and gaiters were somewhat out of keeping with the rest; but luckily they attracted the attention of our host, to whom we were presented by the Doctor; and he, with that urbane courtesy which appears to be innate among the Austrians, desired his head forester to see that the strangers were posted in a good position. Then, with a friendly nod, he continued to give his directions about the drive. Many of the sportsmen had their own *jägers* and personal attendants with them, but they were all ordered to join the line of beaters, or guard certain defiles through which the game might attempt to break instead of passing along the line of ambuscades. The foresters, evidently, were well up in their work—there was no confusion; and the sportsmen being posted at certain intervals with most concise and plain directions to shoot only straight to their front, horns sounded, and the drive commenced. The line of guns was stationed along one side of a prettily-wooded ravine, where clearings had been made which the game would have to pass, within sight of the sportsmen, when driven into the gorge from a circuit of forest some miles in extent. In some places regular stands, screens, and mounds had been raised, that commanded an admirable view of the ground before them; but which could not be seen by the game until they crossed the open ground in their front. Our party were posted in some rocky ground almost at the head of the ravine, the Count himself taking the extreme end, so that although the game had to run the gauntlet of the whole line of guns before we got a chance, still we had certain compensating advantages of position, as the ravine narrowed considerably at our elevated station, and whatever animal escaped the sportsmen below, had to pass within easy shot of us before it could gain the crest of the hill. Our host was the last on the line, so that all his guests got a fair chance at the driven game before he did; but, notwithstanding this courteous concession, I am by no means sure that any sportsman in the line made a heavier bag than he did.

We had not been at our station more than an hour when—crack, crack, crack went the rifles below us; and then a dropping file-firing followed; and, from our elevated position, we had a bird's-eye view of the whole proceedings, and now and again could distinguish the dun sides of deer, and the puffs of rising smoke as the guns were discharged from the different ambuscades. Pipes were laid down, and, with rifles in hand, ready for action, we waited impatiently. A slight rustling sound was heard in the bushes, which added to the excitement, and a fine dog-fox came creeping up: the doctor out of politeness motioned us to fire, but we both had enjoyed too many good day's run after the varmint race, to harm one of them with shot, and we shook our heads at the notion, when he let drive and missed, but one of the Count's friends rolled him over with slugs. Then came a roebuck, which stopped a moment to breathe, and stood with trembling limbs and heaving flanks as if bewildered, within fifty yards of our station; and Elliot dropped him with a bullet through the shoulder. We now heard a rushing in the cover, and three red hinds passed within easy range of us, but they, by the rules of venery, were allowed to go free. They were followed by a wounded boar, who tore along champing his tushes with rage, foaming at the mouth, and bleeding from half-a-dozen gunshot wounds. Crack went the doctor's rifle, and round swung the boar, snorting a vicious defiance towards our position, which his keen olfactories had winded; and he looked as if he was about to charge in our direction, when Elliot and I, firing almost simultaneously, doubled him up in a heap, and "poor piggie" subsided. A rattling of stones and a crashing through the bushes now betokened the approach of deer, and another troop

of hinds tore by, followed by a good stag, with wide-spreading
antlers, evidently sorely wounded. I fired a double shot as he
passed at speed across the vista in front of our station, the first
of which made him wince, and the second brought him to his
knees; but he sprang up again, and was making his way after
the hinds with great difficulty and pain, sometimes falling to
his knees, and then, by a strong effort, recovering his feet, when
the Count gave him a right and left, which tumbled him over,
and he was plunging about on the ground when one of the
jägers rushed up, seized his antlers from behind, and drove
home a small dagger behind the ears, where the back of the
head is set on the neck—which is the usual mode of adminis-
tering the *coup de grâce* to a wounded stag in Germany—and
in a second life was extinct. Strange to say, this stag had
received seven wounds, four of which seemed fairly placed about
the shoulder and withers, any one of which must eventually
have proved mortal; yet such was his strength and tenacity of
life that he managed to scramble up a steep hill before he fell.
Several foxes, and an innumerable number of hares, now made
their appearance, but we let them go unscathed, waiting for
nobler game; and shortly afterwards another party of hinds
came tearing wildly past, and in their rear were five stags, who,
winding the blood of the dead boar, swerved round towards our
ambuscade, and offered easy shots. Elliot dropped the leading
hart with a right and left behind the shoulder, and I managed
to score another with a lucky shot that penetrated the throat
just where it joins the head, when he sprang high up into the
air, and dropped dead, the spinal cord having been severed.
After this came a whole porcine family, and several roe-deer;
and two of the former and three of the latter came to grief
in front of our ambuscade. The fusilade below us now gradually ceased, and a fanfare of hunting horns was the signal
to cease firing and collect the game. In front of our station

DEER DRIVING IN AUSTRIA.

were found two good-sized stags, a fine old boar with good
tushes, and four roe-deer, which we thought was a pretty fair
bag for three guns; but when the game was all laid out for inspection we found some of the other parties had been much
more successful.

We now adjourned to a sumptuous luncheon, laid on a
beautiful bit of short turf under the greenwood shade; and
divesting ourselves of our rifles, we enjoyed one of the
pleasantest *al fresco* repasts I ever sat down to. The doctor,
who had been suffering for some time with a malady peculiar
to the Fatherland, but also well known to most sportsmen, viz.,
Bier-durst, or a craving for malt liquor, recovered his pristine
form after disposing of his sixth mug of the clear, sparkling,
amber-like nectar for which Austria is famous; and especially
directed our attention to the *blue* and *brown* (boiled and
broiled) trout, the Danube Schrill, the salmi of Huchen, venison
pasties, wild boar's head, capercailzie hen, woodcock, grey teal,
or ortolan, quail, and snipe *pâtés*, which, with a profusion of
piéces de resistance, were temptingly laid out before us, flanked
with a goodly array of Gumpoldskirchin, Bisamberg, Vœslaw,
and sundry delicate and luscious Rhine and Hungarian wines,
including both the Ausbrussh and Malzchlap Tokay, beverages
fit for the Gods, that one reads about but seldom sees, for the
vines which produce these wines only grow on the southern
slopes of the Hegy-allia hills, in Northern Hungary, and the
vintage is rarely sold. After we had done ample justice to the
good cheer, pipes were lighted, and hunting yarns told, until a
mort was sounded on the horns, and we went to the place
where the game was collected. The bag consisted of eleven
stags, twenty-three roe-deer, nine hogs, five foxes, a badger, and
a hundred and sixty hares, which we thought was a very good
day's work; but we were told that the same drive the year
before had been very much more successful. Having thanked

our host for our day's sport, we retraced our steps for the
village of Engelhardzell, and the next day returned to Vienna
by steamer.

DEAD HARE.

CHAPTER II.

THE chamois (*Rupi capra tragus*) is no goat, being of the true antelope genus, and the only specimen of that tribe indigenous to Europe. It is larger and more strongly built than a roebuck, a good buck often weighing from 50 to 70 lbs. The head, which is admirably constructed for uniting strength with lightness, is ornamented with graceful black horns, about seven inches long, which rise from just above and between the eyes, and slant forward, forming almost a right angle with the forehead. Their points are very sharp, and are bent back and downwards, and are solid except at the base, in which fits a bony substance that forms part of the skull. The horns of the buck chamois are thicker and heavier than those of the doe, and whilst hers have a semicircular bend towards the back, the points of the horns bend inward. The head is carried very erect, the ears are pointed, and constantly on the move, and the eyes are large and full of intelligence. The engraving represents the head of a chamois buck about three years old.

The hair of the chamois varies in colour with the seasons of the year. In summer it is a reddish brown, in autumn a dark ash, and in winter almost black. The nose, the hair on the forehead, the belly, and inside the legs are of a yellowish tan, and there is always a black stripe extending from the corners of the mouth to the eyes. The chief food of the chamois consists of the young sprouts and buds of the lichen and the mountain herbage. The rutting season commences in November, and at this season des-

HEAD OF THREE-YEAR OLD CHAMOIS BUCK.

perate battles take place between the rival bucks for the favours of the does. The period of gestation in the doe is twenty weeks, and in May the young chamois make their appearance, and when a day old are not to be caught.

They are generally found in herds of fifteen or twenty, the old males remaining alone, except during the rutting season, when they join the herd, from which they expel all the young males. They are very keen of scent, sharp-sighted, and vigilant, uttering a shrill whistling sound when alarmed, which signal sets the whole herd in motion, and they spring from rock to rock and run along almost inaccessible scarps with the greatest ease and security.

There is no animal so timid as the chamois, and few that have the organs of sight, hearing, and smell, so keenly developed. They often become aware of the hunter's presence long before he perceives them, and then with a sharp whistle of alarm they dash along the mountain ridge with a velocity that must be seen to be imagined. The agility of the chamois is proverbial, and the roughest ground, or even rocks of almost perpendicular steepness, seem to offer no impediment to their headlong course. They can stand with all four hoofs together, poised on a pinnacle of rock rising thousands of feet in the air, and scamper at speed along narrow ledges of smooth rock where no hunter dare follow.

" A chamois, when dashing down the mountain, will suddenly stop as if struck by a thunder-bolt some yards from the spot where recent human footprints are to be found in the snow, and, turning scared away, rush off immediately in an opposite direction. A rolling stone or a spoken word at once attracts their attention, and they will look and listen to discover whence the sound has come for an incredibly long time, gazing fixedly in one direction, quite immovable ; and if it happens to be towards something in your neighbourhood that their attention

has been attracted, you must lie still and close indeed to escape
their observation.   The eyes of the whole herd will be fixed on
the spot with a long steady stare, and as you anxiously watch
them from afar, they almost look like fragments of rock, so
motionless are they.   You begin to hope they have found no
cause for alarm, when, 'Phew!' the sharp whistle tells they
have fathomed the mystery, and away they move to the precipitous rocks overhead."

The chamois hunter, to be successful in his calling, must be
a man of no ordinary nerve, for he has often to venture where
few dare follow.   Quoting the words of that experienced sportsman, Mr. Charles Boner, "He is accustomed to have death
stalking beside him as a companion, and to meet him face to
face."   His departure for the mountain—an unknown region
hidden in cloud, and mist, and mystery, his absence for whole
days together, his startling accounts of the wildness, the silence,
and the solitude, and then occasionally the going forth of one
alone who never returned,—all this gave a dim and dread uncertainty to the pursuit ; and where uncertainty is, imagination
will be busy at her work.   His very countenance, his widely-
opened eye, always on the watch, even this must have awakened
strange surmises of sights more fearful than he had yet
heard of.

The chamois hunter has been thus vividly described :—"A
tall man, gaunt and bony, his brown and sinewy knees were
bare and scratched and scarred ; his beard was black and long,
his hair shaggy, and hunger was in his face ; the whole man
looked as if he had just escaped from the den of a wolf, where
he had lain starved, and in daily expectation of being eaten.
But it was his eyes, the wild, staring fixedness of his eyes, that
kept mine gazing on him ; the bent eagle nose, the high flesh-
less cheek-bones added to their power.   There was no fierceness
in them, nor were they greedy eyes, but they were those of a

THE CHAMOIS HUNTER.

man who had been snatched from a horrible death, and in whom the recollection was not effaced, nor likely to be. They were always wide open; the whole creature seemed vigilant, and awaiting at any moment to wrestle with fate. But this was observable in the eyes alone, not in the other features, for the nostrils were not distended, nor the lips clenched, as they must have been to harmonise with the meaning that was in his eyes."
"He is a silent and reserved man," say they who have made the acquaintance of the chamois hunter. Who can wonder at it? Who shall tell the wondrous sights he has seen? Who knows, when he returns at night to his hut in the valley, with the good chamois lading his *Rücksack*, who knows how close the hunter has been that day to death?—by what twig, or accidental stone, or other of God's good providences, he has been saved on the verge of the spiky gulf a thousand feet deep? They can only know it from the hunter's own mouth, and he has long since ceased to regard them as marvels, or things worth relating.

Ischl, more than any place I know, combines the gaieties of a capital with the recreations of country life. Those who prefer society will find balls, concerts, a casino, and, indeed, every kind of dissipation, whilst the lover of nature will be enchanted with the great variety of wild and grand scenery. It is the *beau idéal* of a sportsman's head-quarters, for in the surrounding forests are to be found red deer, roe, wild boar, capercailzie, and black game, whilst chamois are not scarce on the higher ranges, and there is the finest of fishing on the lakes and rivers. The principal fish are trout, grayling, and char. It is a glorious place for those who love the *dolce far niente*, for there is always plenty of agreeable company to help one to do nothing.

I passed some days at this delightful watering-place, doing as other people did, bathing, drinking *molke* (whey) early in the morning, whilst listening to the strains of an excellent band,

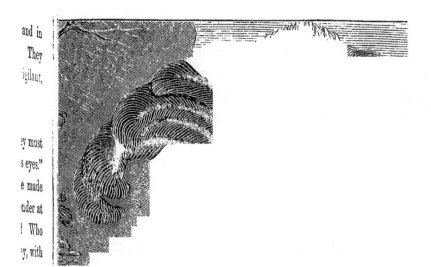

and in
They
igilant,

y must
s eyes,"
e made
nder at
! Who
y, with

in the
t band,

BLACKCOCK DRUMMING.

strolling about the woods, in the society of some of the most amiable of the fairer sex, dining *al fresco* under the shade of an overhanging rock, and joining some *réunion dansante*, or musical party, in the evening. I never once thought of the old fellow bearing the scythe and the hour-glass, for I met with several genial companions whose tastes assimilated with my own ; and, as we are all more or less creatures of impulse, and there seems to be a certain subtle agency, or magnetic influence, by which our feelings become communicated to each other, I was truly happy.

By a stroke of good fortune, I stumbled across an old friend, Herbert L'Estrange, who had served in the Confederate cavalry during the war, and had borne an active part in many of Stewart's raids, and we agreed to have a cruise together amongst the mountains. A day being devoted to preparation for the trip, alpenstocks were got, arms, ammunition, and portable cooking-canteen looked to, and some tins of *pâté de fois gras* and rice bought, in case of any scarcity of provisions *en route*. Leaving our heavier baggage at the hotel, we only took with us a few changes of under-clothing, light mackintosh cloaks, and travelling-rugs, with three of Cording's waterproof blankets, without which I never travel, as they form the best substitute either for tents or bedding.

All being satisfactorily arranged, we left Ischl soon after day-break by a good road, winding along the right bank of the Traun, and, after a walk of about three hours, arrived at the village of Steg, on the Lake of Hallstadt, which is about five miles long, and something less than two broad. Here we took a boat, and pulled over to the village of Hallstadt, where we put up at the "Gruner-baum," a very homely, but comfortable inn. After a substantial breakfast upon *Saibling* (char) fresh from the lake, *Blangesotten* (trout boiled in vinegar and water), and *Gemsfleisch-braten* (broiled chamois-stakes), we clambered

THE COCK OF THE WOODS.

up to the Rudolphsthurm, an antique-looking tower perched on
a projecting rock about a thousand feet above the village, from
whence we had a magnificent view of this wild but gloomy-
looking lake.

After dinner, several guides, hearing of our intention of
making a trip to the mountain, presented themselves; but, at
the solicitation of our Kellnerinn, a buxom-looking damsel, who
did not scruple to show herself *passionée* for my handsome
companion, we engaged a very intelligent and likely-looking
young fellow, named Karl, as our guide, and his cousins,
Hans and Heinrich, to carry our baggage. They did not
belong to Hallstadt but lived in a châlet near the Tannen
Gibirge a high mountain between the Dachstein Range and
Berchtesgaden.

After an early breakfast, accompanied to the pier by our host,
who wished us *Waidmann's Heil* (good sport), we left Hallstadt by boat, and landed at the embouchure of the Gosau,
near an aqueduct which conveys the brine from the mines to
the salt works at Ebensee. Here we entered a narrow, wild-
looking glen, fringed with pines, and, making our way along the
banks of the stream, passed through the village of Gosau, and
halted about two miles beyond for lunch, at a *Gast-haus* kept
by a smith. The landlord of this establishment was a friend of
our guide, and we proposed taking him with us, but, unfortunately, he was away from home, so we had to make the best of
our way without him.

An hour's walk through the pine forest brought us to the
Vorder See, a romantic-looking little lake, at the south-east
extremity of which towered the Thorstein, a mountain over
nine thousand feet high, with glaciers rolling down ravines in
its sides. Continuing our route, after four hours' sharp up-hill
walking, we came to the Hinter See, another small Alp-locked
lake, the waters of which are of a peculiar pale green colour,

except under the shadow of the overhanging cliffs, where they appear almost black. Here we put up at a small *Sen hutte* and, lighting a fire, made our preparations for passing the night comfortably. A hot supper was soon before us, for Karl manufactured a *Schmarren* (a cake, like an Indian chapate, of flour and eggs fried in butter), whilst I made a *rechauffé* of *Geback-enes Huhn*. Having done justice to our good cheer, and washed it down with a hot brew of whiskey toddy, concocted with great skill by L'Estrange, Karl told us some of his adventures whilst poaching in the Baiern Gibirge, and afterwards he and his companions commenced singing "*Jodeln*," and "*Schnadahupfln*," gipsy-like chants peculiar to the mountaineers of Styria and the Tyrol. We then rolled ourselves up in our blankets on some new hay, and were soon asleep.

Afoot at daybreak. After a substantial breakfast we made a start, and in two hours reached the Gosau glacier. Then commenced a stiff ascent up the Dachstein; but our progress was slow, as we had not yet got into climbing condition, and it was nearly noon before we arrived at the summit. We were amply repaid for our exertions by the grandeur of the panorama which then lay before us; for the atmosphere was very clear, and the outlines of even the most distant ranges were clearly defined against the blue sky. At our feet lay the Karls Eis-feld, a vast waste of glacier-ice, which formed a striking contrast to the sombre-looking rocky precipices that enclosed it, or the dense forests of dark fir, from amidst which towered gigantic snow-clad peaks. To the northward were the lakes of Hallstadt, Aussee, and Grundelsee, the peak of the Knippenstein, and the Traunstein and Schafberg in the distance; to the eastward rose the Kammer mountain and the Hohe Gjadstein; to the south were the Gosau lakes, the valley of the Enns, in which the river was seen for miles, glistening in the sun like a silver thread, the Ritterstein peak, and range upon range of the Styrian Alps; and to the westward, in the foreground, was the Hohe-krutze; whilst, stretched out in the distance, were the Tannen Gibirge, the peak of the Ewiger Sehnee, the Steinernes-meer, and the treble-headed Watzmann, which towers over the Königsee in the Berchtesgaden. There is an intense fascination in such scenery, where all is still, and the mysterious silence that reigns is never broken, save by the war of elements or the rumbling of avalanches.

From the elevated position we had attained, a very extensive horizon presented itself; and we sat admiring the sublime scenery for more than an hour, my companions indulging in a pipe, whilst I swept the country with my field-glass, in the hope of discovering chamois. It was, however, too late in the day, and none were to be seen. So shouldering our rifles and baggage, we made the best of our way down a rather steep ridge, and after about four hours' smart walking, arrived at a verdant-looking valley formed by a hollow in the side of the mountain, where we found a log-hut occupied by a couple of herdsmen, to whom Karl was well known. Our hosts evidently did not expect company, and their domicile at first sight did not present a very inviting appearance; but, like good-natured fellows, they at once set to work to clear up the place, and make us comfortable. A heap of new hay was laid down for us in one corner, on which our rugs were spread, a cheerful fire blazed on a clean-swept hearth, the cooking-pots were cleaned, a *Schmarren* made, and I set to work upon the *pièce de résistance* of the repast, a huge "*Pilau,*" after an idea of my own, of which, as it was considered a *chef d'œuvre* of culinary talent, I give the recipe. When the rice has been well washed, throw it in a large pot full of boiling water. After fifteen minutes' hard boiling it will be nearly cooked. When it is so, take it off the fire, and pour in a large cup of cold water, which suddenly stops the boiling, and has the effect of causing each grain of rice to separate from the others; then strain it well; and, whilst the water is running off, melt a large lump of fresh butter in another pan, to which mix a small tin of *pâte de foie gras*. When the rice is well strained, put it again on the fire, add the butter and *pâté*, stir it up well, and allow it to steam for a couple of minutes, shaking the pan every now and then to keep the contents from burning, and you will have a famous dish with very little trouble. When you have any fowls or game, put butter only with the rice, and you can then save the *pâté*.

After supper, to which we all sat down and did ample justice, a brew of grog was made, pipes were lighted, and a solemn consultation was held as to our prospects of sport. By the advice of the herdsmen we resolved to try the Schneewandkogl mountain in the morning, as a fine herd of chamois had been seen two days before. This being decided, citherns were taken down, and songs were the order of the night, our hosts, notwithstanding their somewhat rough appearance, being accomplished musicians, and, joined by our boys, they sang some plaintive mountain melodies with great taste. By particular desire, Herbert and I struck up some of those spirit-stirring Confederate songs that used to ring on the night-air by the James River, on whose banks many of the light-hearted singers now sleep in a nameless grave. Being somewhat tired with our day's work, about eight o'clock we turned in, previous to which I opened the hut door to have a look at the night. The little I could see of the horizon was clear, the stars shone brightly in the firmament, and there was every prospect of fine weather on the morrow. We were stirring long before daybreak in the morning, and having an early breakfast (for it is unadvisable to commence hard work on an empty stomach), we set out under the guidance of Franz, one of the herdsmen. The stars were still brightly shining, but the darkness was waning, and a

peculiar reddish effulgence on the eastern horizon announced
the approach of day.

When we arrived at the foot of the mountain, Karl and I
crept up one side, whilst Herbert, accompanied by Franz and
Hans, took the other, so as to command both sides of a ravine
the head of which was considered almost a certain find for
chamois at this time of the year. As the day advanced the
mist and vapour vanished, and the outlines of every peak were
seen in bold relief against the sky. As the foreground grew
more distinct, whilst looking below amongst the latchen, I saw
three chamois leisurely browsing on the young branches, quite
unconscious of our presence. Although far out of shot, there
was every prospect of my being able to get within range, for the
latchen afforded excellent cover, and what little air there was
stirring blew up the ravine. Desiring Karl to remain motionless and watch their movements, I disencumbered myself of my
Rück-sack, and with noiseless steps crept towards them, hardly
raising my head lest I should attract their attention. This was
not easy work, for it is difficult approaching game in such
situations. After some very careful stalking I got within three
hundred yards' range, and, peering through a clump of latchen,
saw that they had all stopped feeding, and were gazing inquir-
ingly in my direction, which long experience told me was a
certain sign that suspicion was aroused. I lay motionless and
watched their proceedings, for under the circumstances I knew
it was impossible to get nearer. At last I distinguished a buck,
from his horns being thicker and his coat somewhat darker
than the others; and, arranging my sight, I brought the fine
bead of the fore-sight against his shoulder, as he was staring at
the very bush behind which I lay, as if he knew from the taint
in the air that danger lurked there. I pulled trigger, and with
a bound in the air he fell down dead. With a shrill whistle
the rest bounded away, but, without showing myself, I slipped

ONE DOWN.

another cartridge into my rifle, and by a lucky shot, rolled over a doe with a bullet through the neck, as from sheer curiosity she stopped a second as if inquisitive to know what intruder had disturbed their mountain solitudes. Karl was thunderstruck at the performance of my rifle, for he had never seen game killed at such distances, and he had no idea of the range of a Whitworth small bore and the quickness of loading of a Westley-Richards breechloader. Having noted well where both chamois fell, I reloaded, and found the buck lying dead, but the doe had moved away, although I knew that she was hard hit, from the numerous patches of blood, and the slots showing that the toes of the fore-feet were very widely spread, as if she was weak and giddy, and had difficulty to keep on her feet. Following up these signs, I soon saw her staggering slowly along, very sick indeed, and a second bullet entering just behind the shoulder, put her out of her misery.

Having gralloched and cleaned the chamois, the buck of which weighed about fifty pounds, we put them in our Rücksacks, and clambered along the crest of the hill, where we expected to meet Herbert and the rest of our people; but although we waited for some time, and swept the country round with our glasses, we could not get sight of any of them, so we began to descend the mountain, skirting the crest of the ravine, and expecting every moment to meet them. Whilst thus engaged, Karl caught sight of a solitary buck chamois browsing on some herbs between two ridges of rock just below the crest on which we were standing. To slip off my Rück-sack and lay down full length, with my head craning over the brink of the scarp, was the work of a few seconds. He was within range, but it was a long shot, so I took off my felt wideawake, and placing it on a boulder of rock, rested my rifle upon it, and, taking a steady aim, fired. "It was too far," exclaimed Karl; "but no; see, he staggers!"

and his face lighted up—for we could see, from his slow,
unsteady movements, the buck was badly hit. I felt sure my
shot had told, for I was as steady as possible, and I knew
from long experience that my rifle was one of the best that
was ever turned out by my friend " the worthy Bishop."
We had to go along the ridge some distance before we could
descend, and then it was ticklish work clambering down the
face of the scarp with my long heavy rifle. However, at
last we managed it, and had just reached the bottom when
a sharp whistle was heard, and three doe chamois went
bounding up the side of the mountain. My rifle was slung
on my shoulder at the time, and they were far out of range
before I was ready to fire, so we went on towards the spot
where the chamois was standing when I fired. There we
found loose hair, and the aromatic herbage on which he was
feeding was in places wet with deep crimson blood. The
bullet, after passing through him, had flattened on a large
stone, for the splash of the lead was very plain. We followed
up the trail for a few hundred yards, and found him dead,
with his fore-quarters half hidden in a clump of latchen,
where he had fallen whilst making a last effort to escape.
He was not so large as the first I had killed, but had fine
horns, and I felt very pleased with my success. Karl having
cleaned him, slung the body over his shoulders, and we made
the best of our way up to where we had left our Rücksacks. Slinging the venison on to our alpenstocks, we turned
our steps homeward, much surprised at not meeting Herbert
or any of his party. When we arrived at the hut, late in the
afternoon, I found that my friend, in the dark, had sprained
his ankle so severely that he was not able to put his foot to
the ground, and it was with great difficulty that Franz and
Hans managed to get him home. I was very sorry for this
untoward accident, as it did away with all chance of his

killing a chamois, on which he had set his mind.   However, he was not one to be downhearted, and he made up his mind to remain and make himself as comfortable as he could in the hut until he was able to get about.   As his ankle was much swollen and inflamed, I prescribed cold-water bandages without and hot grog within, which gave him considerable relief, and enabled him to sleep during the night.

Dinner over, Karl related our exploits and the extraordinary powers of my rifle, and after some improvised songs we turned in, *happy as chamois-hunters after a good day's work.*

BLACKCOCK.

In the next three days I killed five more chamois, and we then proceeded to the Königsee in the Berchtesgaden, where we had a capital day's sport, and, by good luck, I managed to kill three fine bucks. Unfortunately I was then obliged to return to England, and could not accept many invitations I received to different shooting parties; but I have since heard that as many as thirty chamois were killed by Count Harrach and his friends in a single day.

CHAMOIS STALKING IN THE BAVARIAN ALPS.

The London season was on the wane, and the time at hand when every weary toiler whose duty or greed did not tie him to the shop, the house of St. Stephen, a public office, the Stock Exchange, or barrack square, is contemplating a move either to the country or to the continent, as a change from his ordinary occupation, when the old momentous question once more arises, *Where shall I go?* The hour of freedom is at hand; which way shall I wend my steps? The man who has not a yacht, or a salmon river, an amicable country cousin to cultivate, a wife to consult, or a troop of daughters to get off, naturally meanders in thought over the sea, and considers what unvisited continental capital promises most fun at this season of the year. Perhaps visions of Baden and Homburg flit across his mind as he muses on the past, but they are no more, and he must seek " fresh fields and pastures new."—I was just in this predicament, but to add to my perplexity, an old wound was rankling and threatening trouble, so I did not feel up to much exertion, whilst my physician had not simplified matters by the impracticable advice he gave me for my guinea, " Take your meals at regular hours, go to bed at eleven, and only drink a pint of *sound sherry* to your dinner." In my calling of life it was simply impossible to attempt to follow up this *régime;* for supposing the first two articles in the instructions could be carried out, where—bar miracles—is the sound sherry to come from? Committing the doctor's advice to the winds, I resolved to prescribe for myself the same treatment that the wide-awake farmer gives his land, viz., " rest for a change." I believe that allowing the mind to lie fallow for a season is the best way to get good crops of work out of it. I hold that a good spell of the *dolce far niente* acts like strengthening medicine upon the faculties, and that there is nothing like a long fit of downright unadulterated laziness—call it relaxation if you like—for re-cruiting the mental *physique* and brightening up the ideas. To carry out my prescription properly, the patient must not only be able to abstain from work cheerfully, but also acquire a certain degree of perfection in the art of doing nothing—as no man can thoroughly enjoy a holiday if he has plenty of them : so the real benefit as well as the keen pleasure of a spell of supreme laziness is reserved only for the busy and laborious, who snatches repose as a respite from work. Then a month's saunter amongst strange scenes, men, and manners, with a friend who can be grave and gay at the right times, leaves a green and pleasant oasis to rest the mind's eye upon whilst memory lasts. In a pleasure trip, a good cheery comrade is the great element of happiness, but beware of a fellow who has "no go " in him, who makes mountains out of mole-hills, and who cuts up rough at what cannot be avoided—*Mais revenons a nos moutons.* I was cogitating upon my proposed but yet undefined cruise, when I bethought me of my old friend Elliot, a kindred spirit lately returned from India, who, after wander-ing about the German baths in search of health, was now located at Salzburg, and had lately written me to join him in a trip after chamois, amongst the Bavarian Alps. The wire soon informed me of his whereabouts, and I arranged to meet him on the fifth day at Hotel Nelboeck in Salzburg.

The next morning I started for Cologne by steamer from London Bridge, my sole *impedimenta* being a couple of mule trunks, long enough to contain the barrels of my gun and rifle, and, after a pleasant trip up the Rhine to Mayence, took train the remainder of the distance, arriving at Salzburg in good time for dinner—Elliot and our good host, to whom I had written, were on the look out for me, and the former had obtained permission for us to have three days' shooting in the Royal preserve, from some influential friend at Munich, and the Ober-jäger-meister had been asked to give any assistance we might require.

Starting from Salzburg in a calèche with a pair of horses, a very pleasant drive of about fifteen miles brought us to Berchtesgaden, the scenery in the route being very beautiful, as the road winds round the base of the Untersberg mountain, and then passes through the narrow defile of "the over-hanging rock." After leaving the village of Schellenberg, the valley opens out, and the snow-clad double-headed Watzman mountain rises in all its sublime majesty above the village of Berchtesgaden. The König-See, or King's Lake, is about three miles further on, past the village, and here the scenery is grand beyond description, the pine-clad mountains rising perpendicularly from the water, upon which they cast a peculiarly weird-like shadow.

We spent the greater part of the day in sight-seeing, visiting the jagt-schloss, or hunting-box of the King of Bavaria, and the glacier of the ice chapel, and we had hardly got in the Post gast-haus, at Berchtesgaden, when rain set in which continued until noon the next day, without intermission. This was rather a damper to our spirits, as it would not do to go up the mountain in wet or cloudy weather, but I took advantage of this delay in our expedition, to send to a châlet on the Tannen Gibirge for my old guide Carl, and his cousins, Hans and Heinrich, who had been my companions on a former occasion. Carl and Hans made their appearance the next day, delighted at the prospect of another trip—Heinrich was away—Carl, who had grown into a fine specimen of a Tyrolese mountaineer, introduced his wife, who was no other than the buxom Kellnerinn of the Grunerbaum in Hallstadt, which was my headquarters on a previous occasion, and a better looking couple was scarcely to be found in the Salzkammergat; I need not say how glad I was to see my trusty henchman again by my side, for I had proved his mettle on several occasions, and knew him to be thoroughly trustworthy.

The third morning after our arrival at Berchtesgaden, the weather promising to be propitious, we made a start under the guidance of one of the assistant jägers of the Royal Ober-jägermeister or Head Forester, and, accompanied by four stout mountaineers to carry our stock of provisions, &c., made our way to the Senn Hutten or châlet, where the herdsmen remain during the summer months to avail themselves of the mountain pasturage. Here a small, but comfortable, hut was placed at our disposition, and the occupants of the châlet, the Sennerinnen—a fair sprinkling of good-looking dairymaids brought us any quantity of milk and butter. The evenings are cold at the altitude we had attained, and a blazing fire looked comfortable. To add to our enjoyment the other occupants of the Alm joined our party; a brew of punch was concocted, and as night drew on, the old hut rang again with Schnadahüpfl songs and Jodeln accompanied by the cithern. A dance followed, and long before we separated for the night, good fellowship was established between our party and the other occupants of the *Alm hutten.* Two hours before daylight we were afoot and making preparations for a start, after having done ample justice to a substantial breakfast; and an hour after our departure we were slowly progressing up a romantic and wild-looking gorge, with lofty overhanging cliffs on either hand, and as the day broke we found ourselves at the head of the ravine, where a wall-like mountain ridge, apparently as straight as a house side, seemed to offer an insuperable obstacle to our further progress. On a nearer approach, however, we found—under the jäger's guidance—a point where there was an indentation in the mountain side, and up this we clambered in Indian file, our alpenstocks constantly coming into play. The toil to us was very severe, but the mountaineers strode up without showing the slightest fatigue, although they were laden with heavy ruck-sacken, and we had only our rifles to carry.

After stopping several times to gather breath, we gained the summit of the ridge, where we were told the chamois often frequented. Alas! all appeared blank. Most anxiously and carefully we examined the numerous gorges and corries that opened to our view, and swept the horizon with our field-glasses and telescopes. Not a sign of a chamois was to be seen. This was somewhat disheartening after our exertions, but nothing was to be done to mend matters, so we crept silently along the ridge, halting from time to time and peering into the somewhat misty-looking chasm below. Just as we attained an isolated crag that rose from the steep side of the mountain, the rattle of a stone atttracted the quick ear of Carl, who motioned us to stoop low so as to conceal ourselves as much as possible. Again a slight sound was heard, and in the twinkling of an eye a herd of some twenty chamois, led by a fine old buck, passed in review order before us, at a distance of about 120 yards. As the foreground was very steep, only their heads, necks, and the upper part of their bodies were visible above the latchen, but they were near enough in all conscience, and I was about to aim at the leader when the jäger motioned me not to fire. Although the wind was blowing towards us, they had evidently caught the taint in the air denoting the presence of man, for I heard the sharp whistle of alarm pass more than once from front to rear, and they trotted slowly and hesitatingly along with every sense upon the stretch, for although evidently aware

FLOCK OF CHAMOIS.

of our intrusion upon their domains, they were yet unconscious of the whereabouts of their enemy.

Catching Elliot's eye and seeing that he was ready, I threw up my rifle and brought down the leading buck with a shot just under the ear, and as the herd were rushing backwards and forwards in consternation, I hit a second fairly grown buck in the small of the back. Elliot had dropped a fine buck, and had severely wounded a doe, which was rolling over and over down the mountain, evidently unable to stop itself, until it disappeared in a cleft in the rock. The guides started in pursuit, and soon descried the chamois lying dead in a crevice, from whence, with the aid of a rope, it was very speedily recovered. Elliot now lighted his pipe with great gusto, for the deprivation of the soothing weed was to him the one great drawback to supreme happiness when out stalking. Carl and the jäger gralloched the game, and fastening the legs together by the back sinews, prepared them for slinging. We then drank the *deoch fala*, or death drink, and lightened our packages considerably by demolishing a prodigious amount of luncheon. The day was now well advanced, so, shouldering our rifles, Carl and Hans, each carrying a couple of chamois, led the way, and we retraced our steps down the steep hill-side, which from the top as much resembled a precipice as it did the side of a wall from the bottom.

No description that I can give will portray the surrounding scenery so well as the mighty Minstrel of the North, who says:

> " I've traversed many a mountain strand
> Abroad and in my native land,
> And it has been my lot to tread
> Where safety more than pleasure led.
> Thus many a waste I've wandered o'er,
> Clombe many a crag, crossed many a moor;
> But by my halidome!
> A scene so rude, so wild as this,
> Yet so sublime in barreness,
> Ne'er did my wandering footsteps press,
> Where'er I happ'd to roam."

As we went along, we had ample opportunity of admiring the strength and activity of our mountaineers, who, with a brace of chamois each, and heavy "ruck-sacken," managed to keep ahead of us the whole way down, although we had only our alpenstocks and rifles to carry. We received a hearty greeting at the châlet from the sennerinnen and shepherds, and after a hot supper and a glass or two of grog had put us in good order, we got up another concert and dance, the extempory verses of which bore reference to our skill as marksmen. During the dance the dancer, who leads off the figure accompanied by the cithern, sings a couplet or two and then returns to his or her

GREYHENS.

place, and one after another take up the song. The rest keep time during the dance by a castanet-like snapping of their fingers, every now and then bursting into a peculiarly wild cry. These gatherings serve to promote good fellowship, and he who cannot sing his "Schnadahüpfl" in reply, is heartily laughed at by the rest. During the night heavy rain fell, and it continued the greater part of the next day. The mountain was also so hidden in cloud and vapour, as to leave no hope of the weather clearing up, so we returned to our old quarters at Berchtesgaden the following morning.

IBEX STALKING ON THE ITALIAN ALPS.

He only who has lived amongst the mountains, and participated in the perilous excitement of ibex and chamois stalking, can form a notion of the feelings of delight that the old hunter experiences when a sudden turn in the road reveals to him the glistening peaks of a snow-clad range towering high against the deep blue sky. The heart thrills with exultation at the idea of being once more amongst such scenes with his trusty rifle on his back, creeping up steep lichen-covered ravines, or stepping along narrow ledges of rock, where the sweet-scented, delicate edelweis grows. He recalls to mind the happy days spent on the Alm among the mountaineers, the red-letter days of glorious sport, the pleasant returnings from the chase, the *jödler* of the shepherds, the dances with the buxom *sennerinnen,* and pictures to himself the hearty greetings with which he will be welcomed by his old associates. It was with these pleasurable sensations that, in company with my good friend Carlo Martini, I left the village of Cogne, escorted by a corporal of the king's *gardes-chasse,* who had received an order from Le Chef du Cabinet Particulier de S. M., giving me permission to shoot in the Royal preserves. The districts of Cogne, Campiglia, Val, Savaranche, and Ceresole comprise the king's hunting-grounds; and here the game is strictly preserved, sign-posts being set up in different places, with the inscription, "*Défense de chasse,*"

whilst in every valley keepers and *gardes-chasse* are stationed
to prevent poaching. This district is well-stocked with chamois ;
but its chief attraction in the eyes of a sportsman is that it is
now the only spot in Europe where the steinbock, or bouquetin
(*Capra ibex*), is still to be met with. Being ambitious to shoot
a European ibex, I made up my mind not to fire at any other
game, so as not to lose a chance; and having promised the
gardes-chasse a considerable *douceur* in case of my getting a
shot, they became as anxious to insure success as I was myself.
According to the report of one of their number, three *boucs* had
been seen very lately on the glacier De Tragio, above the
Châtelet du Poucet, on the eastern slope of the Grivola ; so,
after a solemn consultation, it was determined to make the
châlet our temporary head-quarters, and we were now *en route*
for this destination, three mules carrying a goodly supply of
comestibles and bodily comforts, as well as rugs and waterproofs.
The corporal, before leaving Cogne, sent to gather information
from one of his mates stationed at Carasole—a village in the
valley d'Ozca, south of the Grand Paradis—but his messenger
had not returned when we started.

We found the châlet excellent mountain quarters ; and our
appetites were gratified with the luxury of an unlimited quantity
of rich milk and cream, and bowls full of delicious *brousse*. As
we did not leave Cogne until close upon noon, it was too late to
think of doing anything more than a cursory survey of the hill-
side with our telescopes until two of the herdsmen came in;
when, to our great gratification, the favourable report con-
cerning the ibex was confirmed by both ; and one of them
offered to' guide us to a spot which, he said, was a sure find
early in the morning, as he had constantly seen their fresh
tracks on the soft snow, showing that they had passed soon
after sunrise. Highly gratified with this encouraging news,
after a plentiful supper and a glass of hot grog all round, a

quantity of new sweet hay was spread, and, rolling ourselves in our rugs, we slept most comfortably.

At **3** a.m. the corporal and his party, who had passed the night in a kind of loft at the back of the chalet, awoke us, and we found some delicious *café au crême* and a huge *schmarrn*, or·omelette, ready, and, after we had done ample justice to the good cheer, we set off for the glacier. The air, at this early hour, was somewhat chilly; but the exercise of walking at a good pace kept us warm, and I was delighted to find the weather as clear as could be desired, for the sky was cloudless and the stars shone brightly. But dawn was rapidly approaching,· and already the glistening mountain peaks stood out in bold relief against the bluish-grey background. After about an hour's steady walking up a somewhat steep ascent, through patches of flowering saxifrage and boulders of rock covered with soft green mosses, we entered the upper snow regions, where vegetation disappears. Still we travelled on, and after a stiffish burst, which tried our climbing powers very severely, we gained the crest of a high ridge which formed one of the lateral sides of the glacier. Here, in three or four places, the clefts in the side of the mountain were filled with deep snow, which does not melt even at midsummer, and where the ice forms small glaciers. At the foot of these diminutive glaciers, where there is often a low terminal moraine, flow small mountain streams, caused by the melting of the ice, on each side of which are strips of luxuriant herbage, the only signs of vegetation at that altitude. These are the favourite feeding-grounds both of ibex and chamois, and, according to our guide's account, one or other of them was a certain find for *boucs* in the early morning.

One of these snow gullies lay just below us, and a troop of seven chamois were quietly browsing close to the edge of the glacier; the other two feeding-grounds were considerably

higher up the ridge. Having carefully reconnoitred the
ground with my telescope, and made sure that no ibex were
lurking near, I proposed to make a move to the higher altitudes, but my companion, Carlo, was dead beat, and decided to
remain where he was and have a smoke until I returned; so
the corporal, one of the herdsmen who served us as guide, and
myself, commenced clambering along the steep ridge, keeping
just below the crest, so that we could not be seen from the
glacier side of the slope. After about an hour's scramble over
boulders of rock and beds of hard, frozen snow, we came to a
huge level slab under an overhanging cliff, and here our guide
bade us wait whilst he divested himself of his ruck-sack and
shoes and crept on all fours to the brink of the scarp over-
looking the glacier. He had hardly taken a momentary glance
than he began to wriggle back, and I could tell by his action,
as well as from the sudden lighting up of his face, that the
game I sought for was in sight. When he joined us, he said
he could see three ibex, one of which had fair horns, but they
were far out of shot, and were making their way towards the
head of the glacier at a good round pace, so that it was useless
for us to attempt to get near them. This was somewhat provoking after all our trouble, but it could not be helped; we
had got to the ground too late in the day, and the game was off
to a higher altitude. Slipping off my boots, I fastened a rope
round my waist, threw the other end to the corporal, who made
it fast to his belt, and crawled to the brink of the precipice,
which was somewhat ticklish work, as it sloped downwards and
was covered with short, slippery moss, that afforded very insecure foothold. From this point I had, at any rate, the satisfaction of seeing the game I had come so far in search of; for at
about six hundred yards distance a good-sized buck and two
doe ibex were trotting leisurely up the steep side of the mountain with as much ease as if it was a macadamised road, and I

THE BOUQUETIN, OR IBEX OF THE ALPS.

watched them through my telescope get over a terribly rough
bit of ground in five minutes that would have taken me an
hour at least.

Having watched the game until it disappeared behind a
distant ridge, we took a pull of *eau-de-vie*, and made the best
of our way back to the place where we had left the rest of our
party; but they had decamped for the lower regions, and it
was not until we approached the Alm that we caught them up.
They had seen two troops of chamois, but no ibex, and had not
fired a shot. Although we had come back empty-handed, we
passed a very jovial evening, and the corporal related some of ·
his adventures with poachers, several of whom he had shot
down at various times. In some parts of the Alps constant
mountain warfare was maintained between poachers and the
gardes-chasse, and in these encounters many a stalwart forester
has "gone under," and many a bold mountaineer has found a
nameless grave amongst the *latschen*.

The evening was very sultry, and just before we turned in I
noticed the mercury in the barometer had fallen considerably,
whilst the thermometer indicated a degree of heat that seemed
extraordinary when the altitude of our domicile was taken into
consideration, so I felt sure that a storm was brewing; and
later on in the night I was not surprised to hear loud claps of
thunder, and to see a dark mass of gathering clouds rolling
onwards until they obscured the highest peaks, where they
soon commingled in conflict, as the almost blinding flashes of
forked lightning darting from beneath them plainly indicated.
In the mountains the pulse of nature becomes tempestuous only
a very short time before the storm breaks, and often but little
warning is given. On the brightest days mists will suddenly
rise in muffled shapes, like sad ghosts, wrapping the whole
range in their cloud-like folds; and should the hunter be thus
overtaken in the pathless mountains, if the fog lasts he may

GOLDEN EAGLE.

look upon it as his shroud, since in such cases, lone and cut off
from human aid, nothing is to be done but to·lie down and
wait until the vapours lift, and the chances are that in the
meantime he will be frozen or starved to death.   This is,
perhaps, the greatest danger in chamois hunting, although a·
steady·hand and foot, with a perfect absence of " nerves," are
also absolutely necessary.   He has often, in the pursuit of his·
calling, to scramble along narrow ledges of rock or ridges overhanging precipices, when, if he were to allow the peril to cloud
the brain, he would be lost to a certainty.   Luckily, mountain
training not only begets strength in every limb, but it also
endues the mind with self-reliance, and when difficulties
present themselves the whole frame thrills with exhilarating
excitement that, despising danger, enables the hunter to
surmount·obstacles which to the uninitiated appear impossible.
The herdsman who served as our guide was a splendid
specimen of an Alpine mountaineer, and, although he carried
a heavy ruck-sack, he always kept ahead, and continually put
both the *gardes-chasse* and myself to shame by his daring
agility and endurance.   He skipped up˙ steeps we toiled
heavily over, and took in his stride chasms and crevasses that
we hesitated about crossing at all; yet, having had a good deal of
practice in the Himalaya and the Tyrol, up to this time I had
imagined myself to˙be a pretty fair mountaineer, until I found
my powers so vastly exceeded by this simple peasant, who
evidently got over the ground with very little fatigue or
trouble, whereas the corporal was quite done up, and I myself
felt that I had had quite enough for one day.

As rain fell heavily during the night, and storm-clouds still
threatened when we got up in the morning, it was considered
advisable to defer our intended expedition after the ibex until
the weather became more settled ; .so we remained in and about
the *Alm-hütte* all day, amusing ourselves as we best could, by

playing *écarté*, shooting at a mark, or talking to the *sennerin-nen*, when they could find a few minutes to spare from their multifarious duties. The "living roses of the Alps," as some enthusiastic tourists call these hard-working dairymaids, are seldom endowed with much personal comeliness; for the *beauté du diable* of youth soon becomes obliterated by constant exposure to all the vicissitudes of climate, and at an early age they have a premature weather-worn appearance, which, added to their *noli me tangere* costume, that resembles that of a man from the waist downwards, does not enhance their feminine attractions, and whilst in their company one is apt to forget their sex. They are, however, as a rule, cheerful, good-natured lasses, full of irrepressible spirits, fond of a joke, and hospitable to a fault; for I have often known them to put themselves to a good deal of inconvenience in order to make their guests comfortable. The mountaineers themselves are a powerful and handsome race, not particularly learned, and somewhat superstitious, but with head and heart in the right place. They have no illnesses worth mentioning, and rarely require a doctor, except in cases of accident; but it is, nevertheless, true that the same district that can boast of some of the finest specimens of the human race, as regards muscular development, also produces a great number of *crétins*, or idiots, and poor creatures affected with incurable *goître*. I can attribūte no cause for this state of things in such a healthy region, unless it is that these people drink "snow water" that may be more or less impregnated with injurious earthy deposits deleterious to the constitution, or that the disease is generated by "in-and-in" marriages between blood-relations, which is very prevalent in valleys more or less isolated from the rest of the world. In some of these valleys, it is said, that one in seven has some distortion or swelling in the throat, whilst one intellect in fifty is more or less deranged. This is a sad proportion; but, from the number of unfortunates I have fallen in with in these parts, I cannot think it overrated.

Towards evening, the clouds cleared away, and when the sun set there was every indication of favourable weather for the morrow's expedition. My friend Carlo had no ambition to make a second expedition, and the corporal had received a message that obliged him to return to headquarters; so Giuseppe the herdsman, and I, started alone as soon as the moon began to rise, which was about 2 A.M., and we got over the ground much quicker than we had done on the previous occasion, so that we arrived at the first feeding-place before the day had broken. I could easily have got within fair shot of a troop of quite twenty chamois, who, even at that early hour, were afoot and feeding ; but I had come so far expressly to kill an ibex, and did not care to pull trigger at any other game until my object was accomplished. My companion looked at the troop with a wistful and somewhat imploring visage, and his mouth evidently watered at the idea of a roast haunch, for he whispered beneath his breath, "Should I not like to have the picking of the ribs of that fat doe that is so very near us and offers such an easy shot !" But I was above temptation, and bid him lead the way to the higher feeding-grounds. On arrival there, my self-denial was amply rewarded, for the buck ibex we had previously seen, and three or four does, accompanied with their young ones, were quietly browsing beneath us like tame goats. They were perhaps two hundred feet below us, and the buck seemed to be about a hundred and twenty yards from the base of the scarp. Although the distance was not great, the ledge of rock on which we were standing was so sloping, and offered such insecure footing, that it was an awkward matter to get the muzzle of my long-barrelled rifle to bear in his direction. As soon as I got into firing position and felt steady, I gave a low whistle not much louder than a mar-

mot would emit, but it produced the effect I anticipated; for
the buck raised his head, and stood motionless with the exception of his ears, which moved forward as if to drink in the

"THE BUCK RAISED HIS HEAD."

sound, and bringing the fine bead of the rifle to bear against
his fully-exposed shoulder, I pulled the trigger, and the moment
the smoke cleared away, to my intense gratification, I saw him

floundering on his back, with his four legs pawing the air. Fearing, however, lest it should escape or roll into some inaccessible crevasse, I fired a second shot, aiming at his chest, when he rolled over and lay perfectly still. If I had had a breech-loading rifle I might have had a fair chance of killing a doe, as the others, panic-stricken at seeing their leader fall, were some time before they made themselves scarce. I was, however, quite contented, having killed a bouquetin, one of the rarest animals in Europe.

Although my quarry was dead, I doubt very much if I should ever have obtained his horns and skin if it had not been for my stalwart guide Giuseppe, who knowing the ground, soon found a practicable path by which we could descend to the almost inaccessible place where he lay. As it was, we had to use the axe very frequently to cut steps in the steeper slopes and to knock away the icicles formed by the drippings from the snow above. At last, however, we accomplished the descent, and making a circuit under the cliff-like rocks amongst the *débris* that had fallen from above, we reached the spot where the ibex lay, and took the spoils, consisting of the skin head, and horns, leaving the flesh, as it was too rank for food.

Having washed our hands in an ice-cold snow-stream, we lightened the ruck-sack by "lining the inner man" with the greatest portion of its contents; and when our meal was over, Guiseppe, making a compact bundle of the ibex spoils, slung it to the end of his alpen-stock, so that he could carry it over his shoulder. This arrangement completed, we started on our return journey, reaching the Alm-hut at about three in the afternoon, where we received the congratulations our success had earned.

The next day was devoted to chamois shooting, and my friend Carlo was lucky enough to get a brace of young bucks, whilst I had to content myself with a tough old ptarmigan that was stupid enough to stand still after I had missed him once,

and gave me a second chance, when I nearly cut off his head
with a rifle ball. We made an unsuccessful attempt the next
day to stalk a troop of chamois on the eastern slope of the
Grivola, and were returning home, somewhat mortified with
our ill-luck—for we had three times come across our game
without being able to get a shot—when, as we were passing
along a lichen-covered slope under the shady side of a precipitous rock, I heard the peculiar shrill whistle of a chamois,
and I was just in time to knock over a fine buck, with a shot
through the neck, that sprang up from a hollow about fifty
yards in front of us. I fancy he must have been asleep until
our talking alarmed him. He proved to be an old buck, with
thick, wide-spreading horns, which subsequently I considered
good enough to have mounted as a pair of carvers, as a
souvenir de chasse for my esteemed friend, Mr. Baily.
This was our last day's sport in this district, for the weather
again became unfavourable; so we made the best of our way to
Cogne, and from thence by the valley of Aousta to Turin.

GREY PTARMIGAN AND YOUNG.

CHAPTER III.

WILD-FOWL SHOOTING.

TOWARDS the end of October and in the beginning of November, when the cold weather generally sets in, all birds of passage, including wild fowl of different kinds, woodcock, snipe, and plover, begin to arrive and distribute themselves throughout our island and over the continent. All appear to come from the same direction, travelling against the wind, large flights rarely arriving unless the breeze is sharp and bracing. Wild fowl on their first arrival evince much shyness in settling themselves in the tideways and estuaries round the coast, and the first comers may be often seen reconnoitring and making short excursions over the land, flying very high in companies of twenty or thirty together in a double line, like an arrowhead, before they select any particular district for their winter quarters.

Wild-fowl shooting may be said to commence in the month of November, although frequently large flights of widgeon and other species of wild duck arrive in this country much earlier. In some parts of Scotland wild geese have made their appearance before the oats have been taken in, and at such times have committed considerable havoc amongst the grain, but this is a somewhat rare occurrence.

No wild bird is more wary or cunning than wild fowl that have been frequently disturbed, and I have known a flock of wild duck to remain on a sheet of water a whole winter, notwithstanding they were constantly harassed and shot at.

Whenever a gunner came in view, they would assemble out of range, in the middle of the reservoir, or if they were approached in boats, they would rise out of shot, and, flying high, absent themselves until the coast was clear.

He must be an enthusiastic sportsman indeed who systematically pursues wild-fowl shooting at night as a diversion, as there is no sport so uncertain, or more calculated to try his endurance, his patience, and his constitution. In grouse or partridge shooting the sportsman is, at least, dry, and has the amusement of seeing his dogs work. In covert shooting he is cheered by the joyous cry of his spaniels, and in snipe-shooting, although he pursues his sport in cold weather, he can, at any rate, keep himself warm by exercise, whilst the chance of a snap-shot always keeps him on the alert. Not so, however, the wild-fowl shooter's lot. His pursuit is not only carried on at the coldest part of the year, but also during those hours when others are enjoying the comfort of a blazing fire or nestling snugly in their beds. No cheerful conversation of companions enlivens his dull dreary waiting hours, no merry cry of his dogs excites his interest by their instructive sagacity. With him all must be stillness; even his dog couches silently by his side, as he stands, sits, nay, sometimes lies on the frozen ground, listening for the coming flight that in the darker hours are somewhat less wary than in the daylight. Even supposing the fowl to have arrived and alighted, they may have settled down far out of range, and the wild-fowler then has but the choice of two proceedings: to wait freezing in the hope of their approaching within shot, or to wade perhaps thigh-deep in ice-cold water until he can get near them; but this must be done with no little caution—any unusual noise in the water, even the splashing made by his dog if he is not perfectly steady and under command, may cause his ears to be saluted with the " Quack, quack," of alarm, and he has the mortification of

THE ALARM SIGNAL.

seeing the whole flock moving off to some distant part, or hearing the flutter of their wings as they take themselves off to a more secure locality. Thus his hopes as regard that flight are over, and he has only to chew the cud of disappointment and wait in silence for the chance arrival of another. At times small flights will arrive and depart in quick succession, and the fowler may, perhaps, kill a duck or two from each if he has luck; again he may keep a watchful vigil the night through, and return home without having seen or heard a pinion.

The fowler must be as hard as nails, with a constitution that can defy the bleak cutting wintry winds, the soaking rain, and driving sleet; he must be prepared to remain for hours shaking and shivering in his punt, or perhaps, worse still, immersed up to his knees in water, and bent double in a bed of rushes. Supposing the sportsman to have a commodious hut constructed to wait in, and properly trained decoy birds, or a large punt and plenty of rugs, wild-fowl shooting by night may be indulged in with a certain degree of comfort, but even then it is always a very uncertain and precarious sport, that tries both the patience and the constitution; and, in my opinion, even under the most favourable circumstances "le jeu ne vaut pas la chandelle," if any other kind of game is to be got. Duck-shooting from huts is very extensively resorted to on the French coast, but few, if any, *chasseurs* pursue this sport as an amusement; it is purely an affair of business, and hundreds of the poorer classes of peasants obtain their livelihood by it during the winter months. It involves scarcely any outlay beyond ammunition, a gun, a pair of *marais* boots, and requires but little skill in shooting, all the shots being sitting ones, and at short ranges. The huts, which are generally built in the summer season, are warm, dry, and comfortable, being sufficiently large to contain two persons and a dog. The usual places selected are small reedy islands, or promontories commanding a view over a large extent of water, which are known to be exactly in the line of flight of the wild fowl; and this is easily ascertained by the practical fowler, as it is a curious fact that year after year birds come and go in precisely the same direction as if the road was marked out in the heavens for them to pursue. They have also certain lines of flight at night and morning to and from their feeding grounds, and good sport may often be obtained by observing the direction they take, and awaiting their flying over at certain marked spots.

The French *huttiers* generally go to their huts half an hour before dark, and remain in them all night. They seldom kill any other wild fowl than the common wild duck and teal, as widgeon will not drop to the call of the decoy-ducks. From three to five decoy ducks are generally used, and these are tied by the leg, in the water, to stakes driven in for the purpose. The birds used as decoys, although tame and domesticated, are of the wild breed, the eggs being taken from the nest and hatched under hens, and they consequently retain the exact size, shape, and call of their species; hence their efficiency for the purpose for which they are used, and for which the tame variety will not answer, as their wilder brethren will not drop to their call. When a new frost takes place, the *huttiers* break the ice and keep the water open for some distance, and at such times their decoy ducks sometimes attract large flights, which settle on the open water, and a good raking shot amply repays the fowler for his trouble. Some few years ago, I became practically acquainted with the French system of shooting wild-fowl with decoys, as practised in the marshes of the river Somme, which during very severe winters are the resort of all kinds of wild fowl. In the early part of December I started on a fishing and fowling excursion

A NIGHT HAUL.

in a small schooner yacht with auxiliary steam-power, which belonged to a gentleman living at Dieppe, to whom my friend Cameron and myself are indebted for unlimited hospitality and a very jolly cruise. Monsieur Morel was a great fisherman, and perfectly *au fait* in all the detail of piscatorial art in so far as it related to deep-sea fishing, and our craft was accordingly admirably provided with all kinds of rods, lines, and nets. Cameron affected to take to fishing more than shooting, as the weather was extremely cold, and the cabin with its cosy fire and spirituous comforts was always handy, and he really was not fit for any hard work, his health having become completely broken by his cruel incarceration in Abyssinia. We had been old friends in India, and after the Crimean War, had made several shooting expeditions together on the eastern shores of the Black Sea and in Asia Minor, when it would have taken a right good man to keep up with Duncan Cameron in a tramp across country, and a clever scholar to get the best of him in an argument or classical lore. He was comparatively a wreck after his return from Abyssinia, and his health was too much broken to allow him to take much bodily exertion, consequently I did not press him to accompany me upon my wild-fowling expeditions, whether in the punt or ashore. Our crew consisted of a skipper, engineer, four men, including the cook, a most important personage, and two boys, one of whom, Jean, generally accompanied me in my trips. He was rather an odd·fish, and in consequence of his nose having been so badly broken by falling down a hatchway that that organ had assumed almost as many twists as a corkscrew, he was usually hailed as "l'anguille" (the eel) by his mates. He, however, was a hardy, enduring, light-hearted Breton, who never knew what it was to be tired, and an excellent hand in a punt, either for pulling in a sea-way or creeping up to a flight of fowl. Morel had anchored our little craft between St.-Firmin and Le Crotoy, in the *embou-chure* of the Somme, and whilst he and Cameron were engaged in fishing, I and Jean took the punt for a turn amongst the wild fowl, which were flying about in all directions. Amongst a rare gathering of various kinds of duck, widgeon, teal, curlew godwits, and sand-pipers, with the aid of my field-glass, I detected a flock of barnacle-geese, and as they loomed large on the water, I determined to give them my first attention.

The question was how to get near them without being dis-covered, as they were more or less surrounded by a flock of mussel ducks. My punt was just over twenty-four feet long, with good beam in proportion, and remarkably buoyant. She was admirably built and finished, being copper-fastened throughout, and had a strong elm bottom, ash timbers, Norway deal sides, and well-fitted withy deck, which, after being well tarred, was covered over with tightly stretched canvas, which adhered firmly, and gave considerable additional strength, with-out adding much to the weight. Round this the bulwarks were attached, being about four inches forward and gradually declining to two aft, and the stem was covered with stout copper, so as to preserve it when poled through shallow places. The whole punt, both outside and in, was painted a greyish slate colour, so that it was almost undistinguishable at a short distance. The centre opening was about six feet and a half in length, and fitted with a waterproof tent-like covering, so that the occupant could lie down comfortably at full length. The mast was about ten feet long, and fitted into a socket securely fastened to the elm bottom; and when under sail, I carried a brown cotton canvas foresail, sliding gunter mainsail, and leg of mutton dandy.

Two iron spindles fitting in brass sockets were let into the gunwale on each side, and either the oars or short paddles worked upon these props by means of stout leather loops fixed to them. The gunwale and sides of the boat against which the oars worked were covered with sheep's skin, so as to muffle all sound—a very necessary precaution when the birds are wild. In the bow, upon a swivel that worked in a brass socket reaching to a block at the bottom of the boat, and to which was attached a strong spiral spring to ease the recoil, was a double breech-loading gun made by Fuller, with plenty of metal at the breech, having a gauge of about an inch and a quarter, which, with a heavy charge of powder, threw six ounces of shot from each barrel, so as to make a very pretty pattern at ninety yards; and I had besides a double 8-bore Westley-Richards, and a good stock of Eley's long-range green-wire cartridges to stop cripples. I was admirably equipped by Mr. Wilson, the proprietor of Cording's waterproof establishment, then in the Strand, now in Piccadilly, with a most complete fowler costume, which was not only light and comfortable to wear, but also impervious to cold and wet, a great desideratum for wild-fowl shooting when the sportsman is constantly exposed to all weathers, as well as the spray washing over him. The wild-fowler, when punt-shooting, should be careful to have all his under clothes made comfortably large of warm woollen material, paying special attention to have lamb's wool socks, flannel shirt and drawers, with the chest and pit of the stomach further protected by a long chamois-leather waistcoat with sleeves attached. Over this should be worn a long waterproof jacket, reaching a little over the hips, with pockets outside, and having inside the sleeves a second arrangement, which fastens with an elastic band or buttons close round the wrist, and prevents cold or wet from going up the arm. For very inclement weather, or when there is likely to be a sea on, breeches or rather pantaloons of the same waterproof material are required, and these should fit loosely over the knee, but fasten rather closely over the calf and instep. The nether extremities should be clad in

CRIPPLE STOPPING.

Cording's yachting boots, which are admirably devised so as to serve as a boot and gaiter combined. The upper part of the leg is made of stout flexible waterproof cloth, whilst the foot is covered with leather, and along the centre of the sole are four rows of thick flaxen-thread stitching, which swell when wetted and prevent the wearer from slipping. The most suitable head-gear for wild-fowl shooting is a well-ventilated " sou'-wester," of the same colour as your punt, with a peak fore and aft, and a woollen back piece to fasten round the back of the head and under the chin, so as to protect the neck from the cold .and prevent it from coming off, with two holes on each side corresponding. with the orifices of the ears. At the bottom of my punt I had an inflatable air-bed, which was not only most conducive to my personal comfort, but also a precaution of safety, as in case of a capsize it would have proved an effective life-buoy. As a protection against the cold, rain, and sleet, I had a good supply of blankets, rugs, waterproofed on the outside (another of Cording's specialities), which kept Jean and me tolerably cosy and warm whilst waiting for a shot, even when the temperature was enough to freeze one's nose off.

In all wild-fowl shooting the whole paraphernalia of the punt and dress should be of the least distinguishable hue, and long experience has shown that a grayish slate colour is about the best for general work. Jean was provided with a pair of mud pattens, which consisted of thick pieces of flat board, somewhat bevelled off fore and aft, in the centres of which the leathern sandals with straps and buckles were attached, that fastened round the feet and kept them in their place, so that the wearer could walk or rather glide over the soft mud in comparative safety. In some places the false ground is coated with long coarse grass, and much resembles the *terra firma*, so that it is very apt to deceive and engulf the inexperienced if unprovided with mud pattens. I had also a landing net, which proved very useful in picking dead and wounded birds from out of the water, and although I had an admirably broken retriever almost always with me, when in the punt I rarely allowed him to go into the water to recover the birds, as he made us so wet on his return. Master Harry, my canine friend, and constant associate, was a very knowing card, and could keep his watch on the look-out for a flight of wild fowl as well as we could ourselves, for whenever he saw a flock, or heard the sharp whistling, of a flight of widgeon, he would awake us by a low whimpering the import of which I well knew. His usual post in the boat was at my feet, which he kept warm with the heat of his body and long coat, and, unless at my bidding, he rarely moved, so that I found him no encumbrance, whilst at times he proved very useful in recovering game.

Having given some account of my gear and companions, I shall proceed to describe our doings in French waters. Except when a very strong northerly wind is blowing, the marshes at the mouth of the Somme are easy of access to the gunner having a seaworthy punt, but at times the tide runs very strong, and a rough chopping sea gets up in an incredibly short time, which, if he is not careful, will swamp his craft, unless it is constructed with air-chambers. During the winter months the little islands, creeks, and bays are very favourite resorts of widgeon, mallard, pintail, shovellers, teal, and curlew, whilst occasionally, when the weather is more than ordinarily severe, large flocks of geese and wild swans are not unfrequent visitors. When we left the steamer, the sea was tolerably smooth, although the day was dark and lowering as if dirty weather was brewing, but hardly had we pulled in shore than a strong breeze got up, and the water became lumpy, and if it had not been that hundreds of wild fowl were visible, and nice little clusters were temptingly gathered on the mud flats—for the tide was receding, and it was nearly low water—I should have returned

on board.   As it was, I determined to make the most of the
opportunity, and take my chance of getting back.   Luckily
I had a good supply of eatables, and a good-sized keg of *eau de
vie*, snugly stowed in a water-tight compartment, fitted with
sliding panels in the bulkhead, as well as a well arranged
cooking stove, and a store of coffee, tea, and such like *comestibles.*   Feeling myself tolerably independent under the circumstances, I pulled well in shore, and taking advantage of a
sheltering promontory, managed to paddle round a patch of high
reeds, which was almost within long range of the geese.   There
we unexpectedly came upon a small flock of teal, that got up
one by one with a whistle that I was afraid would have alarmed
the geese, but fortunately they were too much engaged in
feeding, and, after waiting a little while, under cover, Jean
noiselessly paddled towards them, whilst I, lying my full length
at the bottom of the boat, brought the sight of my "Long Tom"
to bear upon them, and raked them with a right and left at
about eighty yards distant.   I waited until I saw them gathering
together, with out-stretched necks, before I pulled the trigger
of the first barrel, and the second discharge swept through them
just as they were rising from the water, so that the double shot
committed great havock.   Without, however, waiting to see
the result, I reloaded, and was in time to get a second right and
left among the survivors, who, with a cloud of duck, were
making a circle round their wounded companions, before taking
their departure; a number of splashes in the water followed
the report, and I knew that considerable execution had been
done ; so we paddled up to collect the killed and wounded, and,
after stopping a few cripples and winged birds with my Westley-
Richards, I found we had brought to bag nine geese and twenty-
three ducks of various kinds.   The wind had by this time
increased almost to a gale, and, as the tide came in, the water
became so broken and rough that I determined to run ashore

and take refuge in any habitation I could find—as a mixture of snow, rain, and driving sleet, was anything but pleasant. On looking round not a house was to be seen, for the mists creeping up, our horizon had become very circumscribed, and I had just made up my mind to run my punt upon the nearest mud bank, when I found that I was pretty close to a large flock of widgeon, whom I could hear making a continuous whistling noise, although I could not see them. As we turned round a small point, I caught sight of them feeding, and directing Jean to paddle gently towards them, I got to within sixty yards of the nearest outlying flock before I fired, and the whole swarm flew close over the boat, when I snatched up my Westley-Richards and let drive both barrels right in the thick of them.

. Although many cripples got away in the fog, we picked up twenty-seven widgeon and five pintail, and we were looking out for some stragglers when a distant voice hailed us from a small island covered with reeds. I immediately turned the punt's head in the direction from which the call appeared to proceed, and shouted, for we could see no one, and, guided by an answering "halloo," I found myself in a little creek, on the bank of which a *huttier* had established his ambuscade. Having heard from Morel a good deal· about the skill of the French duck-decoyers, and their mode of calling down flights of wild fowl by imitating their different cries, I determined to take advantage of the situation, and make myself acquainted with their method. Running my punt ashore, I soon fraternised with the occupants of the hut, for they were two, "the *chasseur*" and "his dog," which appeared to be a cross between a setter and a *poodle*, and a very intelligent animal he was, in spite of his cross breed. Fine snow was falling fast at this time, and we were invited to enter the hut, and remain for the night, if we could put up with the scant accommodation.

Having plenty of prog with us, we closed at once with the

DUCK SHOOTING WITH DECOYS.

offer, and, after hauling up the punt alongside the hut, trans-
ferred its contents inside, where we proceeded to make ourselves at home. We were rather closely packed, as the interior
of the hut was not more than ten feet by eight, but the roof
was water-tight, and we stuffed up the embrasures so as to
keep out the cold, and made ourselves very comfortable. After
an abundant supper and sundry tins of hot grog, the *huttier*
showed us his *modus operandi,* which was extremely simple.
He had a double set of decoys, consisting of three drakes and
four ducks, as his hut was situated on a narrow neck of land,
and commanded a considerable extent of water on both sides.
On each of these two ducks were picketted, being fastened by
the leg to a cord fixed to a leaden weight which was thrown
into the stream about eight yards from the shore, and so
arranged that the ducks could swim round in a circle about
three yards in diameter. Two of the drakes were allowed
more liberty, being fastened with a long string by the leg to a
peg driven in near the edge of the water, whilst the third one
was kept in the hut, and only let out now and again with a
light cord secured to his leg, so that his occasional intrusion
amongst the ducks might arouse the jealousy of the other
drakes, and cause them to vociferate when from any cause the
quacking had momentarily ceased.

The decoys were all in position when we arrived, but the
howling of the wind and the roar of the sea prevented our
hearing whether their calls were answered, whilst the darkness
of the night prevented our seeing anything. We therefore
gave up all idea of shooting, and, wrapping ourselves in our
rugs upon the clean straw, slept for some hours like tops.
Towards morning I was awakened by the *huttier,* who bid me
get my gun, as he had heard flocks of duck whistling overhead,
and our decoys were trying hard to get up a flirtation with the
wild birds by calling lustily. Finding the night had cleared

WILD-FOWL SHOOTING WITH A STALKING HORSE.

up, and the fog lifted as the moon rose, I was soon on the alert, and slipping out with my rugs, I ensconced myself comfortably with my bed and rugs in the punt, and training the gun so as to bear on the water, I waited patiently until a rush of wings, followed by a flapping and splashing in the water, announced that a large flight had settled close at hand. "Gardez-vous!" exclaimed a voice from one of the embrasures, and bang went a young cannon from the hut. As the flight rose, I let drive right and left, and followed it up with the "cripple-stopper," and "splash, splash, splash," and "thud, thud, thud," was heard as the stricken birds dropped heavily in the water or on the mud. Out sprang the *huttier* and his dog, and in a couple of minutes the former was in his dingy, that lay concealed in a patch of reeds, whilst the latter was swimming about and retrieving the dead and wounded. Master Harry joined in the fun, and we were just launching the punt to assist, when a loud report sounded at no great distance, which I knew, from the ring, proceeded from the brass signal gun on our steamer. Three-and-twenty duck and teal had fallen from our united discharges, which I begged our host to accept, with half a napoleon and a flask of powder, and then bidding our host adieu, we got all our gear into the punt, and made the best of our way to the steamer, the skipper of which continued to fire his gun and burn blue-lights until we made our appearance. On account of the bad weather, Morel had been rather anxious, fearing that my little craft might have been swamped. So when the tide served, he followed us up the river, and anchored about a mile from the *huttier's* location. It was 4 a.m. when I got on board, and terribly cold; so after a glass of hot grog, and a good warm by the cuddy stove, I was glad to find myself once more comfortable in my snug bunk. We had been very successful and killed a large number of birds, but there was very little real sport in our proceedings, and if we had not had luck, we might have undergone a good deal of hardship and exposure to very little end. I do not like to make a toil of a pleasure, and I do not think I could be again tempted to face a nor'-wester in a punt on a dirty, cold winter's night if I were sure of bagging a ton-weight of wild duck; "mais chacun à son goût."

RUFFS.

CHAPTER IV.

HOG-HUNTING IN INDIA.

"DUM SPIRO, SPERO."

THE Wild Boar has ever been classed amongst the noble beasts in the most ancient annals of Venery; and well he deserves to be so, as none amongst the animal creation has a better right to be styled a cavalier sans peur et sans reproche. Although apparently a coarse, rough, sulky, insolent-looking brute, with a cunning narrow-slitted eye, from which he casts furtive, scowling, and malignant glances, he is gifted with rare metal; and no one can fail to admire his courage, as, regardless of odds, he unflinchingly charges his enemy, maintains his gallant bearing to the close of the contest, and meets his death like a hero, without a cry or a plaintive groan escaping him.

The engraving on the next page represents a "sounder" of wild hog; and it must be allowed that it requires a great stretch of imagination to realize the fact that all the different breeds and castes of the porcine race, which are annually exhibited at cattle shows, are of the same race; for it is almost impossible to trace any resemblance between these gentle, gluttonous, fat, sleepy, bacon-yielding animals, and the formidable tusked monster that roams the jungle at his pleasure, and concedes not his right of way, even to the lion himself—yet unquestionably they came from the same stock; and if again placed in the same condition, their offspring would, after a few generations, become indistinguishable.

A "SOUNDER" OF WILD HOG.

The adult wild boar is generally of a brownish black, which, as years go by, changes to a greyish slate colour. He has also bristles of considerable length about the head, and a shaggy kind of mane. They stand from 25 to 40 inches at the shoulder, have a short head, broad flat forehead, short pricked ears rather round at the tips and lying close to a very muscular neck. The eye is long and narrow, with much display of the white when enraged; and the tusks, in a full-grown boar, average from 5 to 9 inches in length.

Hog-hunting, as carried out in India, is a truly regal sport, being the incarnation of all that is exciting, and it may be said to combine all the attractions of fox-hunting with the excitement of steeple-chasing, heightened by that intense fascination which the presence of danger only can inspire. It is a sport *sui generis*, for it can be compared to no other. In stag or fox hunting, man plays but a secondary part in the game, as the hounds *find, follow,* and *kill;* but in hog-hunting it is widely different. The hunter himself searches for his quarry; he scrambles amongst rocks and ravines clothed with dense jungle to track up the boar, and, when it is reared and fairly started, he has a perilous pursuit before him over an unknown country abounding with holes, rocks, stones, nullahs, steep precipices, and rugged mountains.

After the hunter has surmounted more or less of these obstacles, and by dint of hard riding comes up to close quarters with the boar, he has to depend solely upon his coolness and skill in managing his horse, to prevent their being ripped, as well as upon his dexterity in handling the spear, so as to kill the enraged and desperate animal who shows fight to the last gasp, and who is never conquered until he is slain.

The great secret in attaining success in the hog-hunting field is to *ride straight,* as there is scarcely any ground that a hog can get over where an Arab horse cannot follow. Press him from first to last at the best speed your horse is capable of, *so as to blow him on the first burst*, otherwise he will gain his second wind and run for miles, and there will be tails shaking and heaving flanks amongst those who are in at the death. Those hogs found in hilly countries, that have to take long journeys every night to and from their feeding grounds, exhibit far greater speed and endurance than those bred in the plains, being in far better training for running.

Remember always to ride *with the butt of your spear down and the point well forward, almost in a line with your horse's ears,* so that in case of a fall it is not likely to hurt either your horse or yourself. If you once lose sight of your hog, the chances are that you will not see him again, as he is a cunning brute, and escapes by taking advantage of the inequalities of the ground or some dried-up watercourse.

When closing up with your hog, try and get to his near side, so as to be able to use your right arm freely, and when he begins to tire and his speed to slacken, or when you see him champ his tusks (which prognosticates malicious intent and mischief brewing), touch your horse with your left heel, and spring him alongside of your game at the best pace he can go, taking care to have the point well directed, so that the impetus of your rush drives it well home behind the shoulder-blade and out of the chest. Remember not to let go the butt end ; and, keeping your horse well in hand, pass your antagonist at speed, *wheeling off at the moment* of delivering the thrust, so as to withdraw your spear and avoid a charge. If this is skilfully done the chances are that you will get away scot-free, and leave your enemy rolling in the dust in his last agony. Should the wound not prove mortal, circle round and charge him again at speed as he stands at bay, but be careful how you act or you may come to grief.

Sometimes it happens that the leading spears are thrown

out and baulked of taking the first honours by the boar's doubling sharp round; and, in that case, the second line get a fair chance of taking the spear. The great advantage of having a thoroughly trained horse, with a good mouth, now shows itself; for " the spear is never lost until it is won," and, by wheeling sharply round, the advantageous position may again be gained.

The hunter who has accustomed himself to handle his spear with his left hand equally with the right, possesses a great advantage over a rival who can only work with his right hand. Thus when his opponent has the *spear-hand*—or is riding close on the near side of the boar—ready to spring his horse and take the first blood, instead of jostling his adversary, he dashes up to the off side, and gains an equal chance of getting the spear, being ready to take advantage of the slightest swerve the animal makes if he should attempt to double.

Old boars are proverbially cunning, and after having been once hunted are very difficult to dislodge ; for very often neither noise, nor even the sight of the advancing beaters, will make them budge from their lair and take to the open ground. They break back and charge the line of beaters time after time, and frequently manage to escape in that manner. An old boar " stot" is broad, and deeply indented, from his weightiness of body ; the imprints of the toes are round, thick, and often far apart from one another, whilst his stride is very long in comparison with the rest of the " sounder." The engraving represents an old boar whetting his tushes on the rough bark of a tree, and at the same time scratching his chops and rubbing his head, an amusement which all the porcine race, in common with the clan Argyle, are particularly partial to.

One of our most famous Indian hog-hunters thus describes the different dispositions of the porcine race :—·

AN OLD BOAR.

"There are various kinds of hogs which may sometimes be met with in one morning : I merely allude to their difference in disposition. The young boar is active and incautious, and goes off with amazing speed : fights well, but, from want of sufficient length of tooth, has not the same chance as more aged ones, and, I think, feels the spear more—*i.e.* dies sooner. The boar full grown affords much finer sport : but the grunter, just on the turn, is the one to make a man's blood run brisk. His exertions to save his life, tempered with caution, would surprise a fox-hunter, methinks ! The only way to come up with one of this class is, to press him very hard the moment he bursts, when he will most likely slacken his pace after about a mile. The moment he sees you have the speed of him, he will turn, and then is the time to give him the blow. A hunter should always keep the hog about ten yards a-head of him, a little on the right, so that, the instant he perceives him waver in his direction, he may have him under his spear hand : for hogs in general turn down on the hunter when they come to the stop. This is the time a man's eye and horsemanship tells : if he has a good eye on the hog, and a correct hand on his horse, he does his business for him, and at the instant he delivers his spear into the small of the back (every man has his favourite spot to strike at—mine was always the small of the back, as being the most vital), he has his horse off to the left. The force of the blow checks the hog, and the right spur well put in takes off the horse. People generally get their horses cut at this critical moment. If they miss their aim, the hog gets in on them ; and, unless they have already got their nag away, they get a nasty cut, which sometimes proves fatal, always annoying."

A thoroughly trained horse is a *sine quâ non* in hog-hunting; and a high caste Arab makes the best hunter, as he is the most courageous, the most enduring, and the most sagacious of our

Indian breeds of horses, and is consequently the more easily broken and trained. He should be

> " Full of fire and full of bone,
> All his line of fathers known ;
> Fine his nose, his nostrils thin,
> But blown abroad by the pride within !
> His mane a stormy river flowing ;
> And his eyes like embers glowing
> In the darkness of the night ;
> And his pace as swift as light."

No horse will make a good hog-hunter that cannot do his couple of miles at a fair racing speed ; and the faster he can get off at the commencement of the run the better, as the boar who has been feeding heavily during the night is not in running condition early in the morning, and generally gets blown after being pressed hard for a mile. When he flags, the horse who is in better wind begins to outpace him ; and the rider, springing him up along side, is enabled to drive the spear well home behind the shoulder blade, and passing on at full speed the boar's fore-quarters swing round and he generally rolls over. The horseman, by simply keeping fast hold of the butt end, extracts the spear as the horse moves on, and wheeling round his horse, is prepared for eventualities, having his point ready. If the hunter attempts to make a *waiting race*, and allows the boar to go his own pace, the chances are that he will be beaten in the long run. Some rival will take the first spear, or the boar getting his second wind will escape. "Bul-bul"—the sobriquet of Nightingale of the Nizam's service, one of the best spears in the Deccan—used to give a tyro this advice—-which he carried out to the letter himself,—" Ride straight, make running from first to last, keep your spear point well forward, and never say die." Both the horse and his rider must be gifted with no ordinary qualifications to win the spear of honour in a well-contested field ; and even the finest turn of speed in the horse is unavailing if the rider cannot handle his spear with dexterity, or if either of them have a particle of "the white feather" in their whole composition. A famous old sportsman, Harry Hieover, used to say that, as relates to man, "there are three attributes indicative of a bold manly character, namely, *bravery, courage,* and *gameness.*" I conceive each separately may be looked at in something like the following light. If we see a man breast a wild and heavy sea with the hope of saving the life of another we should call him a *brave* fellow. If we saw another rescue a fellow-man from the attack of others or from the grasp of a ferocious animal, we should admire his *courage.* If we saw a weak, small man, evidently overmatched by a powerful antagonist, but fighting on under every disadvantage, trusting that his determination would eventually bring him off triumphant, we should admire his *game.* Bravery may, I think, be somewhat closely defined as braving the evident risks of life in cases where personal effort, though it may aid cannot secure our safety; courage by facing danger in situations where we have only our own nerve and resolution to carry us through ; and game, the patient suffering and endurance of bodily hurt and pain in either case.

As with men, so in horses, may be found the three characteristics of "high caste;" namely, bravery, courage, and gameness, although they may seldom have the opportunity of showing them. We hold a horse to be *brave* who will leap at any obstacle he may be put at, not knowing what may be on the other side, or who will take his rider in full confidence up to any dangerous animal. We extol the *courage* of a horse who, on the field of battle, amid the roaring and flashing of cannon, and the rattle of musketry, will force his way through opposing hostile ranks, reckless of all dangers. We speak of the *gameness* of a horse, who, although wounded to the death, will carry his rider until his strength fails him, and he drops ; or, again, we frequently hear that such a horse or mare was beaten twice or three times between Tattenham Corner and home, but finally won by a head. This is the *ne plus ultra* of gameness, as a horse so situated must have gone in severe distress; but, the moment he in some degree recovered his powers, he willingly came again and won. Such running is a proof of a generous and willing nature, a voluntary defiance of distress, and *gameness* of the highest order. A perfect hog-hunter must have all three qualities combined.

It is an axiom in the creed of a hog-hunter that a well-trained horse can follow and come up with a boar over any kind of country, and, as far as the jumping is concerned, or even in the scrambling over bad ground, the rule holds good; but there are certain exceptions—for instance, a sounder of hog, when hard pressed, will unhesitatingly throw themselves down the scarped bank of a nullah a dozen or fifteen feet deep, pick themselves up uninjured by the fall, and continue their way; whereas such a drop would bring a field of horsemen to grief, if they were to attempt to follow. Again, some parts of the country are so intersected with rocky corries and ravines that riding hog is impracticable; whilst other districts are so covered with prickly pear and thorny bushes that a horse would be lamed for a month after galloping a mile across country.

Before going further, it would perhaps be as well to give some idea of the nature of the country over which hog are hidden and speared. The "meidans," or plains, the best riding ground we have in the Deccan, are, generally, more or less covered with rank "rumnah" grass and low bush, which hides dangerous holes made by snakes, bandicoots, rats, and other vermin. These often occasion the most terrific spills; for, when getting over the ground at a rattling gallop, it is seldom that either man or horse can see them in time to avoid them. Again, all our Indian riding ground is more or less intersected by *nullahs*, which is the Anglo-Indian term given to the beds of streams or channels, whether they have water in them or not. These sometimes impracticable obstructions have generally steep if not over-hanging and shelving banks; and, in nine cases out of ten, they are too broad to be "*leapable.*" They moreover frequently have beds of rough, loose shingle, boulders of slimy rock, deep sand, and sometimes quicksands, which cause cut legs, sprained fetlocks, and ricked shoulders. The best advice that can be given in riding over such ground is to ride straight, and follow the same line as the hog who, *unless very hard pressed*, is sure to select the easiest place for crossing a nullah; and, wherever a boar can lead, a horse can generally follow. Perhaps the most awkward nullahs to cross are those which are only a few feet wider than a horse can leap, on account of the small space at the bottom scarcely giving the horse room to recover him-self; but an experienced rider can generally form a pretty fair idea of the breadth of the obstruction by marking the time it takes the hog to reappear on the opposite bank. A clever rider, on a thoroughly trained horse, will ride without slackening his pace almost to the *edge* of a nullah; where his horse, which is perfectly in hand, and accustomed to turn round a spear, will "luff up," in case the leap is impracticable, and not much time is lost in seeking for an easier place, and making "an in and out "—

> "Look before you leap if you like, but if
> You mean leaping, don't look long,
> Or the weakest place will soon grow stiff,
> And the strongest doubly strong."

Pulling up is out of the question, if not impossible, when your horse's blood is up: besides it often happens that nullahs, like "sunk fences," are indistinguishable to man or horse until they are close upon them; and then, should the chasm be deep and wide, and the rider not have got his nag well in hand, the chances are that one or both will come to grief; but—

> " No game was ever worth a rap,
>   For a rational man to play—
> Into which no accident, no mishap,
>   Could possibly find its way."

The Deccan hunts have for many years maintained a very high *prestige* in the annals of hog-hunting ; and the different gatherings that have taken place at Poonah, Arungabad, Hydrabad, Jalnah, Elichpore, Sholapore, and Nagpore have generally been well attended, and have produced most brilliant sport. At whatever station the " snaffle, spur, and spear " fraternity met, the tent club was sure to comprise nearly every officer in cantonment, not on duty, who could muster a decent nag, or who loved good cheer and jovial company. Every rank and every branch of the service was fairly represented at these social gatherings ; and some of the most daring leaders and wisest statesmen India has produced have also been famous as the best spears and the hardest riders across country. General Outram—the Bayard of India—the only man, with the exception of Colonel Skinner, who ever speared a tiger to death from his horse—was famous, in that country pre-eminent for good sportsmen, as the boldest horseman, the best spear, and the most experienced large game hunter, long years before he carved his way to fame as a general and a statesman with his sword and his pen ; and the natives still cherish and revere his memory as a sportsman, and extol his daring deeds in the jungle and the hunting-field, although they may have forgotten the many important services he rendered the country.

The following is the system usually adopted by the famous Deccan Hunt, which, in the palmy days of hog-hunting maintained the highest *prestige*, and was ever celebrated for the boldness of its riders, even in a land pre-eminent for the excellence of its sportmen.

The most experienced of its members being chosen Master of

the Hunt, had under his orders a gang of some twenty shekarry scouts, whose sole occupation was to find out the favourite feeding places of hog, and the patches of jungle they gene- rally resorted to at daybreak; and to him was entrusted the general management of the hunt, and all the arrangements for the beat.

The hog-hunters having assembled soon after day-break, as noiselessly as possible, at the jungle-side, the master pairs them off in twos and twos, great care being taken to match the rivals for the spear as equally as possible, due consideration being given to the experience of the riders and the goodness of their cattle; for the great excitement of hog-hunting is not the actual killing the boar, but the great emulation and spirit of rivalry that is engendered in winning the spear of honour from a worthy competitor.

When the line of spearmen have got well under cover, the signal is given for the line of beaters, who are under the guidance of the shekarry scouts to advance. In some jungles it is best to beat silently, and in others, where the bush is thick, it is advisable to make use of tom-toms and other noisy instruments, cholera-horns being sounded only when the game is known to be afoot. We shall suppose ourselves at the jungle-side waiting for the hog to break, and listening intently to the shouts of the beaters, who are evidently approaching the open ground, and driving the game before them, as we can tell by the discordant squirl of the cholera-horns being heard at both ends of the line. Suddenly the yells become louder, and one distinguishes the *"view halloo"* "Soor, jata hy" (There go the pig). Then comes the anxious moment, and the line of horsemen, waiting spear in hand, as if impatient for the fray, peer through their cover, and seek to distinguish the old grey boar from the female and younger branches of his family. Loth to leave his stronghold, and somewhat sulky at being

HOG-HUNTING.

disturbed so early in the morning, he is sometimes difficult to
dislodge, and oftentimes breaks back and charges the line of
beaters, but at last he makes a rush for the open, and is seen
trotting leisurely along, followed by the rest of the sounder, a
short distance in front of the beaters. A report from a pistol,
or "the alarm" on the bugle, announces to the line that the
quarry has broken fairly in the plain, and when the master of
the hunt considers the quarry has gained sufficient law, he
gives the word, and the bugle sounds "*the advance,*" which is
the signal for the line of horsemen to emerge from their cover
and contest the spear of honour.

The old boar, who up to this time has been grunting
savagely, scarcely appears to quicken his movements until the
hunters begin to close upon him, when he bounds away with a
speed that no one who has not been an eye-witness would
conceive. Then comes the exciting moment, the rush for first
blood, and a score of gallant horsemen, with heads up, bridle-
hands down, and the points of their spears kept well forward,
charge at full speed along the plain. Then comes into play
the experience and coolness of the old hunter, mounted on the
best blood of Nedjed, who, enjoying the chase as much as his
rider, follows, *con amore*, every swerve of the boar, and forging
slightly ahead, gains the near side, and enables his master, by
leaning forward in his saddle, to drive his spear well home
behind the shoulder-blade, and cause the quarry to roll over on
his back in the dust. If the spear-point has penetrated the
heart, the grey boar dies—as the brave do—in silence, not a
moan escaping him, but should the vital spot be missed, woe
unto ye that follow if you are not ready, for, in the twinkling
of an eye, the infuriated monster picks himself up, and cocking
his head on one side knowingly, as if to take aim, with a wild
roar, and open-mouthed, charges the nearest of his antagonists,
and unless the onset is promptly met on the point of the spear,

the chances are that one or two horses will be badly ripped, and their riders besmeared with gore.

The boar is one of the most courageous and fearless of forest animals, and when severely wounded, in his desperation, I have seen him charge, utterly reckless of life, against my spear's point, forcing the shaft through his body until he could bury his tushes in the flank of his antagonist's horse. Neither the lion nor the tiger will ever willingly attack a solitary boar, unless they can pounce upon him unawares, which is not often the case, as he is desperately cunning, and can detect the taint in the air at a great distance. His tenacity of life is also very great, and I have seen a boar receive a dozen severe spear-wounds, some of which completely transfixed the body, before he finally bit the dust. The best places to spear a boar, so as to reach a vital spot, are just behind the shoulder-blade, low down, when the point enters the heart or lungs, along the ridge of the spine, when he becomes more or less paralysed, or, if possible, just where the head and neck join.

NUGGER HUNT SPEAR-HEAD.

The engraving shows the Nugger Hunt spear-head, which is now generally used all over India. It is somewhat in the shape of a myrtle leaf, but the curves are very gradual from point to shank, so that it penetrates easily, and is withdrawn without difficulty. Another great advantage of this shape is that the edges and point can be easily ground, and afterwards sharpened on a hone. The Deccan Hunt spear-head, which has four edges, is much used by sportsmen on the Madras side, and some prefer it to that of the Nugger Hunt, because the orifice of the wound it makes is somewhat larger and allows the blood to flow more freely. It is, however, rather difficult to sharpen, which is a drawback in the bush. It is almost unnecessary to add that all spear-heads ought to be made of the best tempered steel, and any showing the slightest appearance of a flaw should be discarded.

A stout male bamboo sufficiently tapering, and with knots pretty close together, makes the best spear-shaft, but when this is not procurable, a close-grained, well-seasoned ash-pole is not a bad substitute. Bamboos for war spears ought to be cut at the close of the hot season, when the sap is in the roots, and they should be hung from the rafters with a 14lb. weight fixed at the bottom for some months to dry straight, and season. The natives say that if bamboos are cut at the new moon, they will endure for any length of time ; if at full moon, that they will decay in two or three years; and that if cut by daylight, then they will get dry-rot before they can become seasoned. They therefore select the straight growing bamboos in the day, and fasten cloths round them, cutting them at night. Although this theory is common in several parts of India, and long experience has proved it to be a correct one, I could never obtain any satisfactory reason why such should be the case. It is, however, certain that in the low lands of tropical countries no attentive observer of nature will fail to witness the powerful influence exercised by the moon, not only over the seasons, but also upon animal and vegetable life, and few people are better aware of this fact than the Carib mahogany cutters of Honduras, as timber cut at the proper time of the year is twice as valuable as that cut out of season.

The spear ought to be well balanced, and it is usual to have the butt weighted with lead for that purpose. In the Bombay and Madras Presidencies, hog-spears are generally nine feet from the extreme point of the blade to the butt, and this was the regulation length both of Nugger and Deccan Hunt Clubs.

NO. I. STARTING FROM THE CAMP.

In Bengal many sportsmen use a spear about six feet in length, weighted with nearly two pounds of lead at the butt. Holding this about a foot and a half from the lead part, they are accustomed to use this like a javelin, or to job down when the horse gets alongside the boar; whereas, in Madras and Bombay, hog-hunters use the spear like a lance, but carried loosely in the hand, so as to allow free play to the wrist in directing the point of the spear. Throwing the spear is considered most unsportsmanlike, on account of the numerous accidents that have taken place both to men and riders by the spear turning, on coming in contact with the ground. No sportsman would throw his spear at a charging boar if he had not his horse's heels to carry him out of danger in case he missed ; besides which, he would have to pull up and dismount to recover his weapon, and in the meantime, the boar is either killed by others, or gets clear off, if he happen to be alone. An experienced hog-hunter directs the point of his spear, and allows the force of his horse's rush to drive it home. In receiving a charge when the boar comes down upon him, he merely holds the point steady, without raising his arm, and lets him run upon his spear—the pace of both, sending it in most effectually. The hunter ought never, if possible, let go his spear, but, after delivering a thrust, bring it out again as he wheels round. For this reason spear-heads should be small, being more easily recovered than large ones that get jammed between the ribs.

The best rig for a hog-hunter is, perhaps, a very easy and loosely cut blouse, of any stout material of neutral colour, reaching some three inches below the hips, and with wide shirt-like sleeves fastening at the wrist, which allows the free action of the arms, and yet is not likely to catch in anything; leather, corduroy, or moleskin breeches, and " Napoleon " boots, which will protect the knees from thorns.

The best head-gear is a fore-and-aft hunting-cap with a two-inch brim all round, built very strong, so as to protect the head, in case of a cropper, and covered with a well-twisted slate-coloured turbaned or cotton-padded cap cover, as a precaution against sun-stroke. Hunting spurs with short necks, and rowels uppermost, and filled with chains and buckles, are best for hog-hunting purposes, and a serviceable seven-inch blade hunting-knife that can be carried in a belt, and worn behind in the hollow of the back, often comes in handy at an awkward pinch. In an inside left breast pocket, should be carried a small flat case, containing lint, plaster, cotton bandage, silk, and a few surgical needles, in case of the boar taking liberties either with man or beast.

I shall now endeavour to portray the usual routine and the different incidents of sport in one of these famous gatherings that took place at Jhoolam Ali durgar, a somewhat famous Mussulman shrine, about fourteen miles from Secunderabad, the head-quarters of the Hydrabad subsidiary force.

For some days previous to the day of the club meeting, Captain Malcolm, the Assistant Resident, then the Master or Captain of the hunt, had gathered every possible information as to the whereabouts of the different sounders of hog from the native scouts and shekarries in his employ; and, in accordance with his directions, the hunting camp was established near the shrine, which was at a convenient distance from the cover intended to be beaten. Here a large double-poled mess tent was pitched, fitted with punkahs and every adjunct of oriental luxury and comfort. On each flank rose smaller tents, *routees* and *bachobas* ef every kind and description, belonging to the different members of the hunt; and behind were picketed long lines of high caste Arab, Mahratta, and Deccan bred horses, many of which were celebrated in story, and showed honourable scars of previous tussles with the grey jungle boar. The

No. II. THE MASTER POSTS THE SPEARS.

opening day of the hunt was devoted to good cheer and revelry, the caterer and *chef de cuisine* being Dr. Riddell, the celebrated *gastronome;* and round the bright polished teak tables a merry party had gathered together to enjoy the good things of this life, and talk over the arrangements for sport. No one who has ever been present on these festive occasions can ever forget them; and even now, after this lapse of time, the sluggish blood rushes through my veins when I recall to mind the enthusiastic, unalloyed happiness and pleasurable excitement that thrilled through every soul, when, after the cloth was removed, and the usual loyal toasts drank, the Master, with the huge silver loving cup in hand, commenced the opening lay :—

THE MASTER'S TOAST.

PLEDGE me woman's lovely face,
Beaming eye, and bosom fair,
Every soft and winning grace,
Sweetly blended, sparkles there.
Is there one whose sordid soul,
Beauty's form hath ne'er adored ?
From his cold lip dash the bowl,
Spurn him from the festal board.

Pledge me next the glorious chase,
When the mighty boar's ahead,
He, the noblest of the race,
In the mountain jungle bred.
Swifter than the slender deer
Bounding over Deccan's plain,
Who can stay his proud career,
Who can hope his tusks to gain ?

Pledge me those who oft have won
Tusked trophies from the foe,
And in many a famous run,
Many a gallant hog laid low.
Who, on Peeplah's steepy height,
And on Gunga's tangled shore,
Oft again will dare the fight
With the furious jungle boar.

The loving cup having gone round, the Master gave out the

NO. III. THE SIGNAL TO RIDE,

programme of the morrow's proceedings, and *paired off the spears*, matching each couple as evenly as he could, taking into consideration their prestige, experience, and the quality of their cattle.

This matter arranged satisfactorily, Tom Morris' chaunt of "The Boar" followed, and then every one round the table gave a song, or a hunting yarn, and kept the game alive until midnight, when the Master broke up the party by starting the closing chorus :—

HURRAH! HURRAH! ONE BUMPER MORE.

FILL the goblet to the brim,
Fill with me and drink to him
Who the mountain sport pursues,
Speed the boar where'er he choose ;
Hurrah ! hurrah ! one bumper more,
A bumper to the grim grey boar !

Hark, the beater's shout on high
Hark, the hunter's shrill reply,
Echo leaps from hill to hill,
There the chase is challenge still ;
Hurrah ! hurrah ! one bumper more,
A bumper to the sturdy boar !

Ride, for now the sounder breaks,
Ride where'er the grey boar takes,
Struggle thro' the desperate chase,
Reckless death itself to face ;
Hurrah ! hurrah! one bumper more,
A bumper to the fearless boar !

See, the jungle verge is won,
See, the grey boar dashing on ;
Bold and brave ones now are nigh,
See him stagger, charge, and die ;
Hurrah ! hurrah ! one bumper more,
A bumper to the fallen boar !

Although these merry meetings were famed throughout India for the joviality and the good fellowship they engendered amongst sportsmen, dissipation was by no means encouraged, although in those days men, as a rule, drank deeper than they do now. The most stupid of popular errors is the constant association of Bacchanalian revelry with sporting pursuits, as if there was any possible natural connection between hard-drinking and hard-riding. Nothing can be more absurd than this preposterous combination, as it is an incontestable fact that drinking and dissipated habits are incompatible with sporting pursuits, which require qualifications that no drunkard ever has. Well-strung nerves, strength, condition, a quick eye, a ready hand, cool calculating courage, and great determination, are the characteristic requirements of the true sportsman, and what habitual drunkard ever possessed these ?

Early the next morning, the shrill bugle sounding "the réveille," woke up the camp, and shortly afterwards a strong muster of sportsmen clad in hunting garments of every shape and hue, gathered round the breakfast table. Before the late-comers had finished their repast, "the boot and saddle" sounded, and the Syces, each carrying a couple of spears, brought up the horses ready saddled and covered with *jules*, whose excited temperament showed that they anticipated the sport with as much pleasure and eagerness as did their riders. Our illustration, No. 1, represents the scene in camp, when "the assembly" sounded, and the hunters, mounting, followed the Master to the cover-side, that might be from two to three miles distant from the camp, and which was carefully watched by our native scouts and trackers.

The Cover-side.—The hunters being told off in pairs, accompanied the Master, who posted them like a chain of videttes along the cover-side, in situations where they would be as little exposed as possible, so that they were not likely to scare the hog and cause them to break back on the beaters. Here each man dismounted, and remained on the *qui vive*, maintaining the utmost silence, and not even indulging in the fragrant weed lest the keen-scented game should wind it. On these

NO. IV.　THE SOUNDER REARED.

occasions, although the hunters have half an hour to wait before the signal is given for the drive to commence, they must not on this account be careless; for one can never know whether some out-lying sounder may not be close at hand; or the game may be on the move, and come out of their own accord before a beater has stirred; and, if the cover is not carefully watched, may steal away unobserved.

No spear may leave his post on any pretence whatever, until the preconcerted signal on the bugle is given. Should a sounder break from the cover near him, he hoists his hunting-cap on his spear as high above his head as he can,—the signal that "the game is afoot" or "gone away;" and every hunter who sees the sign repeats it, so that the whole line is apprised, and the Master orders "the alarm" to be sounded on the bugle, upon which each man mounts and waits impatiently for the sound of the next signal, "the advance" or "ride," when the whole line dart impetuously in pursuit. Our illustrations represent the critical period at the cover-side. No 2 shows the Master and his galloper, or aide-de-camp, posting the spears previous to giving the signal for the "hankwa" or "beat" to commence. No. 3 represents the scene at the exciting moment when the Master orders "the advance" to be sounded, which he only does when he sees the hog have fairly broken cover, and have gained a certain *law*, five hundred yards' lead being always allowed, and sometimes in favourable riding ground nearly half a mile, so that every spear may get a fair start. Then is heard the spirit-stirring cry, as sweet to the ears of the true sportsman as the warbling of Malibran or Patti; and in a few minutes the grey backs of the sounder are seen above the grass and low scrub as they make their way before the beaters, with the old boar champing his tushes and looking viciously inclined as he trots along in the rear of his porcine family. Plate No. 4 represents

NO. V.   TALLY-HO AND AWAY!

a sounder of hog "breaking cover," a sight once seen never forgotten.

The sounder is reared, and last of all to emerge into the open is the mighty grey boar, who suddenly stops in his quick dog-trot to listen. How motionless he stands, as if rooted to the spot; and had you not seen him in motion you might have taken his dark form to be a protruding rock or a mass of earth. Still he stands as immovable as when he stopped, with his head still pointed in the direction in which it was while moving forward; and, if your field-glass is a good one, you will see that he is scowling back inquisitively from the extreme corner of his knowing-looking brown eyes. He need not turn round to look; for his fine sense of hearing detects danger; and, as he snuffs the breeze, his susceptible nose discovers to him the nature of his enemy by "the taint in the air." His ears point backwards; for some unusual sound has attracted his attention: then he gives a sharp whiff, up goes his tail, and away he starts right ahead at his old dog-trot, grumbling audibly as he speeds through the bushes. The sounder, being now dislodged from their cover, made across the plain at full speed, and the line of converging horsemen pressed forward with a mighty rush. The best mounted and the boldest riders soon drew ahead; but for a short time the hog held their own, and made strong running in a bee-line for some distant hills, which if they could only have reached would have saved their bacon. Vain hope, the loud tallyho's and hoarse shouting of their pursuers sounded nearer and nearer in their ears, and louder and louder the old boar grumbled his displeasure.

> "They came with the rush of the southern surf,
>   On the bar of the storm-girt bay;
> And like muffled drums on the sounding turf,
>   Their hoof-strokes echo away."

Scared by these unusual sounds the sounder separated, and each hog took a line of his own, and was followed by a group of horsemen, who slowly, but surely, gained upon their quarry. Our illustration, No. 5, gives a fair representation of such a scene; the hog is still full of running, and the pace is too good to last. Although the "meidan" was comparatively good riding ground, rolling stones and holes had occasioned some ugly spills, and riderless horses and dismounted spears were to be seen every now and again. A broad nullah, full of water, now came into view; and into this the boar dashed without the slightest hesitation, vanishing for a few seconds, and re-appearing on the opposite bank, a little lower down the stream, apparently rather refreshed and invigorated by his bath. Several of the leading horsemen evidently knew the country; and as the stream was not more than fifteen feet from bank to bank, and leapable, they pulled their horses together, got them well between their thighs and crammed them at it.

> " Good Lord! to see the riders now,
>   Thrown off with sudden whirl;
>   A score within the purling brook,
>   Enjoying their early 'purl.'

> " Some lost their stirrups, some their caps,
>   Some had no spears to show,
>   Some few, like Charles at Charing Cross,
>   Rode on *in statu quo.*"

The field now became more select, and although the boar still held his own in the van, and was as yet unscathed, several of the porcine family had succumbed and bit the dust; whilst it was "bellows to mend" with a good many of the horses, as this being the first run of the season, several of them had been short of work, and were more or less out of condition. Four or five were still seen pushing along their jaded horses at their best pace after the boar, whose open mouth, heaving sides, foam-covered flanks, and faltering action, showed that

NO. VI.   THE STRUGGLE FOR THE FIRST SPEAR.

he was blown, and almost run to a standstill. Two noted hard riders, Nightingale of the Nizam's Service, and Shortt of the King's Own, who were well to the front, now closed rapidly upon the boar, and as they rode almost knee to knee, their struggle for the spear was watched with intense interest. They appeared to be very evenly matched; and as they were not more than a couple of spears' length from their quarry, who was staggering about from side to side with exhaustion, it seemed certain that one or the other would obtain the much coveted spear of honour; but the race is not always to the swift, and the spear is anybody's until it is won, for the chances of the chase depend very much on the manœuvring of the hog, which may give the spear to hunters who had been hopelessly left far in the rear. In this instance, when apparently it seemed certain that in another stride or two the spear would be taken, the hog made a sudden double, swerved off past the left of Bul-bul, the near horseman, and viciously charged Captain Madigan, who was following up at some distance in the rear, knocking his jaded horses' legs from under him, and suddenly disappeared in an almost dry water channel, one of the ramifications of the nullah previously crossed. For some time the hog remained unseen as he travelled along the winding bed of one water-channel and up another, but at last he was sighted by one of the hunters, who gave a loud yell and raised his spear, which brought up his enemies *en masse*, when, scared by their cries, he again scrambled up the bank and took to the flat, and his two former pursuers, Nightingale and Shortt, owing to the superior condition of their cattle, were again pounding away side by side in his wake. The boar, again terribly distressed, once more tried to double round, but as he swerved off to the left, Bul-bul, who was mounted on a thoroughbred Arab chestnut mare, made a rush and buried the blade of his spear deep into his brawny neck, and over **the**

NO. VII.   THE BOAR AT BAY.

monster rolled; but in the twinkling of an eye he was again upon his feet, and charged straight at Shortt, who, wheeling round, received him on the point of the spear, which, entering between the shoulder blade and the neck, pierced the heart and ended his career.　Our illustrations represent the struggle for the spear, the last charge, and the death of the boar, being sketched by Mr. H. Bird, the nephew of Colonel "Buxey" Bird, who was always a great gun at Hydrabad meetings, and a recognised authority on all kinds of sport.

The following rules were strictly enforced in the Deccan and Nugger Hunts:—

1. The master of the Hunt must be implicitly obeyed by the whole Club when in the field, and he has the sole direction of the Hunt and the selection of the country for the meet.

2. The strictest silence is to be maintained at the jungle-side, and when Members are once posted they must not mount or leave their cover until the hog have broken and the bugle has sounded "the advance."

3. No followers whatever, or spare horses are to be allowed at the cover-side.

4. When two or more boars break, those who wish to contend for the spear of honour must ride after the largest, and no sow must be pursued if there is a boar in the sounder.

5. The slightest puncture with the spear's point, if it draws blood, constitutes "the first spear," and the owner is entitled to the tushes.

6. Every Member taking "a first spear" is expected to follow up his hog until killed.

7. Disputed spears to be decided by the Master of the Hunt.

8. Disputes, or claims for "the first spear" are to be settled on the spot by the Master of the Hunt, who decides the case according to the judgment of the majority of riders present.　Should there be any doubt upon the subject, the tushes to be divided.

NO. VIII. DEATH OF THE BOAR.

9. In order to prevent accidents through carelessness, any rider jostling another intentionally, or carrying his spear improperly, shall be fined a gold mohur ; and repeated inattention to this rule shall, if brought before the notice of the Committee, render the offender liable to be disqualified from riding for the spear of honour.

10. All fines go to the Hunt Fund.

11. Any Member shooting a hog in the tract of country ridden over by the Hunt, shall be liable to expulsion from the Club.

12. The messing arrangement shall be managed by the Committee chosen by the Members amongst themselves, the Master of the Hunt for the time being President.   Two picnics and two balls shall be given by the Club every season.

A sportsman who would be an adept in hog-hunting must possess strong nerves, a good eye for country, keen sight, firm seat, light hand, and more especially a bold heart and a cool head.

Add to these qualifications a fair judgment of pace, a certain dexterity in handling the spear, and an intimate acquaintance with the habits and extreme cunning of the boar, and you will have an accomplished hog-hunter, such as no other country in the world but India can turn out.

It is considerably over a quarter of a century since I took my maiden spear, yet there are times when every incident of that memorable day comes vividly before me, and in my mind's eye I see the well-remembered forms of my old associates in the forest and the field, and think I hear their joyous voices resounding in my ears, for some of the most jovial nights I ever spent were at these gatherings, at which were collected the boldest riders, the greatest sportsmen, and some of the most distinguished officers that India has produced.

CHAPTER V.

BEAR-HUNTING.

THE common black sloth-bear (Ursus labiatus) is to be met with in most of the hill ranges throughout India; and, although he is a mere pigmy when compared to "Old Ephraim," the grizzly of the Rocky Mountains, he is by no means deficient in pluck; and bear-hunting is, consequently, a favourite pursuit with Anglo-Indians, there being just enough danger in the sport to give it excitement.

The black sloth-bear of the plains, as he is often called, to distinguish him from the hill or snow bear of the Himalayas, is a powerfully-made animal, about six feet in length from the muzzle to the tail—that appendage being only three inches long; while he stands about three feet in height at the shoulder, and his girth round the biggest part of his body is about four feet and a half. When in good condition his weight would be rather over three hundred weight. Like all the rest of the Ursidæ, he is a plantigrade; that is, he plants the whole sole of his foot on the ground in walking, consequently his movements are comparatively slow, and he has not that easy movement bestowed upon the felinæ, and cannot spring on to his prey or bound away from danger. His head and teeth are not nearly so massively made as the tiger's—his skull is elongated, and his jaws do not possess that vice-like strength that all the cat tribe are gifted with. He has a deep, broad chest, and very muscular and powerful fore-arms, but his hind-quarters droop and appear to be somewhat weak. Bears vary very much in shape,

Some are long and low, whilst others have short bodies and great length of limb, but all have most formidable-looking claws, those of the fore-paws being curved, and three inches long; and these claws possess independent movement, each being capable of distinct motion, like the fingers of the human hand. Bears, both male and female, are covered with long glossy coats of thick black hair, without any wool or under-growth at the base, and both sexes have a light cinnamon or dirty-white horse-shoe shaped patch on the chest, reaching from the throat to between the fore-arms, which forms an admirable mark for the hunter to aim at, as a bullet planted in the centre of this goes straight to the lungs and heart, and proves instantly fatal. Both male and female have also grey muzzles, and often a light-coloured blaze up the snout and on each side of the jowl. When the bear is young his fur is generally very long and thick, and in much finer condition than in old animals, and the hide then, if properly tanned, forms a very handsome rug. In walking the toes of the fore feet are turned in, whilst the gait is clumsy and often ludicrous in the extreme, for as the creature jogs along he swings his body in an odd fashion to and fro, rolling his triangular and cunning-looking head from side to side at the same time. The carcass, when stripped of the hide, looks so like that of an immensely muscular stoutly-built man, with short, bandy-legs, that the natives often call the bear Adamzáda, or "the son of man," from the Hindostanee words "Adam," a man, and "zada," born of; and, indeed, he often appears to be a burlesque on the *genus homo.*

As a rule, he is not carnivorous, and does not kill for the sake of flesh : his principal food being the wild fruits of the jungle, pulpy roots, honey, and insects, such as beetles, wood-lice, and particularly white ants, which the prehensile form of his lips and snout enables him to pick up and devour with wonderful dexterity and rapidity. I have on several occasions surprised and killed, or mortally wounded, a bear when digging for white ants in a hole almost big enough to bury himself, which his huge claws and powerful fore-arms enable him to make in an incredibly short time, having been attracted to the spot by the peculiar noise that he always makes whilst sucking up the grubs of the white ants from their tunnelled repositories in the earth. I have also occasionally caught him when up a tree, plundering a wild bees' nest, and watched him gnawing away the wood if the hollow containing the comb was too small to admit his paws, until he had made the opening of sufficient size, when, utterly regardless of the stings of the defending bees, that swarmed round him in hundreds, he would scoop out the wax, honey, and young bees, and devour the whole mass indiscriminately, after which he would leisurely descend and roll himself on the ground to rid himself of any of his tiny antagonists that might have settled upon him. His strong sharp claws enable him to make his way up the trunks of trees to positions most difficult of access, where his keen scent enables him to detect the presence of his favourite food, and he displays great acuteness and perseverance in reaching the nest containing the sweet repast. Nature has been very bountiful in her supply of food for this class of animals; for almost in every jungle, at different times of the year, many species of trees and bushes produce wholesome and palatable fruit in their season, and the earth supplements the supply by many juicy and nourishing roots. Thus the sweet, luscious flowers of the Mhoura are a favourite food for all vegetable-feeding animals and birds; whilst the plum of the wild ebony-tree, the wild mango, the Bhir berries, the bean of the giant Bauhinia creeper, and many other jungle bush fruits, together with wild yams and arrow-root, are also much relished by the various denizens of the forest. When roused in thick bush the bear often rises upon his hind legs, or rather squats upon his hams to listen, and

when in this attitude he stands over seven feet in height. Bears
generally inhabit caves and deep fissures in the rocks, where
they can remain in the cool during the heat of the day; and,
except in very remote districts, they do not leave their mid-day
retreat until near sunset, when they travel considerable distances during the night in search of food, returning to their
caves at daybreak. Any sportsman who can read signs will
easily discover if a cave is inhabited by bears; and, having
assured himself that such is the case, his best plan of proceeding
is to place himself either on one side of the path leading up to the
cave, or in some elevated spot that commands an unobstructed
view of the entrance, early in the morning so as to await their
return. During the rains or in cool or cloudy weather, they
may often be found feeding in the jungle during the daytime,
or hunting for bees'-nests and wild fruit; but if alarmed they
generally try and make for their cave. A bear's temper is very
uncertain; sometimes he will bolt away as soon as he winds
man's presence, whilst at others he will boldly dispute his way
and charge without provocation. As a rule, the female is more
courageous than the male, and she will often fight desperately in
the defence of her young. Bears generally live in families
consisting of a pair and their young, but I have known several
families live in one cave, as if they were gregarious.

HAD been staying some days on the Sheveroy Hills with Burton, enjoying the hospitality of the coffee planters, when intelligence was brought that a very Agapemone of bears had been discovered in some low hills close to the foot of the Sheveroy range. It was therefore decided that we should beat up "their diggings," and having assembled the villagers, who professed to know their haunts, we distributed the usual allowance of grog and tobacco, and gleaned all the information they could give us as to the game in that part of the country. After I had heard all their opinions, I made up my mind to take up a position on the hills where the bears were said to be an hour before the first appearance of dawn, and to await their return to their caves, as in this part of the country, during the hot weather, bears roam about the jungle in search of food all night, and return to their caves in the morning, where they remain during the intense heat of the day, issuing forth again at sunset. They live chiefly on the wild fruits of the jungle, and white ants, which latter insect they devour in thousands by scraping a hole with their claws and sucking them out of their nest. They are also passionately fond of honey, and show themselves wonderfully sharp in finding out wild bees' nests, climbing lofty trees in search of them.

The next morning we were all up, and equipped for sport by 2 A.M., and, after a substantial feed, started for the bear hill on foot, as the villagers said the route was difficult for horses. At this season of the year the night is not at any time dark, and we managed to get along very well in Indian file, although the path was very narrow, and in some places we had to crawl along on our hands and knees. We arrived at the foot of the hill some time before sunrise, and here I halted the party, which numbered about twenty coolies and villagers, and telling Burton to keep as quiet as possible, I went forward to reconnoitre, accompanied by Googooloo, the mulliarry, and two villagers who knew the bears' caves.

Although the hill was not more than 800 feet in height, it was very steep, and the ascent was the more difficult on account of numberless rocky crags which were entwined with thick bush. At last we managed to climb up the dry bed of a watercourse, where we noticed the fresh traces of bears in many places, and after a good deal of scrambling up ledges of rock, we arrived at the summit, which was a small table land covered with tufts of coarse grass and large boulders of rock.

As we were going along, Googooloo suddenly stopped, gave his usual grunt to attract attention, and, tapping me on the shoulder, pointed out two bears at the foot of the hill. With the aid of my glass I could see they were very busily engaged in digging up the earth; so setting the mulliarry to watch their movements, I went on to the caves, and, after a careful examination, found seven entrances, five of which bore marks of being inhabited by bears. I sent one of the villagers and Googooloo to bring up the rest of the party as quietly as possible, so as not to disturb the game I knew was afoot, and by the time they arrived I and the other villager had managed to block up the two smallest entrances with stones and pieces of rock. I posted Burton on a rock which commanded the two entrances of the largest cave, and the coffee-planter by another. The other two I guarded by some of the villagers, who were armed with matchlocks, and I dispatched half a dozen others to different elevated peaks, from which they could survey all the surrounding country and signalize if they saw any game.

When all were posted in their assigned places, I went with Googooloo to the mulliarry, who was watching the two bears, and he pointed them out to me in the same place we had first seen them. Accompanied by Googooloo, carrying my second gun—an eight-gauge smooth bore—I stole down the hill as gently as I could, making for a large rock which appeared to me to be within a short distance of the place where I had seen the bears.

I was some time before I could make my way to it, as the bush and underwood were thick, and we had to make our way through dense masses of entangled creepers, At last we gained the rock, and Googooloo's quick eye soon discovered our friends still hard at work scraping up the earth of the ant-hill. We stole gently up, seeking the cover of rocks and bushes until I got to within fifteen paces of them, still un-discovered. Watching their movements until I got a fair opportunity, I planted a rifle-ball behind the shoulder of one, which rolled over and over on the ground in the agonies of death, and then gave the other the contents of my second barrel, which took effect about the small ribs, tumbling her over

BEARS EATING THE MHOURA FRUIT.

for the moment. She, however, soon got up again, raised herself on her haunches, uttering a peculiarly melancholy cry, and looked round in a most woe-begone manner. This position offered me a splendid shot, and I finished her career with a ball from my second gun.

Having ascertained that both were dead, Googooloo climbed a large tree that was near, and fastened the mulliarry's turban cloth like a streamer to one of the highest branches as a landmark for the coolies, when they came to collect their game. He also cut off a claw from the right forepaw of each bear, so as to mark it as mine, a precaution the gang always took, in consequence of an individual having obtained a deer, which I had undoubtedly shot, at a battue some time previously, and, to the intense disgust of all my people, allowed him to appropriate and carry off.

As we were leisurely returning up the watercourse towards the caves where Burton and the rest of the people were posted, I heard a rolling of stones and a curious grunting noise close behind us. I jumped on a large boulder of rock, and saw three bears making their way slowly up the watercourse in the same direction we were going. I immediately made signs to Googooloo and the mulliarry to hide, and I crouched behind the rock until they were past, as I wished my friends to get a shot, and they were evidently bound their way.

These three had barely passed when Googooloo pointed me out two others making their way up the hill by the same route. Standing behind a rock so as not to alarm them, I let drive right and left as they passed within a few paces of me, both shots telling well behind the shoulder. They were both badly hit, and each must have imagined the other was the cause of his injury, for with a ferocious noise they immediately attacked each other, and closing in a hug, rolled down the hill some short distance. I followed with my second gun, and found one

dead and the other leaning over him in a very deplorable
condition. He was too far gone to take any notice of my
approach, although he continued to make a fearful moaning,
which I put a stop to by a shot behind the ear, which finished
his career.

I had just commenced re-loading, when I heard a loud
straggling volley from the top of the hill where my friends
were posted, and almost immediately it was followed by a shriek
from the mulliarry, whom I saw make a spring into the jungle
just in time to avoid the charge of a huge female bear that
came rushing down the water-course in a most furious manner.
I was directly in her path, and with a roar she made right at
me, when I let drive at her head with my only barrel that had
not been discharged, but it failed to stop her headlong charge
down-hill, and she knocked me down and was on me in the
twinkling of an eye. The slope of the hill was steep, and we
both of us rolled over and over several times until I was almost
breathless, when Googooloo rushed on her with his bill-hook
and endeavoured to attract her attention. Luckily she could
not bite at all, as my shot had smashed her snout and lower jaw
to pieces ; but she kept me locked in her embrace, and squeezed
me more roughly than affectionately. My head was well protected with a bison-skin cap; and getting a tight grasp of her
fur on each side, with my arms underneath hers, so that she
could not do much injury with her claws, I regularly wrestled
with her for some time ; and although I brought my science to
play, and threw her on her back several times, by giving her
the leg, she never let go her hug, and I was almost suffocated
with the quantity of blood and froth that came from her wound
and covered my face, beard, and chest.

Googooloo made frantic hits at her from time to time with
his bill-hook, the only weapon he had, but I ordered him to
desist, as his blows did not appear to do the bear much harm,

and I was afraid of catching one. At last Bruin appeared to be getting weaker, and I saw her wounds and loss of blood were telling; so after a little trouble I managed to draw my knife, and drove it up to the hilt in her body under the armpit. She gave me an ugly hug, and fell over on her side, pulling me with her. It was her last effort, and I picked myself up quite out of breath, but not much injured, having only received a slight claw on the loins, and another rather more severe on the instep. I drew my pistol, which I could not manage to get at before, to give her a *quietus*, but it was not wanted—the game was over, my antagonist was dead.

Being covered with blood and dust from head to foot, I must have presented a comical appearance to Burton and the rest of the people who came rushing down in pursuit of the bear, which had been slightly wounded before she fell in with me. He had met the mulliarry, *en route*, who said he had seen me killed; and no sooner did Googooloo get sight of this individual than he sprang on him like a tiger, for his cowardice in running away, and we had some difficulty in releasing him from his clutches, and preventing him from being strangled. One of the coolies brought me the water-skin, and I washed the blood away from my person, and threw off a part of my soiled clothes. I then bandaged up my loins and foot, which latter bled considerably, and was very painful when I walked, as the claws had penetrated gaiter, boot, and stocking, entering the flesh to the depth of half an inch. Having arranged matters as I best could, I managed to scramble up the hill, though I had some difficulty in doing so, as the back of my head, arms, shoulders, and knees were considerably bruised and raw in places, and I felt shaken and tired after my encounter.

When I arrived at the caves I found that Burton had killed two bears, and the coffee planter had caught a young one alive.

We remained there about an hour and a half longer when another female and two half-grown cubs came rolling along, all of which bit the dust before our united volley. The planter also went after two others which were seen climbing up the hill, but were deterred from coming near the caves, having taken alarm at the firing. He killed one, and severely wounded the other, but somehow or another managed to lose it.

The sun had now risen high above the horizon, the breeze had died away, and not a breath of air was stirring; a mirage was seen spread over the plain, out of which the wooded hills rose like distant islands. The sultriness was getting more and more oppressive, and it was intensely hot before our coolies had managed to collect the game at the foot of the hill, which consisted of eleven bears besides the little one caught alive, not a bad day's work for three guns. Finding myself stiff and sore from my bruises, I mounted my pony, and rode to our bungalow at the top of the Sheveroy hills, leaving the others to continue their sport, whilst I had my foot looked at by the doctor, and got fit for work again.

There are two kinds of bears found on the Himalayan range. The first is the ordinary black bear of the plains, previously described; and the second is the Himalayan, or snow bear, which is only found in the higher regions. They measure about nine feet long, stand about forty inches at the shoulder, and are covered with shaggy hair, which varies both in length and colour according to the season of the year. The winter coat, which is long, and of a grayish, or dirty yellowish shade, falls off in the summer, and is replaced by a shorter and much darker one approaching a reddish-brown, that lengthens and grows gradually lighter as the cold season again approaches. The female and cubs are generally light-coloured, the latter having a circle or collar of white round the neck, which diminishes as they grow older, and finally disappears. In April the female generally gives birth to two cubs, which, when born, are scarcely larger than rats, and of a tawny yellow colour. Within a month their eyes open, and in three months more they attain the size of a poodle dog, and are very playful, always wrestling together. Up to this time they are in considerable danger of being devoured by the male, if the mother does not guard them most carefully. They remain in the den with their parents until more offspring are born, when they are driven out to shift for themselves. Bears attain maturity at about five years of age, and the duration of their lives is estimated at over fifty years. In winter, snow bears retire to caves and clefts in the rocks, where they construct a kind of litter or bed of brushwood and moss, and without becoming torpid, sleep for days together. At this time the Puharries say that they cast the skin from the soles of their feet, but I cannot vouch for the fact. In the spring, when the snow begins to melt, they emerge from their dens, and feed upon young and tender shoots, grass, berries, roots, insects, and herbs. In summer time their favourite food is fruit and honey, in autumn acorns and grain, and at such times they go very long distances to forage. The bear is rarely wantonly ferocious, but when molested and wounded, or when awakened suddenly from sleep, he becomes a dangerous opponent, as he seldom shows any lack of courage. Rising on his hind legs, with head erect, he endeavours to close with his assailant, and strikes tremendous blows with his forepaw, invariably aiming at the face or head, and inflicting most ghastly wounds with his powerful claws. Although a carnivorous animal, the Himalayan bear feeds more on vegetables than flesh, rarely attacking cattle or animals unless when forced by hunger.

Yellow wolves, hyenas, jackals, black-eared foxes, and dholes or wild dogs, are common in some parts of the range; but as their nature and habits much resemble those of their brethren

of the plains, I shall not enter into them. I have frequently
come across packs of the latter animals in the birch forests, and
watched them hunt down gooral, or burrul, always running
against the wind, and often chasing by relays.

CARRYING HOME THE GAME.

CHAPTER VI.

TIGER, PANTHER, AND LEOPARD HUNTING.

ALL forest creatures—with very rare exceptions—are afraid of man, never voluntarily intruding upon his presence, and invariably beating a retreat if they can do so unmolested. None of the feline race, with the exception of confirmed man-eaters, which are few and far between, will attack man, unless provoked, and the taint even of his footstep in the forest will often make them turn aside and leave the neighbourhood.

Although the Carnivora, as a rule, are a cunning, skulking, cowardly, and bloodthirsty set, yet their characters and temperament vary considerably, as some of them, when wounded, exhibit the most reckless, desperate courage, charging fearlessly against their assailants until the last gasp, and others die like curs, without making an effort to resist. The great secret necessary to ensure success in this kind of shooting is *never to pull trigger unless certain of striking the game in a vital spot*, and, again, *always to keep a shot in reserve*, in case of a wounded animal charging. I need not say that extreme coolness is as much required as accuracy of marksmanship, and anyone who feels " that even he has nerves " had better confine his attentions to game that will not retaliate when wounded.

These animals are all very tenacious of life, and the hunter should always endeavour to shoot them either through the brain or the heart. I have often dropped them stone dead with a bullet right between the eyes, or by aiming just behind the shoulder-blade as the fore-arm moves forward in walking,

when, if the heart is missed, the bullet will most likely penetrate the lungs.

THE TIGER.

There is, in my opinion, only one variety of tiger, although
this animal, like all others that I am acquainted with, is
subject to slight variations of appearance, that may generally
be more or less accounted for by his peculiar habits, which vary
according to the locality and the nature of the country he
ranges over. In many parts of India over which I have hunted,
the natives recognise three kinds of tigers, which they distinguish according to their habits and range, by the following
names :—First, the *lodia bagh,* or game-killing tiger ; secondly,
the *contia bagh,* which lives chiefly upon domestic cattle ; and,
thirdly, the *admee khane wallah,* or man-eater, which latter
happily are few and far between.

The *lodia bagh,* or game-killing tiger, such as is shown in the
engraving, lives chiefly in the hills and fastnesses of the forest,
where he subsists upon deer and other wild animals, rarely
showing himself near the haunts of man, and retreating immediately he discovers his presence. The *lodia bagh* may be
again subdivided into two classes, from their different modes of
killing their game. The first prowls about the forest and
tracks up his quarry by scent, approaches him stealthily under
cover, springing upon him when unawares, or running him down
by a succession of gigantic bounds from which even the speediest
deer can hardly hope to escape. The second class of game-
killing tigers depend more upon their cunning than their speed
in circumventing their prey, and are accustomed to lie in ambuscade, by water, or in runs frequented by different kinds of
deer. His usual retreat in the hot weather is to some ravine
amongst the hills where pools of water remain all the year
round, and here under shelving masses of rock, or under the

THE GAME-KILLING TIGER.

shade of overhanging trees, he makes his lair, and lies in wait for any forest creature that may come to quench its thirst by day or night. The regular game-hunting tiger is a small light-made beast, very active and enduring, and his skin is most beautifully and distinctly marked, the black stripes being very close together. He is always very shy and retiring in his habits, and from constantly living on the *qui vive* is very difficult to approach and bring to bay.

The *oontia bagh,* or cattle lifter—so called because his faintly striped coat resembles in colour that. of a camel—is a much larger and heavier animal than the game-killing tiger, being very fleshy, and rarely in the condition to undergo any great exertion. Thus when systematically pursued by hunters, he may be overtaken and beaten out of cover time after time, but a regular game-hunting tiger once lost sight of is rarely again to be fallen in with.

The cattle-lifter, in the cool season, follows the herds of cattle whenever they go to graze, keeping as much as possible under cover so as to escape their guardian's observation, and then striking down any straggler that may approach his ambuscade, which is generally on the skirts of some jungle, in which for a time he has located himself.

In the hot weather he secretes himself in some cover of high reeds, or karinda or tamarask thicket, which are usually found along the banks of the partially dried up rivers, and lies in wait for cattle coming to drink. Watching his opportunity, he kills a bullock by seizing him in his massive jaws by the nape of the neck, as, unaware of danger, he is grazing on the green herbage found by the side of the stream, and with the aid of the fore-paws, which serve as a purchase, he generally manages to dislocate the neck in a moment, and drag him into his cover; the whole affair being so quietly and expeditiously managed that the herdsman rarely discovers his loss until he has collected

THE CATTLE SLAYER.

his cattle to drive them home. The engraving represents the death of one of these wholesale plunderers, whom I shot just as he was about to spring upon a bullock tied up as a bait.

Of course a lazy marauder of this kind also kills a good many head of deer when they come to drink near his ambuscade, but as a rule, as long as he can get cattle, he does not trouble himself to hunt for them.

A single tiger will kill a bullock or buffalo every five days, if he gets the chance, often eating the hind-quarters the first night, and hiding the remainder in a bush, to consume at his leisure. Should he have been fired at, or disturbed on his return to his quarry, he becomes cunning and far more destructive, killing a fresh bullock whenever he wants food; and I have known tigers that have become so suspicious that they would not return to an animal they had killed, although they had only lapped the blood, and the bullock was almost untouched. On the other hand I have known of a tiger returning day after day to the carcase of the ox he had killed and picking the bones clean, notwithstanding he had been twice fired at by a native shekarry. A family of tigers, viz., a tiger, tigress, and two grown-up cubs, are terribly destructive, often killing two or three head of cattle in a day, the young tigers, for practice sake, under their parents' tuition, striking down as many of the herd as they catch in their way.

Of course the damage sustained by these wholesale depredations is immense, but as tigers, as a rule, do not confine their attacks to the herds of a single village, but distribute their favours with impartiality over a whole district, they are allowed to live " on sufferance," notwithstanding their haunts are perfectly well known to all the different village herdsmen. Cattle-lifters seldom molest men, and as long as they confine their attention to occasional bullocks, the apathetic natives are too inert and cowardly to beat up their haunts and destroy them themselves, and when some wandering Englishman on the

DEATH OF A CATTLE LIFTER.

look-out for sport finds himself in the neighbourhood of their villages, unless their cupidity and avarice overcome their natural laziness, in most places they are very unwilling to give any information about tigers, lest they should be compelled to give up their usual occupations and be employed in beating the jungle to drive them out.

The government reward for every full-grown tiger's skin produced was 50 rupees or £5 a head in the old day, and this to some extent served to cover part of the expenses of a hunt, but of late years, by the extreme parsimony of the administration this reward has been reduced to half, consequently tiger shooting has now become a very expensive game, and as a rule the sportsman will find himself about 100 rupees out of pocket for every tiger he bags.

Man-eaters, luckily for mankind, are neither numerous nor invulnerable, but there are several instances on record of villages having been abandoned on account of the ravages that these terrible scourges of mankind have committed. All animals have a natural innate dread of man, but if any of the Felidæ by any chance once happen to taste human blood, either from being rendered desperate by hunger, or by pouncing upon a man by mistake, they acquire a relish for human flesh, and abandon the chase of all other animals. With their change of living their character and habits entirely alter, and they become desperately cunning, skulking and prowling round villages with a noiseless step until they get the chance of springing upon some victim from behind when unaware and defenceless, and carrying him off into the forest before he can raise a cry, so that often scarcely a trace of the ruthless deed remains to give a clue as to the cause of his disappearance.

In India we have three distinct species of the *felidæ*, inferior in strength and size to the tiger, that are often mistaken one for the other, and indiscriminately called panthers, or leopards,

A FAMILY OF MARAUDERS.

notwithstanding they are entirely distinct animals, and differ most essentially both in appearance and habits.

These three species are :—the felis pardus, the true panther, Hindi "*taindwa;*" the felis leopardus, the leopard, Hindi "*bor bucha;*" and the felis jubata, the hunting leopard or cheetah, Hindi "*cheeta.*"

The panther is by far the largest and most powerful of the three species, as it frequently measures eight feet in length from the nose to the end of tail. He has also a well-defined bony ridge along the centre of the skull for the attachment of the muscles of the neck, which is not noticeable in the leopard or cheetah. The skin, which shines like silk, is of a rich tawny or orange tan above, and white underneath, marked on each side with seven lines of rosettes, each consisting of an assemblage of five or six black spots, in the centre of which the tawny or fulvous ground of the skin shows distinctly through the black. The extremities are marked with horseshoe-shaped or round black spots. Few animals can surpass the panther in point of beauty, and none in elegance and grace. His every motion is easy and flexile in the highest degree, he bounds among the rocks and woods with an agility truly amazing ; now stealing along the ground with the silence of a snake, now crouching with his fore paws extended and his spotted head laid betwixt them, while his chequered tail twitches impatiently, and his pale, gooseberry eyes glare mischievously upon his unsuspecting victim.

The panther is much more active than the tiger, making immense bounds clean off the ground, which the tiger rarely does; furthermore, he can climb trees with great agility. The panther, as a rule, is more courageous than the tiger ; and, although he does not weigh half as much, his powers of offence and defence are scarcely inferior, and when a large male panther takes to cattle-lifting or man-eating he is a more terrible scourge than the tiger, inasmuch as he is more daring and cunning. That good sportsman Captain Forsyth states that "a man-killing panther devastated the northern part of the Seoni district, killing (incredible as it may seem) nearly a hundred persons before he was shot by a shekarry. He never ate the bodies, but merely lapped the blood from the throat; and his plan was either to steal into a house at night and strangle some sleeper on his bed, stifling all outcry with his deadly grip, or to climb into the high platforms from which watchers guard their fields from deer, and drag his victim from there. He was not to be baulked of his prey; and when driven off from one end of a village would hurry round to the opposite side and secure another in the confusion. A few moments completed his deadly work; and such was the devilish cunning he joined to this extraordinary boldness that all attempts to find and shoot him were for many months unsuccessful. European sportsmen who went out, after hunting him in vain all day, would find his tracks close to the door of their tent in the morning." The Seoni panther is not a solitary case, several other man-eating panthers having committed similar depredations in other parts of India. Their usual retreats in the daytime are amongst low, rocky hills, overgrown with low bush, and full of hollows and caverns, where they hide when pursued, and from which they issue after nightfall, and prowl round the neighbouring villages in search of prey, retreating to their fastnesses before daylight. They care little for the neighbourhood of water, and only drink at night, even during the hot weather. The black panther is only a variety of the same animal, as I once killed an ordinary female panther, and found two young cubs in the cave from out of which we smoked her, one of which was black, whilst the other was tan coloured and spotted. In holding the skin of a black panther or leopard up to the light, the spots are always more or less perceptible, being more intensely black than the rest of the ground colour.

The leopard is smaller in proportion, and shorter-limbed than the panther, which it much resembles both in form and colour, although the marks on the body are somewhat different, being generally horseshoe or crescent-shaped, and placed much closer together, especially along the ridge of the back. Whilst the former often preys on cattle, and is a dangerous antagonist to man when unarmed, the latter chiefly confines himself to sheep, goats, dogs, and such small animals, although instances of his having attacked adult human beings are not uncommon. I have known villages where children were regularly carried off by leopards if they ventured to sleep outside the huts, even in the main street. The tiger and panther will rarely touch anything that they have not killed themselves ; but the leopard is by no means so particular, and I have on several occasions lost haunches of venison and saddles of mutton that were tied up to the branches of the tree under which my tent was pitched, high out of the reach of village dogs or jackals, that were carried off by leopards allured by the smell of the meat during the night, as I could tell by the footsteps of the marauders the next morning. The leopard is an admirable climber, and will often take to trees when pursued by a pack of dogs, or when lying in ambush for monkeys—his favourite food. The engraving represents an incident of this kind, when, attracted to the spot by the screams of "Master Jacko," I was enabled to shoot his antagonist through the head and secure his beautiful skin. The leopard rarely exceeds 7 feet in length, and stands about 26 inches in height at the shoulder. Very few sportsmen have sojourned for any length of time in the jungle without having been annoyed by these nocturnal depredators carrying off their dogs, and on several occasions I have lost a canine follower in this manner. The illustration represents a night alarm caused

MASTER JACKO IN JEOPARDY.

by the appearance of a leopard in camp ; but luckily his presence was discovered before he could do any harm, and a double discharge of buck-shot from an eight-gauge gun in the back of his head ended his career. The cheetah is smaller, again, than the leopard, but stands high in proportion to his length, which rarely exceeds 7 feet, being 4 feet 6 inches from the nose to the base of the tail, which appendage is $2\frac{1}{2}$ feet long. The felidæ generally have broad rounded paws, armed with sharp, hooked, and completely retractile claws, which can be protruded at will. The foot of the cheetah differs from all the rest of the cat tribe, being long and narrow, and the claws are only partially retractile, and therefore become worn and blunted at the points. The limbs of the cheetah seem formed for speed, being long and slender, whilst the body is slight, compared to that of the leopard, and much drawn in at the flanks. The general colour of the cheetah is a light tan or fawn, covered with round black spots, and a distinct black stripe passes from the inner angle of the eye to the corner of the mouth ; the muzzle is black, and the head rounder than that of the leopard, whilst the male has a kind of mane along the neck and shoulders.

"*Mechaun*" *Shooting.*—The most common way of killing all kinds of feline animals is by shooting them from a "mechaun," or platform built in a tree, about 15 feet from the ground, and hidden from observation by freshly cut branches. This arrangement is constructed in that part of the forest which these animals are known to frequent, and around it, within easy rifle range, are picketed three or four young calves, who, crying for their mothers, attract the spoilers to the spot, when the sportsmen may kill them from their place of concealment, with very little danger to themselves, as shown in the engraving. There is one strange peculiarity about most forest creatures, which is that, however quick they are to detect danger, they seldom or

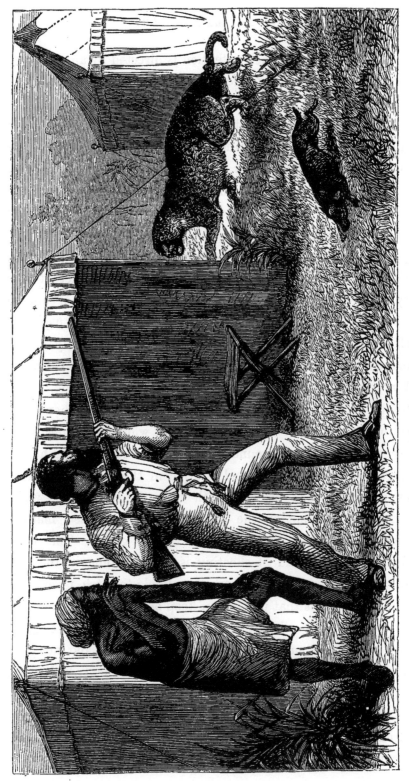

A NIGHT MARAUDER.

never look up, unless their attention is directed by any unusual noise—hence the advantage of building the mechaun in a tree.

"*Moat*" *Shooting.*—Another plan, which is often adopted for killing game of various kinds during the hot season, is the construction of "moats" or ambuscades near the pools where the signs show that wild animals are accustomed to drink. When I was likely to be located in the same spot for any length of time, and had to provide my people with food, I generally built a moat on piles some little distance in the water, as shown in the engraving, so as to command the different runs by which the game approached ; and lest the taint of human footprints in the moist ground should arouse the suspicions of, or scare away, the game, I never allowed any of my people to draw water from the part of the pool they frequented. Should I not have had time to construct such an ambuscade, I used to dig, within a few feet of the edge of the water, when practicable, a hole about 8 feet long, 6 feet wide, and 4 feet deep. Heaping the earth all round like a crenelated wall, and having spread waterproof sheets, and a carpet in the inside, so as to be as comfortable as possible, with four of my people—two of whom always kept on the look-out—I have passed many a night, and killed almost every kind of game. The worst feature of this kind of shooting is that sleeping in the close proximity of water renders one very liable to catch fever ; and the minor evil is that unless you keep on a broad-brimmed hat, with a mosquito veil that will protect your face and neck, you will be severely punished by these small vermin, and not get a wink of sleep, which will unfit you for the next day's work. The party who are going to watch for game at night should go to their ambush at least an hour before sunset, as during a drought many animals come to drink at that time, and the utmost caution should be used in moving about after dark, as

MECHAUN SHOOTING.

there may be other creatures besides the hunters on the look-
out for game.

Beating or Driving.—In some forests it may be advisable to
beat for large game, and I have often made large bags by
taking my station at the head of a ravine, and making the line
of beaters drive the animals towards me.   Previous to beating,
the ground should be reconnoitred, and a good deal of judgment
is required in selecting a position that commands the different
runs up which the animals may come, and it is absolutely
necessary to maintain the strictest silence, and remain as
much as possible concealed. It is very unadvisable on these
occasions to fire random shots, at very long ranges, as the
chances are that the report of your rifle may prevent other
game from coming near you, and lose you a fair chance.
Great care must be taken, also, not to fire in the direction of
the beaters.

The most certain information as to the presence of tigers, or
indeed any of the feline race, is given by monkeys, who directly
the enemy stirs give their well-known cry of alarm, as a warning to the unwary, and continue making a harsh shrieking noise
as long as he remains in sight.   The peculiarly discordant cry
of the *kola balloo*, or solitary jackal, also frequently betrays his
whereabouts, as this animal, who, from old age or infirmities, is
incapacitated from hunting with his fellows, lives upon what
the tiger leaves, and gives notice to his master of any stray
cattle that might serve him as a meal.

In Central India, where trained elephants are tolerably
numerous, the dense covers are beaten with a line of elephants,
and many tigers are thus brought to bag, the sportsmen being
either mounted in howdahs on elephants or posted on some
elevated ground, towards which the game is driven. A good
steady shekar elephant costs about £300 to buy in the first
instance, and about 80 rupees a month to keep, so that

MOAT SHOOTING.

very few military men possess them; consequently coolies hired by the day are generally employed as beaters, every other man in the line having a fire-arm of some kind, or a tom-tom.

The line of beaters, keeping up a perpetual noise, rouse the tiger from his lair and drive him past the ambuscades, behind which the sportsmen lie hidden. When it is possible, elevated ground should be selected for these posts, which command an extensive view of the surrounding country, and watchers should be posted in trees round about the lair to signalise when the animal breaks, and which direction he is making for. These must keep a careful watch, for a tiger that has been hunted before grows very cunning, and when alarmed, instead of breaking boldly forth, skulks from bush to bush and creeps along very close to the ground, taking advantage of every patch of cover that lies in his way. Sometimes when the bush is very thick and he lies close, it is advisable to use rockets to scare him, and make him break into the open. But occasionally even this does not answer, and the tiger will break back through the line of beaters in spite of everything.

SKULL OF TIGER.

TIGER-SHOOTING FROM THE HOWDAH.

THE most favourable time for hunting all kinds of large game in India is during the hot season, as by April or May most of the grass and rank undergrowth is burnt up in the jungle, and the intense heat of the sun has so dried up the face of the country that the water supply is reduced to its lowest ebb; consequently the *felidæ*, driven by thirst, leave the denser forest, and seek the lowest valleys, where pools of water remain all the year round, or frequent the karinda and tamarisk thickets that afford dense and extensive cover in the immediate neighbourhood of most of our rivers in the Central Provinces, and the Deccan. The ·ravages that tigers, panthers, and leopards commit amongst the cattle in India must in the aggregate amount to some hundreds of thousand of pounds sterling per annum; for in many districts the inhabitants suffer a loss exceeding a lac of rupees, or £10,000, in the course of a year. Although in almost every village there is a professional shekarry or hunter, he is generally so inefficiently armed with an untrustworthy matchlock, as to be unable to cope with his wary antagonist; but when he hears of a bullock having been struck down, he proceeds to the spot, and, taking post in the nearest tree, watches by night for the return of the marauder, who, although he may kill and drink the blood during daylight, never feeds before sunset. Sometimes, if he does not bungle at his work, and can get his matchlock to go off, he may succeed in killing or mortally wounding the tiger; but, with his wretched weapons, the chances are that the spoiler escapes unscathed, and becomes far more cunning and suspicious than before. The village shekarry never attempts the system generally adopted by Europeans of tracking up the gorged tiger to his mid-day lair, and driving him out, either with beaters and rockets, or, where the jungle is sufficiently open, with a line of elephants; but in many cases he will be able to give much useful information as to his habits and usual resorts, therefore his co-operation should be secured, and a few rupees will not only loosen his tongue, but also induce him to accompany the tracking party to mark him down. To stalk a tiger on foot in dense cover is often quite impracticable ; as, where there is thick undergrowth, the hunter can rarely see three yards before him, whilst every step he takes is seen and heard by his suspicious antagonist, who can, if he choose, travel round him and take him in the rear without the slightest sound betraying his movements. When the country is covered with high grass, it is almost impossible to drive out a tiger even with a strong gang of beaters : besides this is dangerous and uncertain work, and in many cases the tiger will break back through the beat without giving the sportsmen a chance of a shot. Under these circumstances, little or nothing can be done without the aid of trained elephants, when the quarry can be tracked and followed up to his mid-day lair, and killed with comparatively little danger.

A thoroughly-trained and steady shekar-elephant is invaluable to a sportsman, more especially for beating jungle or high grass ; but unbroken or timid ones are worse than useless, as, in the event of a wounded tiger charging, they become un-governable, and their riders run great danger of being smashed against the overhanging branches of trees.

A well-broken shekar-elephant will beat for his game like a pointer, making his way noiselessly through the brushwood, searching the densest thickets foot by foot, and, at the command of his mahout, throwing stones into the watercourses, where tigers are likely to conceal themselves. When the tiger is afoot, the sagacious animal stands ready at the word of com-mand, so as to allow his master to shoot, and should the animal be wounded and charge, he will stand his ground with the most unflinching courage, as if trusting in the sportsman's coolness and accuracy of aim. Sometimes they display over-eagerness in seeking to kill the tiger themselves by trampling them under foot ; and in such a case the rider is liable to be pitched

A SHEKAR ELEPHANT.

out of the howdah in the struggle. Generally speaking, when mounted on a well-trained and steady elephant, the hunter is exposed to very little danger; and I know of ladies having killed tigers in this manner. I cannot, however, say that I am partial to this kind of shooting, not finding much excitement in it; moreover, I never feel sure of my aim when seated on a jolting elephant, and for my own part much prefer the more sportsmanlike proceeding of killing my game on foot, and giving him a fair chance of defending his skin. I may however observe, that I never myself possessed a thoroughly-trained shekar-elephant; and although I have frequently had at my disposition elephants belonging to Government or native friends, I never felt myself quite safe when travelling at any speed across country in a howdah. Although perhaps endowed with as much nerve as the generality of men, I always felt out of my element in a howdah; and notwithstanding I have been out tiger-shooting upon elephants some scores of times, I always felt far more afraid of the elephant taking fright and bolting, or falling down bodily to the bottom of a ravine, or smashing the howdah and its occupants against the overhanging branches of trees, than I ever did of the tiger.

Every man, let his nerve be what it will, must naturally feel alarm in his first crossing a difficult country; but, after a time, with further experience, the feeling to a certain extent wears off, as he begins to understand the method by which the elephant descends and ascends places that seem, for so ponderous and clumsy-looking an animal, actually impracticable. It is not even reasonable to expect a person, unaccustomed to that sort of thing, to believe in the perfectly surprising powers of this huge animal until he has actually seen them exercised. Let the reader imagine himself seated in a large box on the back of an animal ten feet high, weighing some three or four tons, on the edge of a nullah with steep banks some ten or fifteen feet deep, down which he is about to clamber after a wounded and perhaps infuriated tiger ; and if the situation does not try his nerves, he is more than mortal. Riding over the stiffest country is a mere joke to it, for there you feel that you have a certain command over your horse ; but, when in a howdah, you are helpless, and have to depend entirely upon the *sang froid* of the mahout or native driver, and his capability of managing and controlling the elephant's movements. This he does with an iron instrument, sharp at the point and the crook. This being pressed with the point to his head, is a signal for him to go forward ; on either ear with the crook, to wheel to the right or left ; and on the forehead to stop. By the management of this instrument, accompanied by certain words of command, the paces and the direction of the elephant are regulated. The hind legs of the elephant differ in their peculiar formation from any other quadruped : as, instead of doubling them under him when he lies down, he extends them behind him as a man does when kneeling. The struggle which horses experience in rising from the ground is by this arrangement avoided, as when he wishes to regain his legs he simply draws his hind feet gradually under him, and his enormous weight is levered up without any perceptible effort. Owing to this beautiful mechanism, and the extraordinary development of muscle of the legs and feet, together with his wonderful sagacity and instinct, the elephant is one of the most sure-footed of animals ; and he can ascend and descend the most precipitous slopes, carrying a howdah on his back, with the greatest ease. His method is simple enough. On descending he drops his hind quarters to the ground, while he stands erect on his fore legs, taking each step with the greatest caution ; on ascending the reverse takes place, dropping on his fore whilst erect on his hind quarters; and in this manner, slow but sure, he ascends and descends places that no horse could, even with best and boldest rider on his back.

When he cannot find a safe foot-hold, he sets to work making it
artificially by beating an indentation in the earth with his broad
and heavy foot; and when the fore feet are withdrawn, the hind
feet are inserted in the same place.   From the spongy formation
of the sole of the foot, the tread of the elephant, even when
going his usual pace, a fast swinging walk, is quite inaudible;
and, when travelling over loose sand, where a horse would sink
fetlock deep, an elephant's foot-prints would be scarcely perceptible.

With respect to the best kind of howdah, there are various
opinions.   They are made of as many shapes and sizes as·
the buggies on the Calcutta esplanade, and as *nondescript;*
but perhaps the most convenient one for shekar purposes is
shown in the engraving.   On each corner of the front part of
the howdah should be constructed a perfectly secured gun-rack,
and it is a good plan to have a block of wood some three or
four inches in thickness screwed on the floor, having holes cut
out in the shape of the butt and heel of the gun-stock, stuffed
and padded with leather, to prevent the possibility of accidents
happening from the guns shifting by the jolting motion of the
elephant.   Some sportsmen take large-bore pistols with them
in case of the tiger charging the elephant, and coming to close
quarters with the occupants of the howdah; but, to be effective,
the muzzle must be placed close to the tiger's head, and care
must be taken not to hit the mahout, who is far more exposed
to the brunt of the attack than the hunters in the howdah.
Insignificant as the mahout may look perched straddle-legs on
the elephant's neck and dancing from side to side at every
stride, he has unquestionably by far the most difficult and
arduous part to play in the hunt, and he ought to be a man of
tried courage and *sang froid;* for in the first place he is at no
great distance from the ground, the top of his head being much
lower than the howdah, whilst his feet hang down nearly to the

bottom of the elephant's ears, so that he is far more exposed to danger from a tiger charging, than the occupants of the howdah. Again, he is unarmed except with his iron crook; and, unless he has perfect confidence in the skill of his master as a marksman, he is not likely to bring his elephant properly up when in momentary expectation of the charge of a furious tiger, who is as likely as not to spring and hang on to the elephant's head. The elephant, like the horse, soon finds out what his rider is made of; and however staunch and well trained the animal may be, he cannot be expected to be steady and go ahead when the mahout is trembling and in a state of "green funk." Many an elephant that turns tail and "takes to his scrapers" at the very smell of a tiger, might be brought well up to the scratch by a really good plucky mahout; and, after he has seen a few tigers killed without any accident happening to himself, he becomes perfectly fearless when in their neighbourhood, and seems to enjoy the sport. The late Captain Forsyth, who had much experience in tiger-shooting from the howdah in the Central Provinces, gives the following interesting account of the wonderful sagacity and staunch courage of a perfectly trained elephant:

"A strange affection springs up between the hunter and his well-tried ally in the chase of the tiger; and a creature seeming to those who see him only in the menagerie, or labouring under a load of baggage, but a lumbering mass of flesh, becomes to him almost a second self, yielding to his service the perfection of physical and mental qualities of which a brute is capable, and displaying an intelligent interest in his sport, of which no brute could be thought to be possessed. No one who has not witnessed it would believe the astonishing caution with which a well-trained elephant approaches a tiger, removing with noiseless adroitness every obstacle of fallen timber, etc., and passing his huge bulk over rustling leaves or rolling stones, or quaking bog, with an absolute and marvellous silence; handing up stones when ordered, for his master to fling into a cover; smelling out a cold scent as a spaniel roads a pheasant; and at last, perhaps, pointing dead with sensitive trunk at the hidden monster, or showing with short nervous taps of that organ on the ground that he is somewhere near, though not actually discovered to the senses of the elephant. Then the unswerving steadiness when he sees the enemy he naturally dreads, and would flee from panic-stricken in his native haunts, perhaps charging headlong at his head, trusting all to the skill of his rider, and thoughtless of using his own tremendous strength in the encounter—for a good elephant never attempts to combat the tiger himself. To do so would generally be fatal to the sport, and perhaps to the sportsman too; for no one could stick to an elephant engaged in a personal struggle with a tiger, far less use his gun under such circumstances. The elephant's business is to stand like a rock in every event, even when the tiger is fastened on his head—as many a good one will do and has done."

It is not one elephant in a thousand that is so thoroughly good in tiger-shooting as this; and such as are, command very high prices in the market. From £200 to £400 is now the value of a thoroughly first-rate shooting elephant, though much sport may be had for one purchased for the smaller sum. Captain Forsyth says: "It is difficult to buy horses at a fair, but the difficulty is ten times greater in the case of elephants. Every one connected with the keeping of elephants (and camels) is by nature and training from his youth a consummate rascal, and the animal himself is subject to numerous and often obscure vices and unsoundness." Elephants differ as widely in their "points as do horses, and it is very difficult for an uneducated eye to distinguish these, particularly in the fattened-up condition the animals generally carry at the fair. Furthermore, and

MUSTER OF ELEPHANTS FOR BEATING.

fortunately enough for us, a native's ideas of good points in an elephant (as in the shape of a horse) differ *in toto* from ours. He looks not at all to shape, or good action, or likelihood of standing hard work ; but first of all to the presence or absence of certain accidental marks—such as the number of toe-nails on the foot, which may be five or six, but not four—the tail, which must be perfect and with a full tuft—and the colour of the palate, which must be red without spot of black. Some of the best elephants I have known failed, in each and all of these points. Then a female or a tuskless male is of small value to a native, who wants big white tusks. A rough high action, and a trunk and forehead of very light colour, are greatly in request by the native buyer; who looks entirely to show, and covers up every part of the animal except the face with an enormous parti-coloured cloth. For sporting purposes we look for a small well-bred-looking head and trunk, and a clear, confident eye, devoid of piggish expression, fast easy paces, straight back and croup, wide loins, and generally well-developed muscle—a great test of which is the girth of the fore-arm which should measure three feet eight inches in an elephant nine feet high. A very tall elephant is seldom a good working one, and generally has slow rough paces; so that in a male, nine feet—or a female, eight feet four inches at the shoulder should not be exceeded; a smaller animal than eight feet two inches will be under-sized for tiger-shooting purposes. A female makes the best hunting elephant when she is really staunch with game, as her paces and temper are generally better, and she is not subject to the danger of becoming "must" and uncontrollable, as male elephants do periodically after a certain age. But females are more uncertain as regards courage than males, and it is a risk to buy the former, untried, for shooting purposes. Most *muknas* (tuskless males) can I believe be relied on to become staunch with tigers when properly trained and entered; and for my own part, if buying an entirely untried elephant, I would always select a *mukna*. They are generally more vigorous and better developed than tuskers, though not usually so tall; which may be accounted for because young tuskers, after their sharp little tusks begin to grow, prick the mother in the process of sucking, and are consequently driven off by her and allowed to shift for themselves, whilst females and *muknas* continue to be nourished by her until she has got another young one.

All elephants intended to be used in hunting tigers, must be very carefully trained and entered to their game. A good mahout or driver is very difficult to obtain. They differ as much in their command over elephants as do riders of horses; and a plucky driver will generally make a staunch elephant and *vice versâ*. The elephant should first be accustomed to the firing of guns from his back, and to seeing deer and other harmless animals shot before him, in company with a staunch companion. He must not be forced on at a tiger, or a hog or bear, which he detests even more, until he has acquired some confidence, though in some few cases he will stand to any animal from the very first. When they have seen a few tigers neatly disposed of, most elephants acquire confidence in their human allies, and become sufficiently steady in the field; but their ultimate qualities will depend much on natural temperament. The more naturally courageous an elephant is, the better chance there is of his remaining staunch after having been mauled by a tiger— an accident to be avoided as long as possible. It will occur at times, however, in the best hands; and then a naturally timid animal, who has only been made staunch by a long course of immunity from injury, will probably be spoiled for life, while a really plucky elephant is often rendered bolder than before by such an occurrence.

The finest sport I ever had in shooting from a howdah was in the Deccan, whilst quartered at Secunderabad. Having obtained a fortnight's leave, I was staying at Chuder ghaut, near the city of Hyderabad, with a first-rate sportsman, Captain Mounsey, who had lately retired from the " King's Own," and had established himself in a somewhat palatial mansion near the Resi-dency, when we received invitations from the Shazada Mir-fet-Ali, and Abdoola-ben-Ali, the chief of the Arab and Puthan contingent, to accompany them on a pleasure and shekar party at Shah-nugger which was some twenty miles distant. Otter and Madegan of our host's old corps, Blake of the 36th N. I., and Doctor Riddel, from Bolarum, were also asked to join the party ; and having sent our horses, tents, baggage, servants, and shekarries on before, early one morning we found ourselves at the village where our native friends were encamped.

The camp was pitched under the shade of a fine peepul grove, and at first sight resembled a great fair, as on one flank quite a large bazaar was established, where, from the hubbub and clamour of voices, it might be imagined that a good trade was being carried on. A large double-poled tent, with luxurious furnishings, serving as a *dewan khana* or reception. hall, occupied the centre of the position, and separated our tents from our native friends' encampment; and in the rear were picketed over a dozen fine-looking elephants, a long line of gaily caparisoned native hackeries, and several Persian and Deccan bred horses, fattened up with ghee and jagherry, until they looked in the condition of prize oxen. We received a most cordial welcome from our native friends, who were attended by a large suite, including several taifas or nautch girls, and a band of native musicians, and sat down to an excellent breakfast, at which our prospects of sport were discussed. The Zemindar of that district, who was present, informed us that he was very glad that we had come, as there were several tigers almost in the immediate neighbourhood, and that scarcely a day passed without some of his villagers

A PANIC-STRICKEN ELEPHANT.

losing their cattle. As native reports as a rule are not very reliable, Otter, who was a great linguist, in the course of the forenoon had several herdsmen up, who professed to know the where-abouts of tigers, and questioning them each separately, found their evidence to tally in the main; so it was determined to commence operations the following morning with a grand beat. In the meantime, it was necessary to survey the ground, and determine the line of country we intended to drive; so Blake and I, mounting our horses, with a couple of our own shekarries and some villagers, made a *reconnaissance* of some likely-looking low hills; whilst Otter, Mounsey, Madegan, Riddel, and our native friends on pad elephants, went to examine a nullah, which was said to be the usual haunt of a family of tigers, who had committed terrible depredations on the villagers' flocks and herds. On our return to camp, we had every reason to be satisfied with our prospects of sport, as we had seen several fresh traces of tigers, bears, and hog, whilst the other party had found a broad ravine, clothed with dwarf jungle and intersected with several nullahs, the sandy beds of which were covered with tigers' foot-prints of many dates, from a week old to fresh pugs made that morning. The Zemindar, having assembled the herdsmen of several of the surrounding villages, gave directions that scouts should be sent out in all the most likely places, and all information sent in at once to camp. He also arranged that at daybreak a line of watchers should be posted in trees on the lateral hills, commanding a view of the ravine we intended to beat, so as to notify the movements made by the tigers, and their line of retreat; and a large body of sowars and matchlock-men were to take post at both sides of the head of the ravine, to drive back the game in case it should attempt to steal away unobserved. The next morning, as we were getting up from breakfast, information came in that several tigers had been marked down, and that all the watchers were at their posts, and in fact that only our presence was necessary for the game to commence. We were to take the field with a line of ten elephants, six of which, intended for our use, carried howdahs, and were considered sufficiently staunch for any kind of game we were likely to meet with; whilst the others, bearing pads, each accommodated half a dozen natives, and sundry boxes containing refreshments. We now stored rifles and ammunition in the howdahs, and paired off, Mounsey riding with the Shahzada, Otter with the Zemindar, Doctor Riddel with Abdoola, whilst Blake, Madegan, and I, had only our shekarries with us. We made a somewhat imposing appearance, as we filed out of the village; and forming line as soon as we got into open country, we were soon traversing a fine game country. We first passed a grass-covered maidan, studded with custard-apple bushes, and here we put up great numbers of partridges, hares, and ravine antelope; but they were allowed to go unscathed. Then a couple of sounders of hog were reared, and, as the ground was rideable, "visions of first spears" crossed our minds, and sent the blood coursing through our veins, and we registered a vow to have a spin across country in that district before we were many days older. We were jogging quietly along on the extreme right, when we heard a sudden commotion at the other end of the line, followed by the angry trumpeting of an elephant, which gave warning that game was afoot, and very shortly afterwards a tigress and two nearly full-grown cubs sprang out of a patch of dense cover by the dry bed of a water-course thickly overgrown with reeds and long rumnah grass. Crack, crack, went five or six rifles, and the cubs were soon disposed of; but the tigress was but slightly wounded, as she crouched low in the high grass, and presented very little chance of a fair shot. However, enraged at the pain of her wounds, and her maternal feelings being roused at the death of her young, with a shrill scream of anger she boldly charged our line, and, springing open-mouth at Mounsey's elephant, seized his ear in her teeth and left the marks of her claws pretty deeply scored on his shoulder. Luckily old Hyder was a staunch and well-trained tiger-hunter, and undismayed by the suddenness of the attack, with an angry screech he shook her off, and pirouetting, gave her a kick that nearly knocked all the breath out of her body, as for a moment she lay motionless as if quite bewildered ; and Mounsey and the Shahzada, taking fair aim, let drive, when she rolled over once or twice, stretched out her limbs, and expired.

The game being hoisted on pad elephants, the line was reformed, and shortly afterwards, on passing through a patch of low bush, a magnificent tiger sprang out of some high reeds in the dry bed of a water-course, and I had a fair right and left shot ; but, unaccustomed to shoot from a jolting howdah, I missed clean, and a perfect shower of bullets rattled round about him as he dashed across the open. Although he was manifestly hit, from the short sharp yelps he gave, he continued to bound along through the bushes until he passed in front of Madegan's elephant when he had to cross the open bed of a water-course, and a second discharge rolled him over, dead as we thought ; but on hurrying up to the spot he was nowhere to be seen, having vanished, as it were, into the ground. Closing up our line, we tracked him by his pugs to some dwarf date-trees and custard-apple bush, when, as we were beating the banks of a nullah, Madegan espied him stealing away furtively behind some reeds, and let drive at him, when he crouched, evidently sulky and meaning mischief. Madegan ordered his mahout to press forward, but he had no heart in the game, which did not add to the steadiness of the beast he was driving, who, upon winding the tiger, gave a scream of alarm, turned tail and fairly bolted. Blake and I now hurried

TIGER-SHOOTING FROM THE HOWDAH.

up, and this time I should have got a fair shot had not my elephant accidentally hurt his foot against a sharp stone, and proved so fidgety that I could hardly keep my feet by laying hold of the sides of the howdah, much less take a fair aim; so I reserved my fire, and Blake's elephant charging boldly up to the crouching tiger, gave him the chance, and he hurriedly fired a right and left, which wounded the infuriated beast, but did not disable him; for, before the smoke had cleared away, with a hoarse, angry roar, the monster bounded on a low bank, where he stood for an instant with every hair straight on end, and lashing his sides with his tail; and then with a terrific, guttural, growling noise, he sprang on clean to the elephant's forehead, and with claws and fangs fastening on his head and ears, dragged him to his knees. The poor beast screeched piteously, and made frantic efforts to shake off his relentless foe, whose hind claws were lacerating his trunk most dreadfully; and the huge brute, staggering from intense pain, tried to kneel down and crush him; when my elephant, as if suddenly awakened to a sense of duty by the cries of distress emitted by his companion, pluckily rushed up; and, although I felt somewhat afraid of hitting my friend's elephant or mahout instead of the tiger, the case was critical, and as I brushed by I planted a right and left just behind the top of the shoulder-blade; and Blake, who never for a moment lost his presence of mind, leaned over the front of the howdah, and almost simultaneously lodged the contents of his second gun in the nape of his neck, when the brute relaxed his hold and fell to the ground writhing in his last agony. Hardly was Blake's elephant freed from the worrying gripe of the tiger, than, excited by rage mingled with revenge, he coiled up his trunk, and, uttering a terrific trumpeting noise, knelt down, and literally lifting the prostrate carcase on his tusks chucked it on one side, and commenced dancing a war dance upon it, to the utter discomfiture

AN "UGLY CUSTOMER,"

of the sportsman in the howdah and his attendant, who had to hold on like grim death. The mahout was dislodged from his seat, but, retaining his hold of the ropes, eventually regained it, and guns, rifle, and all the loose gear were pitched on the ground before the frantic animal could be quieted and forced away from the carcase by the other elephants. The sight was ludicrous enough for the spectators, but Blake did not seem to see any fun in it, and to add to his discomfiture the stock of a valuable gun was broken in the fall, a loss not easily made good at an up-country station.

After this little episode we beat some high-grass country for some hours, but only found an occasional sounder of hog or a few straggling antelope ; so we returned to camp fairly satisfied with our first day's work, and finished the night with a *burra khana* (great dinner) and a nautch.

There were sounds of revelry in the camp throughout the live long night, and the nautch was prolonged until the small hours, consequently few showed up at the usual time in the breakfast-tent, notwithstanding one of the Shekarries of the Zemindar of Bhoonghir brought in intelligence that a leopard and several bears were marked down. However, somewhat later in the forenoon Nightingale, of the Nizam's Irregular Horse, joined our party, and as he had only three days' leave and seemed very eager to commence operations, Blake, Madegan and I agreed to accompany him to the Manjharra hills, where the game was said to be.

We took five elephants with us, one of which carried a couple of small hill tents, provisions, stores, liquor, and our servants, whilst our syces followed with our horses and boar spears. We had four immensely powerful dogs—a cross between a huge Polligar dog and a Bringarry bitch—that stood over thirty inches in height and possessed indomitable pluck, but little amenability to discipline, and at Bulbul's suggestion it was

BEAR-HUNTING WITH THE SPEAR.

determined to course the bears into the open and spear them
from our horses. We marshalled our elephants in line soon after
leaving the camp; and in passing through a date grove Madegan
killed a couple of hogs out of a sounder that broke away from
almost under his elephant's feet; and Bulbul and I secured
a couple of ravine deer that, scared at the elephant, ran, as if
bewildered, across our line. The ground was very much broken
and almost impossible to ride over, or we should have mounted
our horses and tried some pig-sticking, as several hogs broke
away within easy range of us; but, having enough pork for
food, we did not molest them. As we were passing a temporary
hut belonging to some toddy-drawers, who make a kind of spirit
called "rakkee" from the fermented sap of the date, one of the
men told us that the bears constantly came down from the hills
during the night and early morning and emptied their toddy-
chatties; and that very often they might be found, half-drunk
in a neighbouring thicket, which he offered to show us. Under
his guidance we wheeled off to the westward, and soon came to
a patch of thick cover where the bears were said to congregate.
Hardly had the elephants got into the cover than one of them
trumpeted, and a couple of bears started up from under the
shelving bank of a dry watercourse, one of which Blake hit
very hard, but failed to stop; and they both set off at a good
round pace for their fastness in the hills, which were about
three miles distant. As they got over the ground much faster than
we could follow on the elephants on account of the over-hanging trees, as soon as we got into the more open jungle again we
mounted our horses, and, changing our rifles for hog-spears,
gave chase. After a spurt of about a mile we came in sight of
them again; and Nightingale, who was mounted on a magnificent little Arab mare, got the first spear, and with Blake's
assistance soon "skivered" the old male, who made a terrible
row before he succumbed. I and Madegan made after the

DEATH OF THE BEAR.

female, and my horse, excited at the chase, although he had never hunted a bear before, carried me right up without the slightest hesitation, and enabled me to drive the spear right home behind the near shoulder, and out of the chest, which grassed her at once, and with a low wailing moan she stretched out her limbs and expired. When she was dead we found that Blake's bullet had entered the fleshy part of the haunch and come out of her side, without, however, disabling her, and from which wound she would doubtless have soon recovered, as bears, being very tenacious of life, soon get over very severe wounds. Having hoisted the game on the elephants, we made the best of our way to Oomrapett, where we encamped.

Oomrapoor is a small village of only a few dozen huts, but beautifully situated near the bund of a fine tank, surrounded by low wooded hills. Several small streams flow from the high background into the lake, and a somewhat larger one issues out of it and forms the principal head water of the Beckullair river, which flows into the Kistnah at Wojerabad. The surrounding country is very hilly, and the jungle was said to be alive with game of different kinds. The head men of the neighbouring villages of Bustarpully, Venkalapoor, Mullapully, and Sydapoor had all assembled to welcome us, they having received information of our coming; and, as supplies of different kinds were plentiful, we sent to the Shah-zada and begged him to join us. After we had heard all the native authorities had to tell us about the game of the district, we gave them their *congé* and a bottle of *eau-de-vie* a piece, which we called " Bulbul's cholera mixture," so as to ease their consciences, if they had any, about drinking the liquor forbidden by the Prophet, and then we adjourned to the tank to perform our ablutions before dinner. Whilst we were disporting amongst the lotus leaves close to the edge, for we dare not venture out of our depth on account of weeds, we heard a howling on the bund, and three or four women came running along with their brass chatties in their hands, screaming "Bagh! Bagh!" (a tiger, a tiger). As we had no guns with us, our situation might have been awkward; so, snatching up our toggery, we made tracks for the tents. We were not long getting into our clothes, and were just ready for a chase, when some of the villagers informed us that the intruder was only a cheetah who was constantly prowling about the village. Being now fully equipped and on our mettle, we determined to make a few casts round about the bund of the tank, where he was said to have taken refuge; and Bulbul and I, taking our hog-spears, mounted our horses for the chance of a run, whilst the others got on the elephants, with their rifles. The ground below the bund of the tank was covered with a second growth of low jungle, chiefly composed of custard apple-bushes and date-palm, so the elephants, who were in line pretty close together, could easily make their way through it. Scarcely had we commenced beating than a rustling in the cover ahead and the angry trumpeting of one of the elephants gave notice that the game was afoot, and shortly afterwards Madegan caught sight of him crouching behind the bushes and endeavouring to steal away. I saw that if we could only get him out of the narrow strip of jungle and make him break into the open we should have a very fair chance of spearing him, as the tank lay between us and the hills, and maidan in front was tolerably good riding-ground, although more or less covered with rumnah grass and baubhool bushes.

I did not anticipate much chance of getting the spear myself, as my friend Bulbul was admirably mounted on a chestnut Arab mare of great repute as a hog-hunter, whilst I had only a galloway 13·3 in height. "Habesh" was, however, a very plucky little beast, and would follow a hog *con amore;* but he had never yet faced any of the felidæ, and I felt uncertain how he would act. As the elephants were carefully beating every yard of bush, we were not much afraid of his making back; so we rode into the more open ground, in order to be prepared for a spurt when he should be driven out of the cover. From the continuous noise made by the elephants it was pretty certain that the quarry was somewhere just in front of them, and he was evidently somewhat sulky at being disturbed, for now and again his tail was seen waving amongst the bushes, and low angry growling was heard.

The line of elephants had now almost got to the further end of the cover, and every rustle in the bush was listened to with anxiety. At last, with a short, angry roar, he sprang into the open, and then we saw at a glance that it was not a cheetah, but a fine male leopard. Bulbul and I immediately gave chase; but for the first half mile, although we were going our best, we scarcely held our own, whilst the leopard seemed to be getting over the ground without any exertion to himself. As we got further out into the plain the ground became harder and more open, and my companion, making a spurt, forged ahead, and began to gain ground, and I soon saw that if the pace continued for any length of time I should "not be in the same field with them at the death." I therefore carefully husbanded my little nag's strength, who, with his ears laid back, was pulling like mad, jealous of being outpaced, and edged off to the left, where there was a clump of nymn-treés and a date tope, which I thought our quarry would most likely make for. In the meantime Bulbul had steadily crept up to within a few spears' length of the leopard, who was beginning to show symptoms of distress, for his pace had slackened and his tongue was hanging out of his mouth; and a few moments more must have decided the affair, when suddenly he disappeared in a blind nullah. The horse my friend was riding was a thoroughly-trained hunter, or both would have had a nasty fall of eight or ten feet; but the little Arab, as if aware of his danger, wheeled sharp round when

LEOPARD HUNTING.

he saw the game vanish and saved himself. The sudden jerk, however, snapped one of the stirrup-leathers and nearly brought the rider to grief; but, luckily, he managed to keep his seat, and shouted to me to keep on after the leopard—who, almost run to a standstill, was slowly trotting along the bed of the water-course and coming in my direction—whilst he repaired damages. As soon as the nearly-breathless animal saw me, he scrambled up the opposite bank of the nullah; and I, jumping off my horse, led him down one side, and up the other, and again gave chase. The game was now all in my favour, and every stride brought me closer, until at last I raced almost alongside the leopard, and, rising in the stirrups as I shot past, drove my spear home behind the withers and out of the chest; when, as I wheeled off sharp to the left, the bamboo shaft broke from the sudden wrench, and I was defenceless, and might have come off but second best, if he had not been too far gone to turn the tables. As it was, he was mortally wounded, and Bulbul put him out of his sufferings as he lay writhing on the ground with a thrust behind the shoulder, which penetrated the heart and caused instant dissolution. He proved to be rather a large leopard, as he measured 7 ft. 8 in. in length from the tip of the nose to the end of the tail; and his skin was in first-rate condition, shining like satin. It was certainly a wonderful bit of luck my getting the spear, which my companion must have had, if he had not been so unfortunately thrown out by the nullah. As it was, we returned to our huts highly satisfied with our sport, for it was a most exciting run from first to last.

THE DEATH OF A MAN-EATING TIGER.

I was hunting in the Deccan, in the neighbourhood of Mulkapore, when I heard that a man-eating tiger, which I had been after for some days, had been seen skulking near the outskirts of the village of Botta Singarum. I had, on a former occasion, tracked this cunning brute to one of his lairs, where the remains of several of his victims were discovered, and had twice beaten all his usual haunts in the jungle; but up to this time had never been able to get a shot at him. Sending my gang of trackers on before I mounted my horse, and, guided by the villager who brought the news, I made my way to the place where the marauder had been seen the evening before, where I found unmistakable signs that the information I had received was true, as his fresh pugs were plainly visible.

I sent my horse back to the village, and, accompanied by the gang, followed his track through a narrow ravine densely wooded. Here the trail became exceedingly difficult to follow, as the brute had evidently been walking about backwards and forwards in the bed and along the banks of a dry nullah, and we could not distinguish his last 'trail. I caused the band to separate, and for half-an-hour or so we were wandering about as if in a maze, for the cunning brute had been describing circles, and often, by following the trail, we arrived at the place we started from.

Whilst we were all at a loss, suddenly I heard a low "Coo" twice repeated, and I knew that Googooloo, who was seldom at fault, was now on warm scent, and from his call I was as certain that the game was afoot as any master of hounds would have been, while breaking cover, to hear his favourite dog give tongue. The gang closed up, and, guided by the sound, we made our way through thick bush to where Googooloo was standing by a pool of water in the bed of the nullah.

Here were unmistakable marks of his having quenched his thirst quite lately, for when we came up the water was still flowing into the deeply-imprinted pugs of his forefeet, which were close to the edge of the pool, and I noticed that the water had still the appearance of having been disturbed and troubled.

After having drunk, the brute made his way to some very thick jungle, much overgrown with creepers, through which we could not follow· without the aid of our axes. Thus, stalking with any hope of success was out of the question, so I held a solemn consultation with Kistimah, Chineah, Googooloo, and the dhoby, as to the best means of proceeding.

I felt convinced that the brute was still lurking somewhere near at hand in the jungle, for, besides the very recent trail we were on, I fancied I heard the yelling of a swarm of monkeys, which I attributed to their having been frightened by his appearance ; besides, this was just the kind of place that a tiger would be likely to remain in during the heat of the day, as it afforded cool shade from the sun, and water. All the gang were of my opinion, and Kistimah observed that, on two different occasions, after a post-runner had been carried off, he had remarked that the trail of the tiger led from this part of the jungle to a bend in the road, where he had been known frequently to lie in wait for his prey. " These man-eaters," added he, " are great devils, and very cunning, and I should not at all wonder if even now he was watching us from some dark thicket." As he said this I carefully examined the caps of my rifle, and I observed some of the gang close up with a strange shudder, for this brute had inspired them all with a wholesome fear, and prevented their straggling. Two or three spoke almost in whispers, as if they were afraid of his really being sufficiently near to hear them conspiring for his destruction.

At length Kistimah said that he had been thinking of a plan which, though dangerous in the execution, might be attended with success. It was for me to go, with a man dressed as a runner, down the main road at sunset, being the time the tiger generally carried off his victims, and to run the chance of getting a shot. At this proposition sundry interjectional expressions, such as "Abah !" "Arrez !" " Toba !" " Toba !" escaped

TRACKING UP A WOUNDED TIGER.

from the lips of the by-standers, and, from sundry shaking of heads and other unmistakable signs, I could see that it had not found much favour in their eyes. Chineah, the dhoby, and one or two of the gang, however, approved of the plan, and Kistimah offered to accompany me as the post-runner. This, however, I objected to, for I thought that I should have a better chance of meeting the tiger if I went alone than in company; besides, I preferred having only myself to look after. The plan of action once settled, I returned to the village and obtained from the patel the bamboo on which the tappal-runners sling the mail-bags over their shoulders. To the end of this is an iron ring with a number of small pieces of metal attached, making a jingling noise as the man runs, which gives warning of the coming of the post to any crowd that might be obstructing the path, allowing them time to get out of his way. Having broken off the ring, I fastened it to my belt, so as to allow it to jingle as I walked; and, arming myself with a short double rifle by Westley Richards, a brace of pistols, and a huge shekar knife, I made Kistimah lead the way down the road towards the place where the man-eater was said to lurk.

About a mile from the village I made the gang and the villagers who accompanied me halt, and went on with Kistimah, Chineah, and Googooloo to reconnoitre the ground. The road was intersected by a narrow valley or ravine, along the bottom of which was a dry, sandy watercourse, the banks of which were overgrown with high rank grass and reeds, intermixed with low scrubby thorn bushes. To the left was a low, rocky hill, in some places bare and in others covered with thick jungle, with wild date or custard-apple clumps here and there. Kistimah pointed me out a clump of rather thick jungle to the right of the road, where, he said, the tiger often lurked whilst on the look-out for his prey, and here we saw two or three old trails. He also showed me a rock, from behind which the brute had sprung upon a post-runner some weeks before; but we saw no signs of his having been there lately. It was, however, quite what an Indian sportsman would term a "tigerish-looking spot," for bold, scarped rocks, and naked, fantastic peaks rose in every direction from amongst the dense foliage of the surrounding jungle, whilst here and there noble forest trees lowered like giant patriarchs above the lower verdure of every shade and colour. Not a breath of air was stirring, nor a leaf moving; and as the sun was still high up, without a cloud visible to intercept his rays, the heat was most oppressive, and respiration even was becoming difficult on account of a peculiar closeness arising from the decayed vegetation under foot, and the overpowering perfume of the blossoms of certain jungle plants.

Having reconnoitered the ground round about, I felt rather overcome with lassitude, and returned to the rest of the gang whom I found sleeping in a clump of deep jungle a little off the road-side. Here I lay down to rest, protected from the piercing rays of the sun by the shade of a natural bower formed by two trees, which were beat down with the weight of an immense mass of parasitical plants in addition to their own foliage. I must have slept several hours, for when I awoke I found the sun sinking low in the horizon; however, I got up considerably refreshed by my nap, and, giving myself a shake, prepared for the task I had undertaken. I carefully examined my arms, and having ascertained that nothing had been seen by any of my gang, some of whom had kept a look-out, I told my people to listen for the sound of my gun, which, if they heard, they might come up, otherwise they were to remain quiet where they were until my return. I ordered Chineah, Kistimah, Googooloo, and the "Dhoby," to accompany me down the road with spare guns in case I might want them; and when I arrived at a spot which commanded a view of the ravine which was supposed to be the haunt of the man-eater, I sent them to climb different trees.

Kistimah begged hard to be allowed to accompany me, as he said this tiger never attacked a man in front, but always from behind; but I would not permit him, as I thought that two people would perhaps scare the animal, and his footsteps might prevent me from hearing any sound, intimating his approach.

The sun had almost set as I proceeded slowly down the road, and, although I was perfectly cool and as steady as possible, I felt cold drops of perspiration start from my forehead as I approached the spot where so many victims had been sacrificed. I passed the rock, keeping well on the look-out, listening carefully for the slightest sound, and I remember feeling considerably annoyed by the chirping made by a couple of little bulbuls (Indian nightingales), that were fighting in a bush close to the roadside. Partridges were calling loudly all around, and as I passed the watercourse I saw a jackal skulking along its bed. I stopped, shook my jingling affair, and listened several times as I went along, but to no purpose.

Whilst ascending the opposite side of the ravine I heard a slight noise like the crackling of a dry leaf: I paused, and, turning to the left, fronted the spot from whence I thought the noise proceeded. I distinctly saw a movement or waving in the high grass, as if something was making its way towards me: then I heard a loud purring sound, and saw something twitching backwards and forwards behind a clump of low bush and long grass, about eight or ten paces from me, and a little in the rear. It was a ticklish moment, but I felt prepared. I stepped back a couple of paces in order to get a better view, which action probably saved my life, for immediately the brute sprang into the middle of the road, alighting about six feet from the place where I was standing. I fired a hurried shot ere he could gather himself up for another spring, and when the smoke cleared away I saw him rolling over and over in the dusty road, writhing in his death agony, for my shot had entered the neck and gone downwards into his chest. I stepped on one side and gave him my second barrel behind the ear, when dark blood rushed from his nostrils, a slight tremor passed over all his limbs, and all was still. The man-eater was dead, and his victims avenged.

My gang, attracted by the sound of my shots, came rushing up almost breathless, and long and loud were the rejoicings when the tiger was recognised by Kistimah as the cunning man-eater who had been the scourge of the surrounding country for months. He was covered with mange, and had but little hair left on his skin, which was of a reddish brown colour, and not worth taking.

I have killed many tigers both before and since, but I never met with such a determined enemy to mankind, for he was supposed to have carried off more than a hundred individuals. He fully exemplified an old Indian saying, " that when a tiger has once tasted human blood he will never follow other game, men proving an easier prey." On the spot where the tiger was killed a large mausoleum now stands, caused by the passers-by each throwing a stone until a large heap is formed. Since that day many a traveller who has passed that way has been entertained by the old pensioned sepoy, who is in charge of the travellers' bungalow, with an account of the terrible man-eater of Botta Singarum.

CHAPTER VII.

ELEPHANT HUNTING IN INDIA.

THE elephant hunter, to be successful in his calling, must have a thorough knowledge of the nature and habits of that sagacious animal, whose keenly developed senses far exceed that of any other denizen of the forest; he must be well acquainted with its peculiar structure and anatomy, or his bullet, however true, will never reach the vital part with any certainty; he must be an adept at "tracking," or following spoor, with a silent foot, and in the understanding of *jungle signs*, which art is only acquired by constant study and long practice; he must be patient and enduring, satisfied with hard fare, short commons, and terrible thirst, as he will often have to subsist wholly upon his gun, with the ground for his bed, and a forest-tree for his canopy. In following up spoor he must be prepared to encounter · considerable hardship and fatigue, weary marches and counter-marches, days of intense heat, and damp cheerless nights, painfully diversified. He should feel that "there is a pleasure in the pathless woods," and "society where none intrudes:" for he must often be content with Nature and his own thoughts as companions, and he must not let his spirits be depressed by the solitude and intense stillness of the deep jungle. The hunter must sleep like a hare, always on the alert, ever prepared and watchful; for he never knows what he may meet, or the danger a moment may bring forth. Inured to peril, he must never be cast down or faint of heart; or he had better not attempt to follow up the spoor of the elephant to his haunts in the dense, deep jungle, where the rays of the sun seldom penetrate, and the woodman's axe was never heard—where the deadliest of fevers lurk in places the most beautiful to the eye; and where, with the exception of certain times in the year, the air and the water are poisoned by malaria, and impregnated by the exhalations of decayed leaves and decomposed vegetable matter entailing certain death to the hunter, were he tempted to follow up his perilous calling out of season.

In Southern India, sometimes herds of elephants are tempted to roam, and leave their homes in the deep jungle to devastate the sugar-cane plantations and rice-fields of the ryots, where they commit great damage; and on such occasions the sportsman is enabled to get amongst them without being obliged to penetrate the dense forests so pernicious to health. In Africa elephants are found alike on open plains as well as in the deepest forest, and I have found spoor denoting their presence in the most inaccessible places on the ridges of high mountain ranges.

The General Character.—My own experience leads me to believe that the elephant—whether of the Indian or African species—in his wild state is naturally a harmless, quiet, shy, and inoffensive animal, as I have frequently watched large herds of these huge beasts for hours together in their own domains, and never saw them assume the offensive, or evince any disposition to attack or molest other animals, such as hog, deer, antelope, or hippopotami, that might be feeding near them. On the contrary, I have seen an old boar successfully dispute the right of way with a herd of five elephants, and, by charging at their legs, drive them away from that part of the pool where his porcine family were drinking. It seemed ridiculous to see these unwieldy monsters shuffle away with cries expressive of terror, as if utterly unconscious of their own immense superiority of strength.

In their native haunts, Nature has provided for them such a rich profusion of food that their wants lead to no rivalry with other animals: they are not compelled, like those of the carnivorous species, to resort to device in order to obtain subsistence, and the consequence is that they rarely have occasion to exercise the extraordinary sagacity with which they are gifted, but roam listlessly about the forest, every action bespeaking inoffensive indolence and timidity combined with wary caution. Should they discover the intrusion of man in their domains, they rarely evince any disposition to become the assailant, and although the herd may number a score, and the hunter be all alone, they will fly his presence with the greatest precipitation. Even when wounded and rendered desperate, they are naturally so awkward, unwieldy, and utterly unaccustomed to use their gigantic strength offensively, that in a tree forest, clear of underwood, they are not difficult to escape from, provided the hunter keeps his head cool, and is tolerably active.

The Social Habits.—A herd of elephant is not a group that accident, or attachment, may have induced to associate together, but a family often consisting of more than fifty members, including grandfathers, grandmothers, mothers, sons, and daughters, and the similarity of features, colour of their eyes, build, and general appearance, attest their common lineage and relationship as belonging to the same stock; although several herds or families will browse and feed together in the open glades of the forest, and travel in company in search of water, or migrate in large bodies to fresh pasturage, on the slightest alarm, or appearance of danger, each herd assembles and rallies round its own leader, and takes independent measures for retreating together. If, from any accident, a bull elephant becomes separated from his own family, as soon as he discovers his lone situation, he rushes frantically through the forest, uttering the most piercing cries

THE INDIAN ELEPHANT.

of distress, for he is not allowed to attach himself to any other troop. The lord of a herd, however, does not object to a stray female joining his seraglio, and amongst a herd I have frequently met with a female who bore no family resemblance to the rest of the troop, and was evidently an outsider. If a young bull cannot find his family, or is turned out of the herd for precociousness, not an uncommon occurrence, .he either attacks the leader of another herd, and fights for the supremacy, or becomes a "rogue." These "rogues," or outcasts, lead a solitary life, and gradually become morose, vicious, and desperately cunning. One member of the herd, usually the largest tusker, but sometimes an energetic and strong-minded female, is, by common consent, implicitly followed and obeyed as leader, and it is wonderful to observe the devotion of the herd to their elected chief.

Elephants utter four distinct sounds, each of which is indicative of a certain meaning. The first is a shrill whistling noise produced by blowing through the trunk, which denotes satisfaction. The second is the note of alarm, or surprise, a sound made by the mouth, which may be thus imitated, "*pr-rut, pr-rut.*" The third is the trumpeting noise they make when angry, which, when they are very much enraged, and when charging an assailant, changes into a hoarse roar or terrific scream. The fourth sound betokens dissatisfaction, or distress, frequently repeated when separated from the herd, tired, hungry, or over-loaded, which may be thus imitated, "*urmph, urmph.*"

The skin of the elephant is very sensitive, and at certain times of the year, when a district is infested by the tsetse fly, a whole herd will coat themselves with mud to protect themselves, as much as possible, from the bite of that poisonous insect. In the forests they frequent, a kind of large horse-fly, also, gives them incessant annoyance; and, consequently, the elephant is rarely ever still; for the ears flap, the tail switches, the body sways to and fro, the trunk is continually on the move, whilst the legs are in perpetual motion, rubbing one against the other, to ward off the attacks of these malevolent torments. Should an elephant, however, be suddenly alarmed, or become suspicious, on account of some slight deviation from the common order of things, or should he detect the taint in the air denoting the presence of man, he will remain motionless as a statue, with his great ears extended, so as to drink in the slightest sound, for hours at a time.

The olfactory organs of the elephant are developed to an extraordinary degree, for their scent is so acute that I have known a troop of elephants, when on the way to their usual drinking-place at night, halt and turn back without quenching their thirst, being deterred from approaching the water, because they detected the taint in the imprints of men's footsteps who had passed along the path in the previous afternoon; when the prints must have been, at least, twelve hours old. Their sense of hearing is also extremely acute, and they can detect unusual sounds in the forest at much greater distances than any other animal. The comparatively small size of the eye seems to protect it from being injured as the elephant forces his way through the bush, and it is furnished with a nictating membrane, which enables it to free itself from dust, dirt, or insects that may accidentally have got in. Small as the eye appears, there is no deficiency of sight, although the range does not extend above the level of the head, or to any great distance; however, his delicate sense of hearing and his remarkably acute smell amply compensate for his somewhat limited vision.

The progressive movement of the elephant is different from the motion of all other animals, on account of the great weight of his body, Nature has formed him with only two bones in his leg; whereas the horse has three, without counting the joint uniting the hoof, which enables him to move along at a springy pace; the gait of the elephant therefore is stiff and awkward, and this want of elasticity renders riding on him for any length of time extremely disagreeable and fatiguing. The elephant kneels like a man, his hind legs going out behind, whereas those of a horse are doubled under his body.

The usual pace of an elephant, when undisturbed and browsing, is an indolent, swinging kind of walk, the body swaying from side to side with the motion of the legs; but if he is under marching orders, and travelling to a fresh pasturage, he quickens his gait, and gets over the ground at the rate of quite five miles an hour. When alarmed, he shuffles along at a kind of ambling pace ; which, for a short distance, exceeds twelve miles an hour, although it never equals in speed the gallop of a moderately fast horse on open ground. The Indian variety is far less speedy and enduring than the African. The former soon gets blown and stops. For a creature of such huge size and ponderous weight it is inconceivable how stealthily and noiselessly he can get through the forest if he chooses, without either breaking a twig or causing a dry leaf to rustle. From the spongy formation of the sole of his foot, his tread is exceedingly light and quite inaudible. In soft sand, where a horse would sink up to his fetlocks every stride, the spoor of an elephant would be hardly perceptible.

THE DIFFERENCE BETWEEN THE INDIAN AND THE AFRICAN ELEPHANT.

The Indian and the African elephant differ most essentially, not only in their general appearance, the shape of the head, the formation of their teeth, the curvature of the spine, and the size of their ears, but also in their habits. By placing their different descriptions in juxtaposition, the chief distinctions between the two species will be better understood by the reader.

THE INDIAN VARIETY.

The Indian elephant has a high concave forehead, channelled in the centre, the facial line being almost perpendicular with the ground when the animal is moving.

THE AFRICAN VARIETY.

The African elephant has a low, receding forehead, the skull being convex from the root of the trunk to the back of the head.

HEAD OF INDIAN ELEPHANT.

The back of the Indian elephant is convex.

The back of the African elephant is concave.

The ears are very small, and do not hang lower than the chin.

The ears are immensely large, completely covering the shoulder when laid flat against the side.

The tusks are set wide apart in the

The tusks are set in the head very

The Indian Variety.

head, and are long in comparison with their diameter, being often gracefully curved. They rarely weigh over 100 lbs., even in the largest bull elephants, which are found in the Wynaad forests.

The females have only small, straight tusks, that rarely weigh more than 8 lbs.

The brain of the Indian elephant is placed somewhat higher than in the African species, and it is not difficult to reach, provided the hunter understands the anatomy of the skull, as there are six vulnerable spots by which the cerebrum can be penetrated with a hardened bullet, if fired at from a proper angle. They are as follows :—

First, the forehead shot, as it is called, when the hunter, getting to within fifteen paces from his game, aims at the shield-shaped depression just over the root of the trunk and in a direct line with two prominent points of bone, some six inches above the line of the eyes. At this spot the bone of the skull is soft and honeycombed, and the bullet, taking an upward course, passes between the cartilaginous substance and muscles that encase the roots of the trunk, penetrates the brain, and causes instantaneous death. The Indian elephant hunter prefers this shot to any other, but it is not always obtainable, as when an elephant charges, the vulnerable spot is more or less concealed and defended by his uplifted trunk. For the forehead shot to be effective, the hunter must be right in front of the elephant, and not more than twenty paces distant, otherwise the brain will be missed.

The next most vulnerable points for the hunter to aim at are the temples, when, if the hunter firing from a short

The African Variety.

close together, being held in their place by a mass of bone and cartilage, in which the roots are imbedded to a depth of at least two feet. The largest tusk I have ever seen, a single one, weighed 226 lbs., and is now to be seen in front of a cutler's shop in St. Paul's Churchyard.

The females have small, straight tusks, weighing from 10 to 20 lbs.

The brain of the African elephant is situated behind the mass of bone and cartilage in which the tusks are firmly imbedded, consequently the forehead shot is rarely effective.

Again, the bone of the skull recedes, and is much harder and denser in substance than in the Indian species ; besides which the tusks almost join about the level of the eyes, and with the cartilaginous substance in which they are set most effectually protect the brain. This is also placed somewhat lower than in the Indian elephant, and is consequently more difficult to reach.

That the African elephant can be killed in the same manner as the Indian variety by the fore-hand shot, *when fired at from an elevation*, I know from personal experience in several instances, but inasmuch as the tusks and their encasement to a great extent protect the brain, it is a very hazardous shot to try on level ground in the open, as on several occasions I have seen the most accurately planted bullets produce very little effect, not even stopping or stunning the animal fired at. Mr. Henry Faulkner, of the 16th Lancers, who has had much experience in elephant shooting both in India and Africa, states that he has frequently killed African elephants by a single bullet in the forehead, and I have heard many Boers say that they have done the same thing with their roahs, some

THE INDIAN VARIETY.

distance, so that his bullet takes an upward course, aims just between the eye and the ear, the brain will be penetrated, and the animal drops, or rather sinks, to the ground stone dead. The

THE AFRICAN VARIETY.

of which carry projectiles nearly a quarter of a pound in weight. Still, I look upon it as haphazard work, and bad policy to attempt.

The most vulnerable parts of the

HEAD OF AFRICAN ELEPHANT.

temple shot is most effective when the position of the hunter is in advance and to the right or left of the elephant.

When the hunter is pursuing an elephant he may sometimes get a fair shot at the point where the lower part of the ear is joined to the head, and if his bullet is accurately planted in this spot, it will either 'prove immediately

skull of the African elephant are the temples, and a bullet entering between the eyes and the upper point of the ear will generally penetrate the brain. This is my favourite shot, and latterly I rarely pulled trigger at an elephant until I had so manœuvred as to get a fair chance of planting a bullet in this deadly spot. I have often found it

The Indian Variety.

fatal, or, at any rate, drop the elephant and render him temporarily unconscious, when a second shot in the temple will give him a quietus.

The sixth vulnerable spot in an elephant's head can only be obtained when the hunter is pursuing an elephant down the side of a steep hill, or if he is on a rock above him, when, if he aims so that his bullet strikes the back part of the skull, just above where it joins the vertebræ of the neck, the shot will prove immediately fatal.

A shot, fired from the right or left rear, just behind the shoulder-blade, often proves mortal, provided the projectile is hardened, and driven with a large charge of powder.

The Indian elephant generally frequents the same tract of jungle, rarely travelling more than twenty miles in a day, and if vigorously chased or followed up, soon shows signs of fatigue.

Indian elephants rarely forsake the forest for the open country, except when tempted to make nightly inroads in the rice-fields, and even then they always return to their jungle haunts on the first approach of dawn. During the intense heat of the day, they resort to the deepest shade they can find, and at this time may often be found fast asleep, or indolently fanning themselves with the branches of trees.

Indian elephants live chiefly on different kinds of herbage, and the young shoots of the bamboo, and may be considered as essentially grass-feeding animals. They are also particularly partial to rice, Indian corn, or, indeed, any other kind of grain, and commit great damage in cultivated tracts near their haunts in the forest.

The African Variety.

quite as effective with the African elephant as the front shot is in the Indian species, having on several occasions killed my game with a single shot.

The African elephant is often killed by a single ball skilfully planted just behind the ear, and again, by the Boer's favourite shot behind the shoulder, the "dood plek," but the hunter must take care to reserve his shot until the forearm is advanced well forward, so that his bullet will not be turned aside in its course to the heart, by glancing off the hard shank bone. I have also often killed elephants instantaneously when posted on an elevation, such as a high rock commanding a ravine or defile, by firing from above either at the top of the forehead, or at the back part of the skull, just where the head joins on the neck.

The African elephant is migratory, and changes his ground continually, as forage becomes scarce or exhausted.

Large bodies of African elephants, consisting often of several herds, in their periodical migrations to fresh pastures, frequently travel at the rate of forty miles in the twenty-four hours; and they get over the ground much faster and with less fatigue than the Indian species.

African elephants are as often found on the open plains as in the woods, and they appear fond of extreme heats, as I have frequently seen them basking in the sun at noon-day as if they enjoyed the warmth.

The African elephant is decidedly a browsing animal, or a tree-eater, as his general food consists of the foliage of certain trees, and especially the Mimosa. He also lives upon such herbage as is to be found in African forests, and different kinds of succulent plants found in the vicinity of water.

THE INDIAN VARIETY.

The Indian species is gregarious, the old bulls often remaining with their families, consisting of females with their calves, and young males, nearly all the year round.

The following are the dimensions of the largest Indian elephant I ever saw, which was killed by Burton and myself on the Annamullai Hills.

	Ft.	In.
Height at shoulder	10	8
Height of head	11	10
Greatest girth	15	0
Circumference of fore-arm	4	10
Circumference round fore-foot	4	8
Length from ridge on top of head along the spine	10	10
Length of tusks	5	10
Circumference of tusks	1	8
Weight of tusks	. 183 lbs.	
Breadth between points of tusks	3	8

THE AFRICAN VARIETY.

In Africa, except during the rutting season, the old bulls keep to themselves, consorting together in small herds, whilst the females and their young keep to themselves, and are sometimes met with in herds of several hundreds.

The following are the dimensions of the largest African elephant I ever saw, which I killed on the Longwee River, one of the tributaries of the Zambesi.

	Ft.	In.
Height at shoulder	13	2
Height of head	12	9
Greatest girth	17	6
Circumference of fore-arm	5	10
Circumference round fore-foot	5	4
Length of back from crown of head to tail	12	4
Extreme width of ears from tip to tip across forehead	14	0
Length of tusks	7	2
Circumference of tusks	2	4
Weight of tusks	246 lbs.	

ELEPHANT HUNTING IN THE COIMBATORE DISTRICT.

I DO not know a more jolly military station in all the Madras Presidency than Coimbatore for a sportsman, as the forests round the Anamalai and Neilgherry ranges are perhaps the very finest hunting-grounds in India for all kinds of large game, and they are both within a day's march from cantonment. Burton and I had been enjoying the *dolce far niente* for about a week with the 3rd Light Infantry, whose comfortable bungalows were close handy to a lake round which snipe were to be found in thousands during the season, when one morning, just as we were preparing to start for a day's snipe-shooting, Kenny, of the 84th Foot, came in with the headman of Moodoonoor, who informed us that a herd of elephant had been committing great depredations in the grain fields near his village during the night-time;

and that, although large fires had been lighted at sunset by the villagers, they still continued in the neighbourhood, and visited the cultivated lands almost every night. Here was a chance not to be met with every day; so Burton, Kenny, and myself, resolved to avail ourselves of it at once. The village of Moodoonoor, which was about 15 koss (30 miles) distant, lay amongst the low spurs of the Anamalai range; so we sent on our two head servants, with Chinneah and Googooloo, my two shekarries, in a hackerry, so as to make preparations against our arrival, and gather whatever information they could about the elephants.

Kenny had a retinue of low-caste servants, picked up promiscuously at Madras, who bore a most unenviable reputation in the cantonment, although they had only arrived a few days previously; and as they were almost in a state of mutiny at the idea of going into the bush, it was resolved to give them an extra month's wages and discharge them instanter. They were accordingly summoned, and Joakim, the butler, was the first to make his appearance. He was rather unprepared for his sudden dismissal, and wanted to argue the case, for, assuming the mien of injured innocence, he exclaimed, " You tink I thief man. Oh, Kenny Sahib! how many shirt you got in box when you come from Madras ?"—"Three dozen," said Kenny. " Yas, Sar; now go look for box. Master got more than six dozen, and plenty, plenty sock. Now you tink I robber man."—"Well, you scoundrel," said Kenny, rather taken aback at the fellow's insinuation, "where did the other shirts come from then ? Did you steal them ?"—" No, Sar, I no robber man. I makee changee business with washerman; give one old shirt no good and take two new. Make proper changee for changee." In spite of this somewhat knowing defence of his reputation, he failed in convincing us of the desirability of retaining him, so his services were dispensed with, and Ramasawmy, the Khidmuhgar, was called in. He was a pariah of the lowest caste, although he called himself a Christian, which signified that he eat pork and would get drunk whenever he had a chance. When asked as to what sect he belonged to, he somewhat cheekily replied, " I Gor almighty man, same caste like master. Suppose I tink my master go for make this business him catchee cold." What he meant by this ambiguous threat, deponent knoweth not, and he had not time to explain, for in the twinkling of an eye he was flying through the air with his master's toe very near his western point. The last of the triumvirate, the maity or cook boy, taking warning by this ignominious ejection, came in with a salaam, took his money without a word, and retired. Luckily, Kenny was able to engage a couple of very decent-looking servants, who were well known in the regiment, having been for several years in the service of an officer who had gone to England on sick leave ; so he was put to little or no inconvenience by the change.

Whilst we were making preparations for the expedition and superintending the packing up of tents, supplies, and such like gear, Kenny's sacked triumvirate came up, prepared for the road, having been ordered out of cantonment by the magistrate, and had the cheek to ask for written characters and three bottles of brandy, as medicine for their journey to Madras, and both applications being refused, they went away highly indignant. Having seen them clear off the premises, we sent our baggage, horses, and servants, on in advance. I had given my head boy directions to engage three sets of bullocks at the different villages as he went along, so that we might have relays of fresh animals every five or six miles, and after dinner a couple of bundles of straw and our mattresses being spread at the bottom of country carts, well covered over with matting, as shown in the engraving, we rolled ourselves up in a blanket, and made a start, sleeping comfortably all night, and finding our-

COUNTRY CARTS.

selves at the choultry at Moodoonoor when we awoke in the morning.

Soon after daybreak our hut was pitched in a small clearing outside the village, and after we had a refreshing tub and substantial breakfast, we set off, under the guidance of several villagers, for the fields of "bargee" that had been devastated by the elephants. Here we had palpable evidence of the damage that these animals can commit even in a single night, for several acres of ripe grain had been more or less destroyed, a small part of which had been torn up and eaten, whilst much more had been trodden into the earth by their ponderous feet. From the spoor I estimated the herd to consist of about nine animals, of which one was evidently a good-sized bull, as his stride was longer, and the imprint of his foot was much larger and further apart, than the rest. I could also see places in the banks of a nullah where he had used his tusks in endeavouring to uproot a small bush, bearing a fruit like a wild plum. One of the ryots, who was watching his crops the night before when they came, said that he heard them in the forest tearing down the under-wood and crashing through the bamboo jungle soon after sunset, but that they did not come out into the open fields until past midnight, when the villagers' fires had burnt almost out. He could not say how many they were, for he was only too anxious to keep out of their way, as they were rushing wildly about all over the clearing until close upon daybreak. As they came and returned by the same route unmolested, I thought that they would most likely choose it again on their next visit to their feeding grounds; so bidding Chinneah and Googooloo follow me with their spare guns, I stole gently forward to reconnoitre in case they might still be lurking in the neighbouring forest. There was no difficulty in following up their trail, as a regular pathway was made up the hill, bushes being levelled and bamboos torn up in all directions; and they had evidently travelled very leisurely, as they had broken off and browsed on the young shoots and tender roots along the whole of the route.

Having satisfied myself that the spoilers had not been scared and frightened away in spite of the villagers' fires, I felt convinced that they would return by the same path; so I returned to the rest of the people, and began to make my preparations accordingly. I noticed from certain marks that the herd had paid several visits to a group of three large jamun trees, and had broken off some of the lower branches, so as to get at the fruit, whilst they had also picked up the fallen berries from below; and as these trees were of great size and commanded a good view of the surrounding clearing, I determined to rig up a couple of "mechauns," or platforms, at some 20 feet above the ground, and after two hours' hard work, I managed with the aid of my people and the villagers to accomplish my object, and two substantial bamboo platforms were erected far out of reach of the elephants' trunks.

Here Burton and Kenny elected to pass the night, and having constructed a bamboo ladder to get up and down with more comfort, they had their rugs and mattresses carried up, and fenced round the sides of the mechaun with a kind of rough basket-work, so as to prevent their guns or gear from falling out.

Having seen that my pals were comfortably settled, I reconnoitred the ground to select my own post, and as I observed that the herd had feasted upon a patch of pumpkins and gourds that were only a short distance from the outskirts of the forest, I determined to build a moat, or skarm, in the middle of this cultivation, but close handy to two large trees, against the trunks of which I fastened two bamboo ladders, in case of being unearthed, and obliged to beat a retreat. The moat is generally constructed in the following manner. A pit about 14 feet long 4 feet wide and 5 feet deep, is dug out, and, if there is time, the sides and bottom are lined with bamboo and covered with date-leaf matting so that two people can lie down comfortably in it. About 8 feet of the centre part is strongly flat-roofed over with stout logs, strong enough to bear an elephant's weight, which are again covered with earth, and young bushes are often placed over it. Thus it resembles a burrow having two entrances, which are left open at each end, and here the hunters sit with only the upper parts of their heads above the ground. Great care must be taken that the general appearance shows no deviation from the common order of things, and that there are no signs of human occupation about it. The more natural it appears the better chance the hunters have of close shots ; and of course great attention must be paid that the moat is constructed to leeward of the track or run by which the game is likely to come, otherwise their keen sense of smelling will instantly detect the atmosphere tainted by man's presence. There is always a certain smell perceptible in freshly turned up earth ; so to kill it, I planted several strong scented bushes round about, and covered it with sand from a neighbouring nullah and creepers, taking care to have a good show of ripe pumpkins all round about the ambuscade. It was three o'clock in the afternoon before every arrangement was made for our passing the night, and then we adjourned to the tent for dinner, taking all the people, villagers included, with us.

After dinner we carefully cleaned our rifles and loaded with hardened bullets made of one part quicksilver to nine of lead, and, accompanied only by Chinneah, Googooloo, and Burton's shekarry, carrying our spare guns, some prog and a large supply of cold tea, we adjourned to our ambuscades. Having seen Burton, Kenny, and the shekarry comfortably settled in their eyrie, and warned them against firing in the direction of my moat, I ensconced myself with Chinneah in my own diggings, and, leaving Googooloo in the tree to watch, slept

like a top for some three or four hours, when Chinneah awoke
me and bade me listen, for there were suspicious noises in
the forest.

Although the moon had not yet risen, the night was clear,
and the sky was studded with stars, so that after a little time I
could distinguish the surrounding objects pretty well with the
aid of my field-glass. The continuous buzzing noise of the
insect world after nightfall in the forest, when every bush and
tree gives forth some sound, and life is everywhere audibly
manifest, presents a remarkable contrast to the strange, weird-
like stillness that reigns during the intense heat of the day;
and in the early part of the night the Cicadæ kept up a
ceaseless melody, which was only broken by the hum of some
enraged, bloodthirsty mosquito as he vainly attempted to find
an entrance in the thin silk gauze veil I wore round my hat
and shoulders to protect my face and neck from the ruthless
attacks of these night marauders. As the night advanced, the
cries of various wild animals resounded through the jungle, and
a sounder of hog and a couple of porcupine came so close to my
ambuscade that Chinneah had to pelt them with earth in order
to drive them away, and prevent their eating the pumpkins we
intended for nobler game.

Scarcely had they gone when a troop of sambur made their
appearance, and they were followed by a score or so of green
monkeys, who came close upon us before they detected our
presence, when they scampered jabbering away. Now and
then a crashing of wood was heard on the hillside, and a low
"Urmph, urmph," followed soon after by a faint whistle or
blowing sound assured me that a herd of elephant were afoot
on the hillside. Every sound an elephant makes has a signifi-
cant meaning to a hunter well versed in woodcraft, and from
constant observation I knew by the "Urmph, urmph," that
one of their number was distressed at having lost the run of

the rest, and that the low blowing sound that followed it denoted his satisfaction at having again fallen in with them. For fully three hours every now and again we heard those unmistakeable sounds which denoted their presence in the bamboo forest that clothed the lower spurs of the hillside ; but, as if suspicious of danger, they seemed to avoid breaking into the plain, and I began to fear that we should none of us get a shot, as the moon was rising, and I thought that, if they were afraid to venture in the open during the darker hours, they certainly would not come now that it was light enough to distinguish any conspicuous object on the plains. My surmise was, however, wrong, and soon after midnight a big female showed her great massive forehead at the edge of the jungle, and shortly afterwards moved stealthily and noiselessly forward, where for quite five minutes she stood like a statue, only moving the ears backward and forward, as if to drink in any sound that might be carried on the night breeze, which was laden with the most delicious perfumes of wild flowers, which perhaps prevented her from being scared by the

" Frouzy pores that taint the ambient air,"

and winding us in our subterranean retreat. Having made up her mind that the coast was clear, she turned her raised trunk towards the opening in the jungle from which she issued, and made a curious blowing sound that nearly resembled a low whistle, and at this signal she was joined by seven others, who stalked in a majestic manner in single file up to her, and then scattered over the plain and began to feed on the grain. Although they passed midway between Burton's mechaun and my post they did not detect our presence. Shortly afterwards, two females and a fine stately bull with decent-sized tusks, made their appearance, and followed in a bee line the track of the rest, evidently quite oblivious as to all recollections of past feeds on moura plums or pumpkins, for they gave both our positions a wide berth, and began to browse quite half a mile beyond Burton's mechaun. For three mortal hours we impatiently watched their proceedings, and about an hour before day-break, my stock of patience becoming exhausted, I called down Googooloo from his perch, and we crept towards Burton's post, having first taken the precaution to give a single whistle, which was answered, so as to prevent any chance of our being mistaken for game. Burton had had a visit from a female and her young one, but he did not care to fire at her, having seen two young bulls in the herd, beside the tusker who came last. It was therefore decided that, as the herd would not come to us, that we should go to them, and I arranged that Burton and Kenny should try and stalk the tusker in the open, whilst I and my people should cut off the line of retreat, in case they should make for the same gap by which they entered the plain. Having looked to our arms and put on fresh caps, my companions began to creep cautiously towards the herd, taking advantage of any cover they could find, whilst I made tracks for the opening in the fence through which the herd had forced their way, and took up an admirable strategic position between three or four large clumps of stout bamboos which commanded the path quite close to the edge of the clearing. These clumps of bamboo grew so close together that, although there was space for a man to creep between, an elephant could not easily squeeze his carcase through, so that the enclosure formed a kind of natural fortress in which we could take refuge, in case of being hard pressed or charged by the herd. Cutting away some of the young shoots and creepers that might have tripped us up, I had hardly finished my arrangements when a running fire was heard, and Chinneah, who had mounted a high tree which commanded an extensive view of the plain, announced that one elephant had fallen, whilst the big female leader and

ELEPHANT SHOOTING.

the tusker were heading in our direction at full speed, followed
at some distance by the rest of the herd, who, being impeded
by the young ones, could not get so fast over the ground. . In a
little while we could hear them blowing and tearing along
through the grain, but they must have winded our position, for
they suddenly halted and stood perfectly still at the extreme
edge of the bamboo jungle ; and although they could not have
been more than thirty yards away, for nearly five minutes not
a sound nor a movement betrayed their position, until the rest
of the herd came close up, when they cautiously moved forward.
By stooping low I could see their great legs moving in our
direction ; so creeping round a thick clump of bamboo as the
bull passed within six yards of my *cache*, I got a fair view of
his temples, and gave him a right and left between the eye and
the ear, which rolled him over luckily right in the path of his
watchful mate, who, with a vicious scream of revenge, charged
straight at me, when, as she stumbled over the legs of her ex-
piring lord, who was struggling convulsively and writhing in his
death throes, I was enabled to end her career with a couple of
two-ounce bullets right between the eyes, and she fell doubled
up in a heap close to the tusker. The report of my rifle, or
perhaps the scream of alarm made by the female at seeing her
mate fall, scared back the rest of the herd, and Burton hit a
young tusker twice as he broke back across the plain ; but as
both shots were fired at long ranges, they did not penetrate the
brain, and although severely wounded, he made his way into
some thick jungle, followed by the rest of the herd.

As the day broke, several of the villagers, hearing the shots,
came to see what we had done, and one of the village shekarries
brought with him some of the Mulcher bush tribes, who,
always living in the forest, are well acquainted with the haunts
of different kinds of game. After we had eaten some breakfast,
and procured refreshment for our people, Burton and I set out

TRACKING UP A WOUNDED ELEPHANT.

to track up the wounded elephant, and after cutting our way through some dense jungle, we found him drinking at a small river. Although he winded us before we saw him, and dashed splashing through the river, Burton brought him down by a well-directed shot just behind the back of the head as he was clambering up the opposite bank. Burton and Kenny had killed an old female between them, who would persistently show fight and prevent their getting near the tusker they were trying to stalk ; so amongst us we had killed four elephants, not a bad night's work considering the circumstances under which we were placed. The ivory, however, was not of much account, as the largest pair of tusks did not exceed 41 lbs. in weight ; but in the old days the Honourable John Company disbursed 70 rupees for every elephant's tail and tip of the trunk produced at the cutchery, so that these rewards helped to pay our shekar expenses, which were very heavy at times, as we had so many people to feed.

Whilst we were tracking up the wounded elephant, we came upon an open glade or natural clearing, through which a mountain stream flowed, and as it was much trodden with bison and sambur, and there were also pugs of a large tiger freshly imprinted in the moist sand of a nullah at no great distance, we ordered some of our people and the Mulcher folk to construct a comfortable hunting-lodge of three huts, and surround it with a stout *abatis* fence, strong enough to keep out intruders from the adjacent forest. Having myself selected the spot and marked out the ground, I left Chinneah to carry out the arrangements, and we adjourned to the tent, where we found Kenny had been extremely thoughtful of our requirements, and an admirable tiffin and well cooled bitter beer was awaiting our arrival. I distributed among the ryots, through the curnum or headman of the village, 100 rupees, as some compensation for the loss they had incurred through the elephants destroying their crops, and by this act established myself thoroughly in their good graces, so that they kept my camp well supplied with rice, grain, ghee, sheep, fowls, vegetables, and milk, and furnished carriers without any hesitation. In consideration of my *largesse*, they would not allow any extortionate prices to be asked for what supplies I required, and they kept me furnished with every information they could gain as to the haunts of different kinds of game. When my forest bivouac was finished and stored with provisions and various requirements, I superintended the cutting of a practical bush path to it, and made it my temporary head-quarters.

Our first precautionary arrangement on arrival at the new hill camp was to summon all our people and tell them off into watches, as with jungle all round it was very necessary to keep a good look-out in case any of the marauding Carnivora should visit our cattle-shed. A large quantity of dry wood was also collected, so that those on watch could keep up the fires without going outside the fenced enclosure. On examination of the ground round about our encampment, the fresh pugs of tigers and wolves, and several spoor of elephants, some three or four days old, were distinctly visible, besides numerous slots of different kinds of deer ; so we had every prospect of good sport in our new diggings without going far from home. W had hardly our little stockaded fortalice in defensible order when one of the jungle wallahs came in somewhat scared, having seen two tigers making their way towards the stream about five or six hundred yards distant from our station Burton and Kenny, accompanied by Googooloo and Chinneah carrying spare guns, started off at once in pursuit, whilst I remained behind to superintend the strengthening of the fences. Hardly had they been gone five minutes when one of my servants called me and directed my attention to a peculiar whimpering noise, the import of which I well knew, that seemed to proceed from a patch of olibanum bush scarcely a hundreds yards away. My two trustworthy shekarries were with my pals, and there was no one at hand whom I dare trust with a second gun ; so slipping the strap of a short double S-gauge smooth-bore by Westley-Richards round my shoulder, and taking my favourite double 10-bore rifle in my hand, I gave a couple of other guns of large calibre to my horse-keeper and dog-boy, and sallied forth, my staunch old veteran Ponto leading the way by half a dozen yards, and showing by his precautionary actions that he thoroughly understood the nature of the game he was after, for he carefully reconnoitred and winded every bush that might afford concealment to a foe, and made casts from time to time to try and discover a trail, all the time peering watchfully ahead in the direction from which the suspicious noises appeared to come. All at once he gave a slight whimper and crouched down close to the ground, and I then knew that the game was afoot and in sight, but I was scarcely prepared for what followed ; for a magnificent full-grown tiger, with a tremulous roar, sprang over a low bush and alighted between the dog and myself, where he crouched as if about to spring on me. At this moment his attention was attracted by a vigorous attack from Ponto, who, fearing his master was in danger, flew at him. Immediately I let drive right and left, one bullet entering his head just below the ear, whilst the second entered his chest and came out far behind the shoulder, so that death was instantaneous, and if I had been quick enough with my second gun, I might have had a fair shot at his mate, who came skulking round the bush to see what had so incensed her companion, but who bolted with a sullen growl when she saw what had happened. Her subsequent career was, however, a short if not a merry one, for in her confusion—at becoming so suddenly a widow—she made tracks by the same route by which she came, and consequently fell in

JUNGLE WALLAHS.

with Kenny and Burton, who were following up her pugs from the stream, and who greeted her appearance with a volley, which broke her spine and disabled her, when a third shot stretched her lifeless.

The only reason to which I could attribute the tiger's aggressive line of action was that this was the beginning of the rutting season, and that hearing the dog giving tongue, and not seeing him, his jealousy was roused, and he must have fancied the sound came from one of his own species, who had the audacity to interfere with his domestic arrangements. Luckily my noble dog was unhurt by my double shot, and after walking round his foe two or three times, and smelling him all round, he vented his spleen upon him, " after the ancient manner of his species."

THE DEATH OF A ROGUE ELEPHANT.

I was staying at Ootacamund on the Neilgherries, when one morning soon after daybreak my head shekarry Chineah, awoke me with the intelligence that a Curumber had come into the cantonment to say that a large herd of elephants had been seen the day previously near a nullah that flowed into the Moyaar river, about three miles from the foot of the Hills. Wedderburn, who had also received the news, came to my bungalow, and it was arranged that he should go down the Seegur, or northern ghaut, and work towards the eastward, whilst I went down that of Coonoor and made for Gujelhutti, where we were to meet on the third day. This was a capital hunting-quarter, close to a narrow belt of jungle between the Hills and Moyaar river, through which elephants had to pass whether en route for the Ballyrungum Hills or for the southern forests.

Having completed my preparations I sent on the guns, &c., Chineah, Googooloo, the Gooroo, and a horsekeeper, also two coolies laden with prog; and after they had started four or five hours, I mounted my nag Gooty, and caught them up at the bottom of the ghaut just as the sun was setting. We passed the night at the Metrapolliam bungalow, after having ordered the headman of the village to send to Seremogay and have a boat prepared for us. The next day we went down the Bhowani as far as the confluence of the Moyaar, and here we hunted for three days, but, as we could not find any fresh spoor of elephants, we made the best of our way to Gujelhutti, the village where Wedderburn was to have joined me. The village consisted of only seven bamboo and grass huts : but no sooner did the inhabitants understand that I was going to remain in that neighbourhood, than they all, men, women, and children, turned out to cut bamboos and gather dry leaves and long grass, for the construction of a hut, under Chineah's directions.

Whilst these preparations for passing the night were being made, two men of the Mulcher village, who had just returned with a load of roots which they had gathered for food in the jungle, came up with the intelligence that they had been chased by a *rogue* elephant that afternoon near a shallow tank about a coss distant. Although somewhat fatigued by my long walk, as it yet wanted a couple of hours to sunset, I determined to go after him, and leaving Chineah in charge of the camp, accompanied by Googooloo and the Gooroo carrying spare guns, I set out under the guidance of the two Mulchers. Their coss proved a very long two miles, for I found myself close to the foot of the hills before they pointed me out a fresh spoor, evidently that of a solitary elephant of no great dimensions.

After tracking it up for a short distance, I came to a jheel, or marsh, full of high reeds and stunted bush, and there, in the centre of a shallow pool, I saw the object of my search, evidently enjoying the luxury of a bath. At first sight I thought it was a huge female, as no tusks were perceivable, but on a closer inspection with my field glass I found it to be a bull, although of the kind called by the natives "*hyjera*," or "barren males." The Mulchers told me that he was a very vicious brute, as not only had he repeatedly charged them without provocation, but when he found they had eluded his pursuit by climbing up a large tree and hiding themselves amongst the foliage, he wreaked his fury on a bamboo which he plucked up and trampled to pieces under his feet, screaming with rage the whole time. Such being the case, I did not care to have more people about me than was absolutely necessary, so giving the two spare guns to Googooloo, I bade all the rest climb into high trees, from whence they could see the sport without danger.

This matter arranged, I tried the wind by a feather, which, when after elephants, I generally kept pinned by a bit of fine silk to my hunting cap; but as circumstances turned out, this precaution was hardly required. I now put fresh caps upon my guns, taking care to see that the powder was well up in the nipples, reconnoitred the ground carefully, and made a half-circuit of the marsh, in order to get behind the cover of a patch of high reeds which appeared about seventy yards distant from the spot where the elephant was standing. We both kept well under cover, making as little noise as possible, and approached *up wind;* but the keen-scented animal, although he had his back turned towards us, perceived the taint in the air when we were three hundred yards distant, and with a hoarse scream of rage, came rushing, tail on end, in our direction, flourishing his trunk about and sniffing the wind. Luckily, the loud splashing of his great feet betrayed his movements, for we were knee-deep in the mud, and the reeds in some places were considerably higher than our heads. This was an awkward position to be in; moreover, the setting sun shone right in my face, and as I was much afraid that it would dazzle my eyes and prevent me from taking proper aim, I pushed on until I came to a place where the reeds were only up to my waist, when I halted, looked to see that my guns were dry, and then told Googooloo to get on my shoulders to look round over the reeds for the enemy. Scarcely had he mounted than I knew my foe was discovered by the hoarse appalling scream of rage that rang through the air, sounding as if close at hand; and barely had Googooloo time to reach the ground and catch hold of the spare guns, than the infuriated monster burst through a patch of high reeds in our rear that had hitherto concealed him from our sight, and charged splashing up towards us. When I first caught a glimpse of him, he was certainly not more than five and thirty paces distant, and I immediately raised my trusty rifle ; but life and death were on the shot, and it did not belch forth its deadly contents until he had charged to within fifteen paces, when I let him have it, aiming full at the centre of the hollow just over the trunk. The ragged bullet flew true to the mark, burying itself in the brain ; but the impetus of his headlong charge carried him on, and with a mighty splash that might have been heard at a quarter of a mile's distance, he fell with outstretched trunk close to my feet, covering us over with mud from head to foot. I felt sure that my aim was fatal, but had it not been so, we should have been in a pretty predicament, for we were both completely blinded for the moment, and if he had not been very severely hit, he might have caught us, one after the other, before we could have cleared the mud away from our eyes. Poor Googooloo got much the worst of it, being also nearly choked ; but after some spluttering and coughing, he wiped his eyes on the tail of my shooting coat, and we simultaneously burst out into a loud laugh at each other's queer appearance.

This elephant was evidently a most dangerous rogue, for he had not only tracked us up entirely by his extraordinarily keen scent (in following the taint in the air), but had also showed desperate cunning in *doubling* before he made his attack, so as to take us in the rear and cut off our retreat.

Having washed off some of the extraneous mud in a neighbouring pool, I went to examine the dead elephant, whose almost rabid state I could now easily account for, as besides the hole my bullet had made, from which the blood was still oozing, there were three other recent wounds in nearly the same place, with a fourth that had passed through the off ear, and two more in the off shoulder. What astonished me more particularly was, that none of the three wounds which the animal had previously received should have proved mortal, although all were planted in the most vital part of the elephant's skull, and one within an inch of my own shot, from which death was instantaneous.

On my attempting to probe the previous wounds with a ramrod, in order to ascertain the direction the bullets had taken, I was much surprised to find them plugged up with red clay, which operation, I have no doubt, was performed by the sagacious animal himself, in order to stop the hæmorrhage. However, as night was drawing on, and I had a good hour's walk through the jungle to my camp, I deferred all further examination until the morrow ; and having looked to my arms, in case they might be required *en route*, cut off the elephant's tail and the tips of his ears, to send to the collector's cutcherry for the Government reward, and joined the Goorco and Mulchers, who, hearing the shot, were approaching us. We then made the best of our way to the village, which we reached safely, after nearly missing our way once or twice from the darkness of the night. I was regularly tired out when I arrived, but a bath, clean clothes, and a good dinner soon set me up all right again.

On the morrow at daylight, I sallied out, accompanied by the gang and a large party of Mulchers, taking my course towards the jheel where I had killed the elephant the day before. Here I found that a pig had been paying a visit to the remains, for a bit of the hind quarters had been eaten away, and there were no fresh traces of animal life except the broad slots of a large boar, besides which I could plainly see the rips made by his sharp tusks in the flesh. The gang then set to work with their axes to cut out the tusks, which, although considerably thicker, much resembled those of a female, being only about sixteen inches in length, and hardly protruding from the lip. They were, however, perfectly solid,* the cavity at the end being only an inch in depth, and much heavier than ordinary ivory. I then cleared out the mud, and with an iron ramrod probed the wounds in the forehead, when I found that, although they had all struck the vital spot, not one had been delivered at the proper angle so as to penetrate the brain, although they were, I imagined, sufficient to have caused the animal to die a lingering death.

As the ground about the jheel seemed a very likely-looking haunt for elephants, I and Googooloo took a stroll round, looking out for spoor, but not a fresh one was to be seen, except that of the rogue killed the day before, although there were signs of almost every other denizen of the jungle having drank lately at the pool. Whilst we were away, some of the gang, who were curiously inclined, with their axes extracted the bullets from the forehead of the dead rogue, and presented them to me on my return, when to my surprise I recognized two cylindro-conical projectiles, made of a mixture of lead and pewter, as belonging to Wedderburn's two-grooved double rifle. The third was a round brass bullet that exactly fitted my Westley-Richards' two-ounce smooth bore, of which Wedderburn had a sister gun, so that I knew that he had fallen in with the elephant before I did. My friend was an admirable shot, and used to fire at elephants at very long ranges, when it was almost impossible that his bullet could reach the brain, not being fired

---

* Their weight was just under eight pounds each.

at a proper angle. I halted at Gujelhutti for four days, when, finding that Wedderburn did not put in an appearance, I returned to my head-quarters at Ooty.

Here I learned that my friend had been killed by an elephant; and it appeared from the testimony of those who were with him and witnessed the catastrophe that they had fallen in with fresh spoor soon after descending the ghaut, and had early in the day come across a solitary elephant, apparently without tusks, who was standing fanning himself in a patch of open tree jungle, knee-deep in undergrowth. Wedderburn, in the first instance, tried to approach him to leeward, but finding that he could not get a shot, the animal's back being turned towards him, crept round from tree to tree until he got a fair view of his forehead, when he let drive right and left with his double rifle, and dropped him. However, the elephant, who was only momentarily stunned, began to recover his knees, when Wedderburn, snatching his second gun from his shekarry (a double two-ounce smooth-bore), again brought him to the ground with a third shot, and fancying he was dead, rushed forward, but the animal with a scream of rage regained his feet, and perceiving his antagonist, charged upon him tail on end, with his trunk thrown high up in the air. At this moment, Wedderburn either lost his presence of mind and fired without aim, or finding that the mortal place in the centre of the forehead was hidden by the upraised trunk, must have endeavoured to bring him down by a side shot, but his fourth bullet (most likely the one that passed through the ear) produced no effect and in the twinkling of an eye, before he could get out of the way, the infuriated animal was upon him, twisted his trunk round his legs, and hurled him to the ground ; Wedderburn, although much injured, and doubtless with some of his limbs broken, still moved, and at this moment one of the shekarries, who carried a loaded gun, fired two shots into the animal's side; but nothing attracted his attention from his victim, whose piercing shrieks rang through the forest, for regardless of the shouts and cries of the natives, he again seized him, placed his huge foot upon his chest, and trampled and knelt upon him until almost every bone was broken, when he flung the mangled and lifeless body on one side, and rushed trumpeting through the forest. Such was the melancholy fate of one of the best shots that India ever produced; and I must have fallen in with his vindictive adversary about eight hours after the fatal rencontre, for I am convinced, from the circumstantial evidence of the recognized bullets, that the " *rogue* " I slew was the guilty party, although each of the half-dozen elephants that were killed round about the Hills was supposed to have had something to do with the transaction.

STRATEGY *VERSUS* FORCE.

Many of my most successful hunting trips took place before the introduction of breech-loading arms, and in those days I was often put to severe shifts, and had to think twice before I fired at an animal that might turn the tables. The following incident will explain the tactics I found necessary to adopt upon one occasion. I was elephant-shooting in the Wynaad forest, when I came across an unusually fine tusker standing alone by several large boulders of rock, against one of which he was rubbing his hind quarters, as if he belonged to the clan of Argyle. Immediately I caught sight of him I dived into the deeper jungle, and, by taking a circuitous route, got well to windward of him. I then regretted that my staunch Yanadi, Googooloo, was not with me, as I had no spare gun, and felt nervous lest my prey might escape. However, there was no help for it, so after carefully reconnoitring the ground, in order to avail myself of any cover it afforded, I crept forward on my hands and knees, and, after a few minutes of intensely exciting stalking, managed to wriggle up and ensconce myself behind a low ledge of rock, whence I could observe every motion the elephant made.

He was standing on three legs, the off hind-foot being raised from the ground, and leaning carelessly against the other, whilst the fore-part of his body was swinging to and fro. Although he was not more than twenty paces distant, I could not get a fair shot, as his head was turned directly away from me. I waited nearly ten minutes for a chance of his altering his position, during which I had ample time to admire his stately proportions and magnificent tusks, but he never moved an inch. I could not get round in front of him on account of the wind, and as I did not like to risk the chance of losing so fine a fellow by an uncertain shot that might not prove mortal, after a few seconds' deliberation I determined to try another plan, which, as I had not a spare gun, was attended with considerable danger.

I examined the ground carefully, so as to be prepared in case I had to make a run for it, and then taking off my leathern gaiters and extraneous clothing, so as to have my limbs as free as possible, noiselessly crept on my hands and knees behind him, and placing the muzzle of my gun almost close to the centre of the hind-foot which was raised, I pulled both triggers almost simultaneously, and sprang out of the way. A shrill shriek of agony followed the double report, and I just escaped a ferocious blow aimed at me with his trunk, being fortunately out of reach. I ran round to the back of the rock before I ventured to look over my shoulder, when, finding he was not on me, I re-loaded as quickly as possible; this done, I felt secure, and again approached the scene of action.

I found my plan had proved completely successful, for my antagonist was entirely disabled. My gun—a double two-ounce smooth-bore, by Westley-Richards—had been heavily loaded,

having about six drachms of powder in each barrel; and the
bones of the foot were so completely shattered by the double
shot that he could not put it to the ground, and every time he
attempted to make a step forward he fell heavily. He must
have suffered intense agony, for he uttered most piteous cries
between his bursts of rage. As I approached, he strove to
charge with a shriek of despair, but fell heavily to the ground,
and, as he was rising to his knees, I stepped up and dis=
charged both barrels into the hollow over the trunk, the contents of which penetrating the brain, he fell "never to rise
again."

THE DANGER OF RANDOM SHOOTING.

Young sportsmen are apt to become over-excited when large
game is afoot; and, in their eagerness not to let a chance escape,
will not wait until a fair shot presents itself, but fire at random.
This is a mistake that should be guarded against, or it may
bring the hunter to grief. Except in very exceptional cases he
should not pull trigger unless he feels pretty certain of hitting
his game in a vital spot, and I think I may attribute my own
immunity from accidents to my constant observance of this
rule. Out of 876 bull elephants I have killed in India and
Africa, I never had but one serious accident, and this occurred
when I was a mere tyro, and may be attributed to my own
carelessness. As the incident may serve as a warning I shall
relate it.

I had been shooting with some success in the Wynaad
forest, and had just killed an elephant, when a mighty bull,
the patriarch of the herd, and seven females, dashed
hurriedly past at a distance of about fifty paces. I threw up
my rifle, and, aiming behind the ear, let drive a couple of snap-
shots for the chance of stopping him, the last of which took
effect, for it brought him to his knees; but he immediately

regained his legs, and, separating from the females, tore frantically through the forest, which he made resound with his angry roar.

I snatched my second spare gun—a heavy two-ounce double rifle—and, jumping down the bank, ran with all speed to cut him off at the gorge, which was extremely narrow, as the torrent made its way between a huge cleft in the rock, through which I knew he must pass in order to join the rest of the herd. I was running down the bed of the stream, on either side of which rose high banks, when I heard a rattling noise among the stones behind me, and on turning my head I saw the wounded bull tearing after me, with his eyes flashing fire and his tail straight on end, about forty paces distant. Speed I knew would not avail me ; he would have been down upon me before I could have clambered up the bank, so I swung round and dropped on my knee, to take a more steady aim. On he charged with a fiendish shriek of revenge ; I let him come to within fifteen paces, when I let drive, aiming between his eyes (my favourite shot) ; but whether it was that I was unsteady, being breathless from my run, or that my rifle, which weighed sixteen pounds, was too heavy, I know not ; but my left arm dropped the moment I pulled the trigger, (not from nervousness, for I was perfectly cool, and never lost my presence of mind for a moment,) and my shot took effect four inches too low, entering the fleshy part of the root of the trunk instead of penetrating the brain. It failed to stop him, and before I could get out of the way the huge brute was on me; I saw something dark pass over me, felt a severe blow, and found myself whizzing through the air : then all was oblivion.

When I came to, I found myself lying on my face in a pool of blood, which came from my nose, mouth, and ears. Although nearly choked with clotted gore, a sense of my perilous situation flashed across my mind, and I strove to rise and look after my antagonist, but he was nowhere to be seen. I picked myself up, and although fearfully bruised and shaken, found that no bones were broken. I was lying on the top of the bank, although quite unable to account to myself how I got there. In the dry bed of the nullah I saw my rifle, and after much painful exertion managed to crawl down and get it. The muzzle was filled with sand, which I cleared out as well as I could; and then, sitting by the edge of the stream, began to wash away the blood and bathe my face and head. Whilst so employed I heard a piercing shriek, and saw Googooloo rushing towards me, closely followed by the infuriated elephant, who was almost mad from the pain of his wounds. Luckily a hanging branch was in his way, and with the agility of a monkey he caught hold of it, and swung himself up the steep bank, where he was safe.

The elephant, balked of his victim, rushed wildly backwards and forwards two or three times, as if searching for him, and then, with a hoarse scream of disappointment, came tearing down the bed of the nullah. I was directly in his path, and powerless to get out of the way. A moment more and I saw that I was perceived, for down he charged upon me with a fiendish roar of vengeance. With difficulty I raised my rifle, and taking a steady aim between his eyes, pulled the trigger— it was my only chance. When the smoke cleared away I perceived a mighty mass lying close to me. At last I had conquered. Soon after this I must have become half senseless, for I hardly remember anything until I found myself lying in my hut, and Burton leaning over me.

It appears that Chineah and the gang had carried me in on a litter, and, finding my body very much swollen from the severe blow I had received, my back being black from the waist upwards, had applied a native remedy, and covered the bruised part with leeches, which had the effect of counteracting the inflammation, although I shall carry their marks to the end of my life. This was a close shave, but it taught me a lesson, and since that day I have never had an accident through random shooting.

SKULLS OF THE AFRICAN AND INDIAN ELEPHANT.

CHAPTER VIII.

BISON AND BUFFALO HUNTING.

THE gaur, or Indian bison, which is the largest of the Bos tribe, is found in the dense forests of Southern and Western India, as far north as the Nerbudda river, but the finest specimens I have seen were shot in the Wynaad and Canara districts, and in the dense forests on the slopes of the Neilgherry and Anamullai Hills. Bison are generally found in the extensive tracts of bamboo forest that form a kind of terai or belt round many of our hill ranges in Southern India. Their home is on the densely wooded hillside, where they graze upon the young shoots of bamboo and the succulent grasses that clothe the slopes of the ravines. In the hot weather they may be found during the day on the plateaux lying down in some shady retreat sleeping and chewing the cud, but towards evening they make their way downwards towards their feeding grounds, graze all night, and return to their day-haunts soon after day-break; except during the rains, and in cloudy weather, when, if they are not much disturbed, they may be found grazing at all hours. In the intensely hot weather, when the mountain streams dry up, herds of bison may be found wandering in the plains far away from their usual haunts, being compelled to quench their thirst at some large river, and during a general drought I have known bison to travel twenty miles in search of water, and return to their mountain fastness in the early morning.

During the rutting season, which is in the cold weather, the large herds break up, and each stalwart bull retires to rusticate with his seraglio, consisting generally of from eight to fifteen cows. At this time free fights amongst the bulls are of common occurrence, and those who are in the sere and yellow leaf, or weakly, being worsted in the combat, are ignominiously driven out of the herd by their younger rivals. A bull once tabooed is never again allowed to join the herd, and the lonely life he leads does not improve his temper, for solitary bulls are generally morose and vicious brutes.

Shortly after the rains, towards the end of October, the cows begin to calve, and for this purpose they separate from the bulls, and retire to some secluded ravine until the calves are about two months old and strong enough to follow the herd. Immature bulls are allowed to remain with the cows unmolested by the lord of the harem, and from this time until the commencement of the rutting season the old bulls are often found alone, but in the vicinity of the herd, so as to be at hand in case of danger. Single bulls always lie looking to leeward, trusting to their keen sense of smell to guard the windward quarter.

Except on the Sheveroy Hills, where driving has been resorted to with considerable success, bison are generally killed by stalking, and inasmuch as they are gifted with remarkably keen scent and hearing, and are very quick to detect the presence of man, it requires considerable cunning and very careful tracking in order to get near them.

In stalking a herd of bison the hunter should always make his way up *against* the wind, taking advantage of any cover that may offer itself. Having got within range, and managed to conceal himself behind some friendly bush, he will watch the movements of the herd and wait his opportunity of getting a fair shot at the bull, as no sportsman would fire at a cow if he has a chance of killing the lord of the herd. The great secrets of success in bison-stalking are coolness and discretion, and in the long run a sportsman who will bide his time, and wait patiently until he can get a fair aim at a vital spot, will kill far more game than he who, in a state of nervous excitement, fires at anything and everything he sees, trusting more to good luck than good shooting. The following are the dimensions of one of the largest bison I ever killed :—

	Ft.	in.
Height at the shoulder, not following the curve of the body*......	6	4
Height to the top of hump	6	9
Length from tip of nose to the insertion of tail	10	4
Length of tail	3	4
Girth of body	9	3
Girth of fore-arm...	2	10
Girth of neck	4	10
Breadth of forehead..	1	5
Circumference round base of horns	1	9
Length of horns	1	4

General colour—black along the back, light dun under the belly and inside the thighs, and the legs below the knees and hocks dirty white, but cleanly made and finely proportioned as those of a deer. The frontal bone is nearly two inches thick and exceedingly hard, and the bullet must be hardened and driven with a large charge of powder to penetrate it. I have seen leaden bullets flattened on a bull bison's forehead a score of times, so massive is the skull, and in some cases I have known the animal to go off apparently not much the worse, although the shot has been fired at point-blank range.

BISON AND TIGER HUNTING IN THE WYNAAD FOREST.

There is certainly no part of India where such a diversity of game is to be found as in the great Wynaad forest, surrounding the Neilgherry and Anamullai ranges ; but, except during the intensely hot weather—when the stagnant swamps and decomposed vegetation, which generate malarious vapours and

---

* Bison are said to have been killed measuring twenty-three hands at the shoulder.

BUFFALO SHOOTING.

fever infecting miasma, are dried up and rendered temporarily innocuous—this belt of jungle, which varies from five to thirty miles in width, is extremely unhealthy, and there are certain seasons when it is almost certain death to sleep a single night in the "terai." The healthiest season of the year to hunt in those forests is March, April, and May, and at this time the best sport is to be had, as the trees are tolerably clear from leaves, and the scarcity of water drives all kinds of game to the proximity of the rivers and pools. Elephants, tigers, panthers, leopards, bears, hogs, sambur, spotted deer, and bison, are drawn by the drought from their usual haunts in the densely wooded. ravines and impenetrable forests on the sides of the hills to the more open jungle through which the Bowani and its tributaries flow.

The dense teak and bamboo forest which clothes the Anamullai range near Coimbatore is one of the finest hunting-grounds in Southern India, and here in their vernal home may be found vast herds of bison, as well as elephants, tigers, leopards, sambur, and sundry other game. Perhaps the finest bison stalking in the world is to be had in this district, and Burton, my old *camarade de chasse,* and I have had many a glorious day's sport in these primeval woods. The following description of a day amongst the bison in this forest will give some idea of the manner in which this animal is generally hunted in India.

In the latter part of the month of April, during intensely hot weather, Burton and I, accompanied by a large gang of trackers, were out in the bamboo forest that covers the lower slopes of the Anamullai Hills, when we came across the trail of a herd of bison. From the freshness of the "sign," I knew that no great length of time had elapsed since they had passed, but the deep impressions of their hoofs on the soft soil showed that they had travelled past without browsing on the most tempting looking herbage ; so I concluded that they had either been alarmed or had been to the Bowani river to drink, and were impatient to get to the deeper shades of the forest before the intense heat of mid-day. After following the trail for some miles, Chineah and Googooloo, who were creeping along a rugged hollow, which appeared to have been the bed of a mountain torrent, some little distance in front, made a sign to us to keep silent, and shortly afterwards they beckoned us to advance. With great caution we crept noiselessly forward, stopping from time to time to listen, and after crawling on our hands and knees for nearly a hundred yards, we gained the crest of the hill, where we had the satisfaction of seeing a large herd of bison quietly browsing on the green herbage in a patch of open teak forest.

Having satisfied myself that we were well to leeward, and in no danger of being discovered by their remarkably keen scent, I raised myself cautiously behind the trunk of a tree to recon- noitre, and after pointing out to Burton a fine bull, who, sur- rounded with cows, was lazily nibbling the young and tender shoots of a clump of bamboos, about a hundred yards distant, I begged him to reserve his fire until he heard my signal, as I intended to try and stalk the patriarch of the herd, a stately fellow with enormous dewlap, and immensely deep shoulders, who was pawing the ground fretfully, and uttering deep cries, as if impatient for the herd to retire to the depths of the jungle for shelter from the rays of the sun, which were beginning to feel oppressive. I descended a short distance down the side of a hill, and crept along the brow until I got under cover of a clump of bamboos, whence I again caught sight of him. Here I had nearly been discovered, for two cows and a young calf sprang up close to me, and rushed, tail on end, towards the rest of the herd, who, lifting up their heads, seemed to gaze anxiously in my direction. I therefore remained a few moments perfectly quiet, keeping my eye on the mighty bull, who was standing about three hundred yards distant; and when I saw that their alarm had in some degree subsided, I crept gently forward, and, taking advantage of any cover I could find, managed to ensconce myself behind a large rhododendron bush within a hundred and fifty yards of him. I then blew a shrill blast on a silver call I always wore round my neck as a signal to Burton, and shortly afterwards heard a double shot followed by three others. The first report attracted the bull's attention, and he trotted forward a few paces to reconnoitre, tearing up the turf with his hoofs, and lashing his tail, as if indignant that his sylvan retreat should be intruded upon. Whilst in this position, he offered me a fair view of his brawny shoulder, and I planted a heavy cylindro-conical bullet just behind it, which brought him to his knees with a surly roar. Mad with pain, he regained his feet, and staggered forward on three legs, when I gave him the contents of my second barrel in nearly the same place, which rolled him over. Chineah now handed me my other rifle, and I quitted the cover; when no sooner did he catch sight of me than, again springing up, with a deep tremendous roar, he charged headlong at me, tail on end, his eyes flashing fire, and his mouth covered with blood and foam. I let him come within six paces of where I was standing, when I stopped his mad career with a ball in the centre of his broad, massive forehead, which again made him bite the dust. He gave a desperate plunge forward, and rolled heavily over on his side, dead. The others, alarmed, were now tearing frantically over the plain, so I slipped behind the cover of a bush to reload, and, again stealing forward, managed to bowl over a cow, and wound another badly, before the terrified herd sought safety in flight by rallying in a body and crashing through the dense bamboo-jungle which clothed the side of the hill. After reloading, I despatched the second cow with a bullet behind the horns, as she was lying disabled by my first shot, which had passed through the small of her back, and paralyzed her hind quarters.

I now looked out for Burton and Googooloo, who were nowhere to be seen, but a dead cow and a bull calf showed that they had not been idle. Whilst I was examining the latter, and cogitating upon veal cutlets and marrow bones, I heard two double shots in some cover just below the crest of the hill, which was immediately followed by a loud whoop from Burton; and on running up, I found him standing breathless over the carcase of a huge bull which was evidently just killed.

"By Jove! Hal," he exclaimed as I approached, "I'm regularly done up; this bull has led me such a chase. I hit him fairly between the eyes with my first barrel, and he dropped without a struggle, dead, as I thought; so I paid no more attention to him, but, letting drive at the herd as they bolted away, I killed a cow and a calf and wounded a third, when suddenly my friend, as if brought to life by the sound of my last shot, picked himself up, shook his head savagely, gave an angry roar, and charged right at me. Every barrel being discharged, I stepped on one side and got out of his way, when he directed his attention to Googooloo, who dodged him amongst the trees easily enough; for, half blinded with blood from his wound, he reeled and tumbled about as if he were groggy, every now and then falling heavily. As soon as I had reloaded, I gave chase, but all at once missed him, and it was only just now that the Yanadi trailed him up to this clump of grass, where he had cunningly laid down to conceal himself. As I came up, he again charged desperately towards me, when stepping aside, I allowed him to pass, and gave him the contents of both barrels well behind the shoulder, which brought him up, and to make certain, I administered two more shots in the back of the head as he lay writhing and gasping on the ground, and here he is safely landed at last."

On examination we found that the first shot had flattened on the thick bone of the forehead, without penetrating the skull, the bullet being of unhardened lead driven by 4 drachms of powder from a 12-gauge smooth-bore. After having cut out the tongues, and packed up a few marrow bones for supper, we superintended the bushing of the game, and, shouldering our rifles, made a start for our bivouac, well satisfied with our sport, for we had that day bagged three sambur and six bison to two guns, and furnished our people and the Mulcher tribe with a grand supply of meat.

Whilst hunting in the jungle between the Bowani river and the Goodaloor pass at the foot of the Nedineallah Hills, my friend Burton and I witnessed a most gallantly contested fight between a bull bison and a tiger which is worth recording. Night had scarcely set in when a loud bellowing noise was heard, followed by an unmistakable roar which caused no little commotion amongst the horns and bullocks that were picketed round our tents, and from the ominous sounds that followed we knew that a mortal combat was raging at no great distance from our bivouac. Having arranged for the safety of our camp, Burton and I, armed with rifles and pistols, followed closely by Chineah and Googooloo, each carrying a couple of spare guns, sallied forth, and, keeping along the bank of the river for some short distance, entered a dense cover, from which the sounds of the contest seemed to issue, by a narrow deer-run. Here we could only get along very slowly, having to separate the tangled brushwood with one hand and hold the rifle cocked and ready with the other. Having proceeded in this manner for some distance, guided by the noise of the contest which sounded nearer and nearer, we came to an opening in the woods where we saw a huge bull bison, evidently much excited, for his eyes

FIGHT BETWEEN A TIGER AND A BULL BISON.

flashed fire, his tail straight on end, and he was tearing up the ground with his forefeet, all the time grunting furiously. As we were all luckily well to leeward, the taint in the air was not likely to be winded, so I made signs to Chineah and Googooloo to lay down their guns and climb into an adjacent tree, whilst Burton and I, with a rifle in each hand, by dint of creeping on hands and knees, gained a small clump of bush on a raised bank, not more than thirty yards distant, from whence we could see all that was going on. When we first arrived the tiger was nowhere to be seen, but from the bison's cautious movements I knew he could not be far off. The moon was high in the heavens, making the night clear as day; so not a movement could escape us, although we were well concealed from view.

Several rounds had already been fought, for the game had been going on a good twenty minutes before we came up, and the bison, besides being covered with white lather about the flanks, bore several severe marks of the tiger's claws on the face and shoulders. Whilst we were ensconcing ourselves comfortably behind the cover, with our rifles in readiness for self-defence only—for we had no intention of interfering in the fair stand-up fight which had evidently been taking place—a low savage growling about fifteen paces to our right attracted our attention, and, couched behind a tuft of fern, we discerned the shape of an immense tiger watching the movements of the bison, who, with his head kept constantly turned towards the danger, was alternately cropping the grass and giving vent to his excited feelings every now and then by a deep tremulous roaring, which seemed to awaken all the echoes of the surrounding woods. The tiger, whose glaring eyes were fixed upon his antagonist, now and again shifted his quarters a few paces either to the right or the left, once coming so near our ambuscade that I could almost have touched him with the muzzle of my rifle; but the wary old bull never lost sight of him for a second, but ever followed his movements, with his head lowered to receive his attack. At last the tiger, which all along had been whining and growling most impatiently, stole gently forward, his belly crouching along the ground, every hair standing on end, his flanks heaving, his back arched, and his tail whisking about and lashing his sides; but before he could gather himself together for a spring, which might have proved fatal, the bison, with a shriek of desperation, charged at full speed with his head lowered, and the horns pointed upward, but overshot the mark, as his antagonist adroitly shifted his ground just in time to avoid a vicious stroke from his massive horns, and, making a half-circle, sprang a second time, with the intention of alighting on his broad neck and shoulders; this the bull evaded by a dexterous twist, and before his adversary could recover himself, he again rushed at him, caught him behind the shoulder with his horns, and flung him some distance, following up to repeat the game, but the tiger slunk away to gather breath.

Round after round of the same description followed, allowing breathing time between each, the tiger generally getting the worst of it, for the bull sometimes received his rush on his massive forehead and horns, and flung him a considerable distance, bruised and breathless, although the skin seemed too tough for the points to penetrate; once, however, I thought the bison's chance was all over, for the tiger, by a lucky spring, managed to fasten on his brawny shoulder, and I could hear the crunching sound as his teeth met again and again in the flesh, whilst the claws tore the flank like an iron rake. With a maddening scream of mingled rage and pain, the bull flung himself heavily on the ground, nearly crushing his more nimble adversary to death with his ponderous weight; and the tiger, breathless and reeling with exhaustion, endeavoured to slink away with his tail between his legs, but no respite was given, his relentless foe pursued with roars of vengeance, and again rolled him over before he could regain his legs to make another spring. The tiger, now fairly conquered, endeavoured to beat a retreat, but this the bison would not allow, he rushed at him furiously over and over again, and at last getting him against a bank of earth, pounded him with his forehead and horns, until he lay motionless, when he sprang with his whole weight upon him, striking him with the fore feet, and displaying an agility I thought incompatible with his unwieldy appearance. I have attempted to depict "the last round" in my sketch.

The game, which had lasted over a couple of hours, was now over, for the tiger, which we thought, perhaps, might be only stunned, gave unmistakable signs of approaching dissolution. He lay gasping, his mouth half-open, exposing his rough tongue and massive yellow teeth; his green eyes were fixed, convulsive struggles drew up his limbs, a quiver passed over his body, and all was still. His conqueror was standing over him with heaving flanks, and crimsoned foam flying from his widely distended nostrils; but his rolling eye was becoming dim, for the life-blood was fast ebbing from a ghastly wound in his neck, and he reeled about like a drunken man, still, however, fronting his dead antagonist, and keeping his horns lowered as if to charge. From time to time he bellowed with rage, but his voice became fainter, and at last subsided into a deep hollow moan; then his mighty strength began to fail him, and he could not keep his legs, which seemed to bend slowly, causing him to plunge forward. Again he made a desperate effort to recover himself, staggered a few paces, and with a surly growl of defiance fell never to rise again, for, after a few convulsive heavings, his body became motionless, and we knew that all was over.

BISONS IN A SALT JHEEL.

On examination we found the throat of the bison so lacerated that the windpipe was exposed, and several large arteries cut, an ear bitten off, and the flesh on the shoulder actually torn away in strips. The tiger, on the other hand, had one eye gouged out, several ribs broken, and the lower part of the belly ripped open, from which wound the intestines were protruding. I ordered Chineah and Googooloo to collect some dry wood, and light a large fire to keep the jackals and hyenas away, which, being done, we returned to our camp, and were soon in the arms of Morpheus.

Refreshed and invigorated by sound repose, the next morning at daylight we revisited the battle-ground, where we found the gang already busily engaged in despoiling the combatants. The tiger had been so mauled and mangled by his furious adversary that the skin, although beautifully marked, was hardly worth taking, great patches of hair having been rubbed off on all parts. He was a splendid fellow, and had he been able to have got a fair blow with his immensely muscular fore paw on the bison's neck in the first instance, it would have told with fatal effect. The ground, besides bearing numerous traces of the recent combat, was so torn up that it appeared to have been ploughed in patches, and I found it to be strongly impregnated with salt ; consequently I was not at all surprised to find numberless slots of sambur and spotted deer, as well as the fresh traces of a herd of bison, well knowing the partiality of these animals for that article, which they seem to be able to smell from extraordinary distances. The engraving represents young bull bisons gambolling in a salt jheel at night.

The dense thicket of jamen and korinda bushes bordering the Bowani river was a favourite resort of tigers during the hot weather, and continually during the night were we reminded of their proximity either by their calling and answering each other

TIGER SHOOTING ON THE BOWANI RIVER.

or by the bark of alarm of sambur or spotted deer when they detected their presence.   One night, before the moon rose, these nocturnal marauders had prowled for some hours round about our camp, and had caused no little commotion amongst our horses and cattle; so as soon as the moon was well up, Burton and I, with two of our people carrying spare guns, sallied forth, and, guided by the shrieking and jabbering of a troop of monkeys, made our way to an open spot of ground in a ravine near the Bowani, where we fell in with a tiger, just as he had stricken down a doe spotted deer.   Burton caught sight of him first, and rolled him over stone dead with a bullet admirably placed just behind the ear, and we were just stepping up to examine the spoiled foe when, with a long tremendous roar, his mate sprang into the open, and knocking down Burton's horsekeeper, seized him by the shoulder.   Luckily at this moment the moon was unobscured by clouds, and I got a fair aim at the tigress's massive chest, as she stood growling above her shrieking victim. As I pulled trigger, Burton also fired, and she fell dead with one bullet through her heart, and another in the vertebra of the neck, either of which would have proved fatal.   Luckily the horsekeeper was not dangerously hurt, although he had a severe bite in the fleshy part of the shoulder, which took some weeks to heal up.   This place was infested with tigers at this time of the year, and for the best part of two months we made it a practice to sleep during the day and watch for game by water at night.   Besides killing some of the finest specimens of the feline race, and enough venison for camp use, we occasionally fell in with elephants, and had famous sport.

On one occasion we witnessed a grand combat between two tigers for the possession of a deer; and this episode forms the subject of our sketch.   Our goat-boy saw a tiger strike down a buck whilst watching his charge, and scared him from his prey

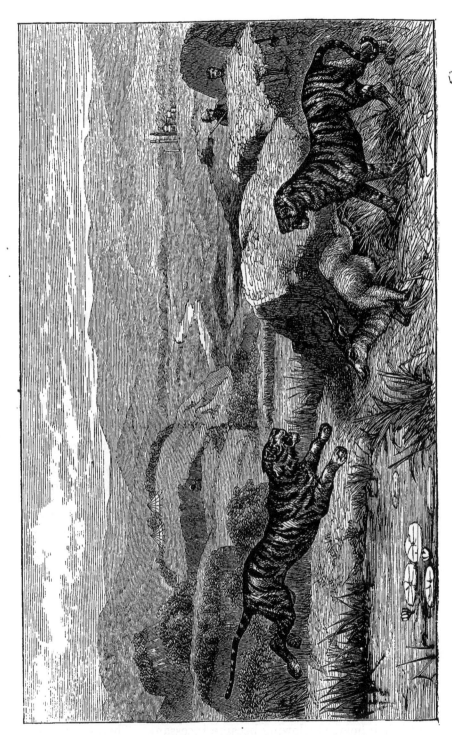

FIGHT BETWEEN TWO TIGERS.

by shouting at him and throwing stones. When the coast was clear, he gave us the information, and towards evening we took post behind some rocks, that commanded the spot. We had hardly spread our rugs to make ourselves comfortable when we heard a rustling in the bushes, and a fine male tiger came crouching along the edge of the water, smelling the ground like a pointer on scent. Although he was within point-blank range, and offered an easy shot, his proceedings seemed so unusually strange that we forbore to pull trigger, and watched his manœuvring for some minutes. At last he perceived the dead deer, and made his way up to it with great caution, sniffing the air at every step he took, as if he could detect some danger threatening. Scarcely had he time to smell his windfall when with a ferocious roar a second tiger sprang from some cover close at hand, and a tremendous fight ensued which we watched with intense interest for several minutes. The second comer, which was much the largest tiger, was gaining the mastery, as he had his opponent hard and fast by the throat, when we fired a right and left simultaneously, and ended the fight, one of the combatants falling dead, whilst the other lay writhing in his death throes, and he was soon put out of his agony by a bullet in the back of the head from my companion's spare gun. This night's work had a peculiar kind of charm both for my companion and myself, for besides being very successful in killing several kinds of game we added very considerably to our "forest lore," and gained much insight into the habits of the different nocturnal animals. Hardly had the sun gone down before the forest seemed to ring with strange wild cries, and among the voices which resounded together we could only distinguish those that were heard singly during momentary pauses that from time to time took place in the chorus. The sambur uttered their loud cries of defiance, which were answered on all sides until their hoarse bellowing became incessant. Then the hollow roar of a tiger would re-echo through the arches of the forest, and for an interval all was still save the noise of the great cicade in the trees. Then the howling of a troop of jackals, or the melancholy wailing of the hyæna, would pierce the night air, and again the almost deafening chorus would recommence.

CHAPTER IX.

SOUVENIRS OF SPORT IN INDIA.

THERE are few countries where such a diversity of game is to be found as in British India, and the facility with which a traveller can now visit all parts of that immense empire has added considerably to the number of sportsmen who have made hunting expeditions to different parts of the country. Besides being a most interesting field for general travel, India offers to the sportsman incomparably the finest accessible hunting-grounds in the known world—except perhaps certain parts of Africa—and there is no other country that can show such a list of large game, or compare for minor sport with the endless array of bustard, pheasants, partridges, and water-fowl. If sport or the collection of trophies be the traveller's object, he can gratify his passion to the utmost extent in this the greatest of our dependencies, for here may be found the elephant, rhinoceros, buffalo, four species of wild bovines, including the mighty gaur, the largest of the race ; and in felines the lion, tiger, panther, and two varieties of leopard ; three varieties of bears ; nine species of antlered deer, and fourteen species of antelope, ibex, wild goats, and wild sheep ; to say nothing of almost innumerable varieties of other wild animals of less account, whose name is legion.

India is now so easy of access that in twenty-one days the traveller lands in Bombay, where he may at once complete his outfit, get camp equipage, stores, &c., and, by the help of a well filled purse and the railways, see almost the whole country

INDIAN TROPHY.—No. 1.

south of the Himalayas, and enjoy magnificent shooting during the cool weather between October and March; when he would finish his tour by a month's cruise amongst the ibex, *Ovis ammon*, and other mountain game in Kashmere and Thibet, returning to England for the best part of the season in May.

The annexed engravings accurately represent most of the trophies which he would be likely to obtain in the way of large game during his trip. The first on the list, by right of his royal rank, is the lion of Guzerat, called in Hindi "aslan," which is certainly an inferior species to the African lion, or at any rate a much smaller variety. It differs also from the African lion in having a comparatively scanty mane, short tail, with a more conspicuous tuft. Underneath are the horns of the axis, spotted deer, or cheetul, a skull and antlers of the bárá-singhá, or twelve-tined deer, and the antlers of the sambur, or rusa deer. These three are common throughout Central India, in the jungles surrounding the hill ranges. The axis (*Axis maculatus*) very much resembles the fallow deer, both in size and general appearance; but the horns have only one basal tine, and the beam branches in a terminal fork. The bárá-singhá (*Rucervus Duvaucellii*), which is about the size of a Scotch red stag, is one of the handsomest of the deer tribe. His antlers differ from any other species, having but one basal tine over the forehead, no medium tines at all, and all the other branches diverge from the terminal fork of the beam. The extreme spread of a fine pair of antlers is about 36 inches, whilst the measurement along the curve of each horn will be about 33 inches. The sambur (*Rusa Aristotelis*), the largest of the Indian deer, is unsurpassed in appearance by any of the race. His antlers very much resemble in form those of the spotted deer, except that they are much more massive and heavy. The horns of a fine full-grown sambur vary from 30 to 40 inches in length, are 10 inches round the base, and often exceed 30 lbs. in weight.

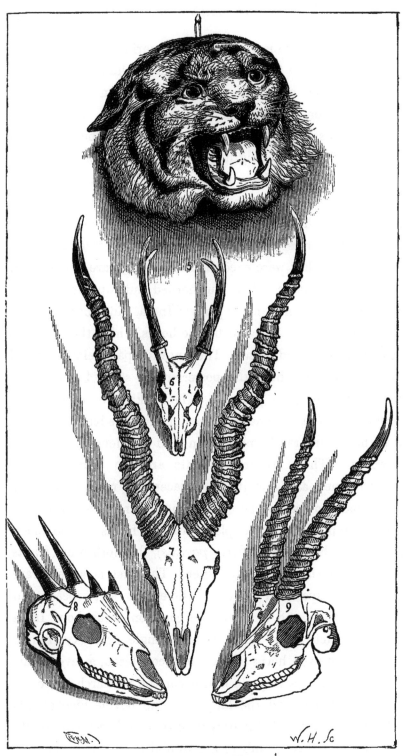

INDIAN TROPHY.—No. 2.

In the second plate is a rather nicely marked head of an adult tiger, and below are the skulls and horns of the kakur, or barking deer, a black buck, the male of the Indian antelope, the four-horned deer, and the chikara, or ravine deer. The barking deer (*Cervulus aureus*) is about the size of a roebuck, and has horns about 9 inches in length. The Indian Antelope (*Antelope cervi-capra*) is one of the most graceful and elegant of the great antelope family. The horns are spiral, ringed from the base to within a few inches of the point, and diverging considerably at the tips. The largest pair of horns I have seen were 29 inches in length ; but they were exceptional, and it is rare to find them more than 26 inches. The four-horned antelope are retiring little things, common in many parts of India, and generally found in pairs or families. The doe has no horns, whilst the buck has four distinct sheathed horns. The anterior pair seldom exceed 2 inches in length, whilst the posterior are some 4 or 5 inches long and set on high pedicles. The chikara, or ravine deer (*Gazella Benettii*), is somewhat smaller than the black antelope, and its horns are rarely more than half the length, and bend backwards. Their favourite haunts are the thinly wooded shallow ravines, and low jungle adjacent to rivers, and they are very hard to stalk on account of their extreme watchfulness.

At the top of the third plate are the heads of the black panther, or kala taindwar (*Felis pardus*), the sloth bear (*Ursus labiatus*), and the ordinary panther. The first is a very rare and beautiful specimen of the Felidæ, but sloth bears and ordinary panthers and leopards are common throughout India in most districts where there is any jungle or rocky ground. Underneath are the horns of an adult cow bison, a seven-year-old bull bison, and a very old bull bison, the patriarch of a herd. The bison (*Bos gaurus*), the largest of the bovine race, affords excellent sport, but unfortunately their range is becoming greatly contracted, and their numbers are diminishing. The horns of

INDIAN TROPHY.—No. 3.

the old bull represented in the engraving measure 28 inches in
length round the outside curve, and the extreme girth at the
base is just under 20 inches. It was shot by my friend Burton
in the Wynaad forest, and considered a magnificent specimen.

In plate 4 is the skull of an Indian bull elephant, the head
of a wild boar, and the skulls of the ibex of the Himalayas
(*Capra ibex*) and the Neilgherries (*Capra neilgherri*); the
former, being 42 inches round the curve, are nearly four times
the size of the latter, which rarely exceed 10 inches in length.
The heads and horns from which these sketches were made
were most of them picked specimens, remarkable for their size.
and symmetry, having formed part of a collection that took
several years to get together ; and they will give a very fair
idea of the kind of game a sportsman may expect to meet with
in a hunting cruise through India.

The next point to be considered is the preservation of the
skins of such of the denizens of the forest as may be brought to
bay.

The Treatment of Skins.—Animals should be skinned as
soon as possible after death, whilst the carcass is still warm, as
the hide is then easily removed. In the larger Carnivora, such
as a tiger, the animal should be lifted to the nearest level spot
of open ground, and laid on his back with his four feet fastened
spread-eagle fashion to the neighbouring trees. Then with
your skinning knife cut from the corner of the lower jaw along
the middle of the belly to the vent, and again four cuts from this
centre line down the inside of each leg as far as the cushion of
the paws, taking care to leave intact the natural features of the
foot. You then commence removing the skin, beginning at the
hind legs and tail, and then going to the fore ones, and when
this and the belly and sides are finished, the ropes should be
undone, and the animal turned on his belly and the hide
removed from the back and head. Great care must be taken

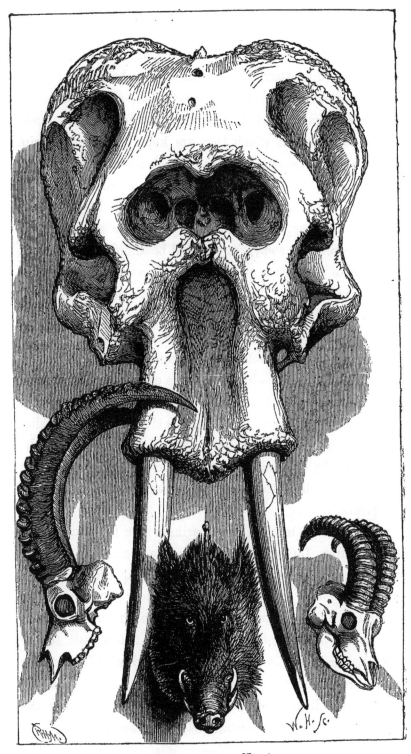

INDIAN TROPHY.—No. 4.

in separating the eyes, the lips, and the roots of the ears, if the skin is intended for stuffing. It must always be borne in mind that the value of the specimen preserved depends as much on the completeness with which all its natural features are saved as on the condition in which they are kept. Thus, if the rim of the eye-lids be severed by the scalpel, the injury is almost irremediable, as it completely changes the natural expression and cast of countenance. The lips must be also very carefully dissected from close round the gums, and after all the superfluous fat is scraped away, they should be thoroughly anointed with spirits of turpentine or arsenical soap and finely powdered. alum. If possible, the skull, after being stripped of the flesh, should be kept for some days soaked in water, when the bones will become clean and white. If the skull is boiled, the component parts are very liable to come apart, and the teeth will crack and fall to pieces, which mars the effect when the animal is mounted. By exposing the skulls of elephants, the Carnivora, deer, or even the entire skeletons of the smaller mammals, near a nest of termites, or white ants, I have had the whole beautifully cleaned both inside and out in an incredibly short time, and when cleaned in this manner, the skulls do not fall to pieces.

Perhaps the best method of preparing a skin for transmission to England from India is simply to remove it carefully from the carcass, and, after having scraped away all superfluous fat and cleaned it, to cover the flesh side with finely powdered alum, and immerse it in a barrel of strong brine, the ingredients of which should be six pounds of alum and two of salt to the gallon of water. This is perhaps the best and most inexpensive mode of preserving a skin which is intended to be sent any distance, as the brine does not affect the colour or cause the hair to fall off, which all preparations of lime are apt to do.

The ordinary mode of dressing a skin is as follows. The

hide is laid on the ground with the fur side downward, and kept stretched out by driving a number of wooden pegs or long nails round the edge. All the fat adhering to the skin is then removed, and wood ashes are well rubbed in, after which it is left exposed to the air to dry. In India, sometimes, a preparation of turmeric and cocoa-nut oil, or milk if procurable, is then worked in with the palm of the hand, and its effect is to make the hide pliant.

The Bedouin Arabs and the Abyssinians are the best hands at skinning I have yet seen, as they will draw off the entire skin of a large antelope, ibex, or goat, by only making one incision at the neck, so that the hide formed an excellent water mushuck, or flour bag.

If any of the Carnivora are killed during a sporting excursion, when, from constantly moving about, the skin cannot be kept stretched for two whole days consecutively, the usual application, after removing all the fat and flesh as carefully as possible, is a little huldee (turmeric) and water; it is then thrown on a camel or any other mode of conveyance at hand, and perhaps never looked at again till the return of the party to cantonments.

It is then that the tanning process commences. First, have the hide steeped in clear water for some hours; put a layer of wood ashes on a level piece of ground, and when the hide is beginning to dry, peg it down, hair undermost, with numerous pegs (to prevent that unseemly Vandyke kind of edge, the result of an insufficiency of pegs), in just proportions; not too long for the sake of an extra foot of measurement, and thereby too narrow; or too broad, making it shorter than it was originally; about 18 inches longer than the measurement before skinning will be about the mark, as all skins stretch to some extent.

Next lay a coat of wood ashes (which are always attainable

in the vicinity of the cook-room) and powdered alum in equal
proportions, made into a paste, on the hide, about the thickness
of a rupee. When this is well dried in the sun and begins to
crack, get the shank bone of a buffalo, being the larger animal,
and presenting a greater surface than that of a cow or bullock,
saw off half the knuckle joint, and with this make your men
rub off all the ashes and mixture, by dint of hard labour, and,
when removed, let all the small fibres and ragged pieces of the
skin be picked off; then lay on a second layer of ashes and
powdered alum, which, after drying, is to be removed in the
same manner. Should the skin be that of a very old tiger,
perhaps a repetition may be necessary, but in most cases twice
is sufficient; the skin now becomes pliant as a glove, and no
vicissitude of weather will affect it. Be very careful to protect
it from night dews, covering it with mats or dry grass, and
removing them at sunrise.

When the heads of bison or stags are to be preserved, the
neck should be cut off close to the body, as they can then be
much better mounted than if severed close to the jaws.

On the Measurement of Animals.—As the comparative size
of different specimens of the same variety of animals is an
object of curiosity to the sportsman, and of value to the man of
science, it would be as well if a regular orthodox system of
taking the various dimensions were adopted, as, whilst one
measures the length and girth of the animal as it lies where it
fell, another contents himself with taking the measurement of
the skin when flayed, stretched, and pegged out, not being
aware that between these two modes of measurement there
exists a difference of at least two or three feet in an animal the
size of a tiger. Again, one will ascertain the length from the
nose to the end of the tail over the head; another carries
the string along the cheek, so as to have a perfectly straight
line, thereby causing a difference of several inches.

Perhaps the following system is about the best for taking the measurement of any of the Mammalia :—

1. Length from the muzzle to the end of the tail, taken from the tip of the nose, over the crown of the head, the tape being carried along the centre of the neck and spine to the extremity of the tail.
2. From the muzzle to the insertion of tail (as before).
3. Length of tail.
4. Height of shoulder taken from the heel to the top of dorsal ridge.
5. Height at the croup.
6. Girth of body behind shoulder.
7. Girth of neck.
8. Girth of fore leg above the knee.
9. Circumference of head.
10. Breadth of forehead.
11. Length from toe to heel and across widest part of sole.
12. Length, girth, spread, and weight of horns.

If this system of measurement were adopted before the animal was skinned, we should hear no more of 14-foot tigers. The average length of a full-grown male, from the tip of nose to end of tail, is about 9 feet 6 inches, and of a tigress 8 feet 6 inches; and although tigers measuring 11 feet have been killed, like giants among men they are few and far between. The skin of a 10-foot tiger will easily stretch to 13 or 14 feet if required, and all skins of the Felidæ stretch considerably in the process of dressing. An ordinary tiger will weigh about 500 lbs., but large cattle-lifters have turned the scale at 800 lbs.

CHAPTER X.

THE Himalaya, the great natural barrier between India and Central Asia, is a mountainous district, about 1400 miles in length and varying from 70 to 120 miles in breadth, consisting of a succession of snowy ranges rising one behind another, unassailable to man except in those places where the beds of rivers intersect it and afford him access to its wild fastnesses.

Every variety of temperature, from tropical heat to the cold of the arctic regions, is to be found in the Himalaya; and, as the nature of the forest changes with the climate, the variety of game the sportsman meets with in this district is something extraordinary.

A dense belt of forest, from ten to twenty miles in width, usually called "The Terai," skirts the base of the mountains, and thickly-wooded spurs, jutting far out into the plain, form hot, damp, swampy valleys covered with long grasses, that at certain times of the year are almost impassable for Europeans on account of the pernicious exhalations and fatal malaria there engendered, which bring on the most deadly of jungle fevers. These virgin primeval forests, which in many parts have never been explored, consist chiefly of sâl, send, sessum (valuable timber), kuldo, cheer (Scotch pine), bamboo, the leguminosæ and elephant-creepers, tree-ferns, wild banana, vines, ferns, high grasses, parasitical orchids, and convolvuli of several varieties; and are the home of herds of elephants, rhinoceros, tigers, panthers, leopards, cheetahs, black bears, hyenas, lynxes, boars, jackals, foxes, wild dogs, tiger cats, sambur, spotted deer, muncjak kakur or four-horned deer, hog-deer, pea-fowl, jungle-fowl, kaleege or silver-pheasant, spur-fowl, black and grey partridge, chickore, bustard, florikin or lesser bustard, quail, and hares.

This tropical belt ceases at from four to five thousand feet, and the forest begins to wear quite a changed aspect, the trees being of a different character, for from this elevation to about eight or nine thousand feet we have beautiful woods of oak of three kinds (the banj, the khurso, and the mohra, all ever-green), walnut, chestnut, sycamore, horse-chestnut, maple, rye and morinda pines, alder, holly, cedar, cypress, ash, poplar, yew, apple, quince, peach, apricot, cherry, filbert, bramble, red and black currant, raspberry, strawberry, with groves of box, laurel, myrtle, white and purple magnolia, camellia, rhododendrons with blossoms of every shade from white and bright yellow to dark purple, fuchsias, geraniums, woodbine, honeysuckles, pep-pers, dog-rose, ivy, violets, primroses, anemone, cowslips, and mosses and lichens as in England. Here, in addition to many of the animals of the tropical belt, we find several species never to be met with in the plains—viz., the brown and yellow bear, the yellow solitary wolf, the gooral or Himalayan chamois, the jerow or hill stag, the thaar or wild sheep, the surrow or goat antelope, the eagle, the moonal or blue pheasant, the koklas or mottled pheasant, the peura or hill partridge, the Himalayan grouse, the woodcock, thrush, blackbird, cuckoo, goldfinch, chaffinch, mountain sparrow, flying squirrel, otter, marten, pine cat, lungoor or black-faced grey bearded monkey, black hill-monkey, boa, and gigantic damium, or rock-snake.

At an elevation of about nine thousand feet we get to a third zone, and, with the exception of a few cedars, khursoo oak, and stunted pine, no trees are to be seen but the white birch, dwarf rhododendrons, a kind of willow, and three varieties of juniper. Here we find a third class of animals— viz., the kustooree or musk-deer, the markhor or serpent-eater (a kind of wild goat), the ibex, the black-eared fox, the cheer or brown pheasant, and the argus or horned pheasant.

At from twelve to thirteen thousand feet the limit of the forest generally ceases (although in some more sheltered places I have found it at over sixteen thousand feet, or about the height of the summit of Mont Blanc), and is succeeded by a fourth zone of grassy pastures, which rise to the snow line. Here in the summer the turf is enamelled with myriads of lovely flowers and aromatic herbs, which are nourished by the melting of the snows, and this is the habitat of the burrul or snow-sheep, the nyan (*Ovis ammon*) or gigantic snow-sheep, the sna and sha, varieties of wild sheep (*Ovis montana*), the bonchour or wild yak, and the kyang or wild horse.

Above the snow line, the elevation of which varies consider- ably, is found a fifth class of animals—viz., the snow-bear, the snow-leopard, the white wolf, the white fox, the white hare, the lammergier, the kungul or snow-pheasant, and the snow partridge.

The above description will show the general nature of the forest at the different altitudes, and the usual habitat of each animal; but the elevation of the line of demarcation varies in different parts, as some places are more or less exposed than others, and some animals change their place of abode to a higher or lower temperature, according to the season of the year, or as they may find food and pasturage. I shall now give some description of the various wild animals peculiar to the higher altitudes—viz., the ovis ammon, the burrul, the ouriar,

THE LAMMERGIER.

the markhor, the ibex, the thaar, the gooral, the surrow, the musk-deer, and goa.

THE OVIS AMMON, or nyan, is the largest wild sheep known, as it measures from twelve to thirteen hands at the shoulder, and weighs over 400lbs. when in good condition. The ovis ammon has enormous horns, much resembling those of a domestic ram, but they make only one curve. They sometimes exceed 50 inches in length and 20 inches in circumference, but are rarely found perfect. The horns shown in the engraving are very perfect, measuring 16 inches in circumference at the base and 46 inches round the curve. The fleece is about 2 inches in length, and of a fulvous grey colour; and round the neck is a ruff of long, coarse hair, which is dark brown in the rams and light ash in the ewes, which are very small and insignificant-looking creatures, compared to the rams. The flesh is of good flavour, and tender. Ovis ammon are common in the valley of the Sutlej, above the Niti Pass, and in the Chusul district; but they are wary and difficult to stalk on account of the open nature of the ground on which they are usually found.

THE BURRUL, or snow-sheep (*Ovis Nahura*), is a gregarious animal, found only upon the loftier ranges. The male stands 38 inches high at the shoulder, and is about 4½ feet in length, often weighing over 200 lbs. The female is scarcely half the size. Their general colour is a light ash with white under the belly; but an old male has also black breast and points, as well as a narrow stripe between the ash on the upper part of the body and the white of the belly. The horns of the male are about 22 inches long by 11 inches in circumference, and they have a single curve, like a ram's, but the reverse way. The female has small flat horns, half the size. Burrul are generally found on the grassy slopes between the limits of the forest and the snow-line; and there, in unfrequented regions, they may be seen, several score together, browsing like tame sheep. They

THE BURRUL.   THE OVIS AMMON.   THE THAAR.

are not difficult stalking, except in places where often disturbed, then they become shy and wary. When alarmed they
utter a shrill kind of snort, retiring rather leisurely, and stopping at times as if to satisfy their curiosity as to the cause of
alarm. They breed in June and July, the males and females
associating all the year round, although flocks of young males
are occasionally met with in the summer. On the Ladac side
of the Himalaya there is a variety of this species called the
Napor.

THE OURIAR is another kind of wild sheep, found on the
Attock range and in many parts of Thibet. It is a fine-looking
animal, of a light-brown colour, with a long shaggy beard, which
in winter covers the chest. The rams have curved horns, generally averaging 24 inches in length, and 12 inches round the
base. The females have very small horns. They are wary,
and extremely active, so they afford good sport stalking.

THE THAAR, a most noble-looking animal, is gregarious,
being often found in large flocks. A ram, before the rutting
season, frequently weighs over 300lbs., measuring 5½ feet, including the head, and 46 inches at the shoulder. The female
is a most inferior-looking animal in comparison with the male,
not being one half the size. The ram is generally of a
brownish-dun colour, almost deepening to black on the head
and points, the neck and shoulders being furnished with long,
shaggy hair. The female and young are of a reddish-brown
colour, rather lighter under the belly. The thaar has horns
about 12 inches long and 10 inches in circumference, curving
backwards, with flat sides. Those of the female are smaller.

THE MARKHOR, or serpent-eater, is unquestionably the most
game-looking animal of the Himalaya, being the last of the
goat tribe, and having magnificent, gracefully-curved horns,
often exceeding 60 inches in length, resembling those of a
koodoo, but twisted in the opposite direction. The markhor is

THE WILD DOG.
THE MARKHOR.
THE MUSK DEER.   THE IBEX.   THE RAVINE DEER.

considerably larger than the ibex, and the hair, which is of a light greyish slate colour, is extremely long and coarse, hanging like a mane on each side of the neck in the winter months. The beard is long and flowing, and often nearly black, so that the head and horns make a conspicuously handsome trophy, as shown in the engraving, The female is of a reddish dun colour, has insignificant horns, and is very much smaller than the male.   There are said to be four varieties of the markhor on the Himalayan range; but as the distinction only consists in a slight difference in the shape of the horns and in their measurements, I think they are all of the same genus, for I have often noticed that in the higher altitudes animals of the same class frequently vary both in the shape and massiveness of their horns, and in size according to their condition, which mainly depends upon the nutriment they can find and the quality of the pasturage in the locality where they are found. Their colour also varies considerably, according to their age and the season of the year.   Markhor are only found on the loftiest and most precipitous ranges, which are almost inaccessible to any wingless animals except themselves. They frequent the steep, grassy slopes and rocky ground above the highest belts of forest; and if the ground has lately been disturbed they are difficult to find, as they seek the cover of the woods during the daytime and only come out to feed in the open early in the morning or late in the afternoon. They are also very wary and suspicious, and, although the ground on which they are found is rocky and broken, it requires very careful stalking to get within range of them. Old male markhor are now not only very scarce, but, from being frequently hunted are generally desperately cunning, so that a head with a fine pair of horns is not often to be got without a good deal of exertion.

THE IBEX of the Himalaya (*Capra Sibirica*) takes the foremost place amongst the varied game of that district, being one of the finest of the goat species.' The male measures 42 inches in height at the shoulder, and is about 5 feet in length, including the head. The female is very small in comparison. The horns of the buck vary from 3 feet to 50 inches in length, and from 8 inches to 13 inches in circumference; those of the female are round, and rarely exceed a foot in length. The general colour of the buck ibex is a yellowish grey, with a darker stripe along the centre of the back, ash-coloured muzzle, and black beard about 8 inches long. The females and young are uniformly of a reddish-grey colour. The head of the ibex is rounder and the nose shorter than any other of the goat tribe, and the ears are placed farther back. Ibex seem little affected by cold, for in the day-time they remain in the most secluded and rugged spots above the limits of vegetation, and in the evening move downwards towards their feeding-grounds, which often lie at a great distance. In summer the males separate from the females, and in a body resort to the higher regions, where they may sometimes be met with in troops of fifty.

The ibex is found in Koonawur, Lahoul, Spiti, Cashmere, and on most of the higher ranges of Thibet.

Although excessively wary animals, ibex are not difficult to stalk if the hunter takes care to keep well above the herd. He must also be sure and keep to leeward, or they will detect the taint in the air, and become suspicious, and then, however favourable the ground may be, it it very difficult to get within range. When after ibex, the best plan to adopt is to sleep as near their haunts as possible, and to get above their feeding-ground by day-break, as the denizens of the mountains are not suspicious of danger from above, although they keep a bright look-out on the hill-side below them. As with all other mountain game, the hunter should not show himself after firing, as if he lies hid he will most probably get another fair chance. Srinugger is not at all a bad head-quarters for ibex-hunting, as there are several ranges within four or five days' march where plenty of sport may be had.

THE GOORAL, or Himalayan chamois, is a gregarious animal, about the size of an ordinary goat, with rough coat about 2 inches long, of brownish-grey colour, rather lighter under the belly and inside the legs, and white under the throat. Both male and female, which are much alike, have black ringed horns about 8 inches long and 3½ inches in circumference, tapering to a point, and curved backwards. They breed in the end of May, the female rarely having more than one at a birth. Gooral are generally found feeding at dawn and near sunset, lying under bushes and rocks during the day. They frequent the steepest grass-covered hills and rugged ground, and never forsake a district, however much they may be disturbed. When alarmed they give a peculiar hissing grunt.

THE SURROW, also a kind of chamois, stands about 3½ feet at the shoulder, and is about 5½ feet long from the point of the nose to the end of the tail. The general colour of the fur is of a reddish grey, deepening to black on the back, head, and hind quarters, with yellow and dirty white under the belly and inside the legs, and a light ash muzzle, with a white streak running along the sides of the lower jaw. Having large coarse ears, the expression of the head resembles that of an ass more than a deer, and the legs are thick and clumsily proportioned, occasioning an awkward gait. The male has a black forelock and mane, which he erects when alarmed, and a large and fiery black eye. Both male and female have highly-polished, black, tapering, sharp-pointed horns, about 12 inches long and 4 inches in circumference at the base, annulated for the first 5 inches and curved backwards almost on to the neck. The surrow is rather a rare animal, and is generally found in the most inaccessible parts of the forest in the vicinity of water. He is a dangerous customer for dogs to bring to bay, often killing and maiming several with his horns before being pulled down.

THE MUSK-DEER, or *kustooree,* a solitary animal, is about the size of a roebuck, measuring 40 inches in length and 22 inches in height. The male is furnished with a sharp-pointed canine tooth or tusk, curving backwards on each side of the upper jaw, which, in a full-grown animal, is about 3 inches in length. The general colour is speckled grey, approaching to black on the shoulders, back, and outside of the legs; reddish fawn along the lower part of the sides and inside the thighs, and dirty white under the throat and belly and inside the legs. The fur is very thick, coarse, and brittle, the hairs being nearly white at the roots and becoming gradually darker towards the end, not unlike the small under-quills of the porcupine. The head is delicately formed, the ears broad and erect, and the tail very small, not being over an inch in length. In males this appendage is quite naked, except a small tuft at the end, caused by continual shaking about; but in females and young it remains covered with grey hair at the top and white underneath. The legs are very slender, the hoofs long and pointed; and they always go in bounds, all four feet leaving the ground, except when grazing. The female and young are rather lighter in colour than the males, and have no tusks; otherwise they are much alike. The musk-pod, which is only found in males, is situated between the skin and the flesh, close to the navel, and much resembles the gizzard of a fowl, having a small orifice through the skin, but no apparent internal connection with the stomach. The musk is found in dark-brown rounded grains, and the pod of a full-grown animal may yield about an ounce on an average. Scarcely any is found in animals under two years old, and more in proportion as they become aged, although this is not always the case, as at times the musk is discharged

THE GOA, OR RAVINE DEER.

through the orifice in the skin. Musk-deer much resemble hares in their habits, making forms in the same manner, and generally choosing to feed early in the morning or towards the evening. Their food chiefly consists of young leaves, grass, tender shoots, herbs, berries, grain, and moss seeds. The female generally gives birth to twins, which are deposited at some distance from each other, the dam only visiting them at times during the day. Thus are those habits of solitude and retirement engendered which continue through life, for they are rarely seen two together, and the fawns never associate with the dam. Musk-deer are found in all kinds of forest, but seldom at lower altitudes than 8000 feet. The flesh is fine-grained and well flavoured.

THE GOA, or hill antelope of Thibet, very much resembles the chikárá, or ravine deer of the plains, if, indeed, it is not the same animal. The only distinction that I know of, and I have killed scores of both, is that the reddish brown fur of the goa is somewhat longer and closer than that of the chikárá. They are alike in size, colour, and habits, and the bucks of both varieties have tapering curved horns, varying from 10 inches to 15 inches in length, and ringed to within 3 inches of the points, which are very sharp. The doe is much smaller than the buck, and has much slighter and shorter horns, that scarcely show any indication of rings, and are often nearly straight.

CHAPTER XI.

SPORT IN THE DOON.

THE Dehra Doon is, perhaps, the *ne plus ultra* of tropical hunting grounds, as the Damun-i-koh or Terai that skirts the lowest spurs of the Himalayan range, abounds in almost every variety of large game usually found in Indian forests. The valley of the Doon is about 40 miles in length, 16 in breadth, and is bounded on the north by the Moosoaric hills, on the east by the Ganges, on the west by the Jumna, and on the south by the Sewalek hills, a densely wooded range about 3000 feet in height, and from 8 to 10 miles across. My party, a triumvirate, consisted of an old school chum, Fred Graham, and Doctor Singleton, both of whom were ardent sportsmen and excellent companions.

Three is, in many respects, the best number for a shooting party, as it not only allows all the members to participate in any conversation that may take place, but, in case of argument or indecision of action, gives a majority; besides, three cots can be stowed very comfortably in a hill-tent, but not four: three can, in most cases, hunt well together; and lastly, three well-armed Europeans, with their attendants, form a little army in themselves, and, in case of need, can hold their own against any marauding attempts by predatory hill tribes.

Our programme was arranged as follows: first a fortnight or three weeks hunting in the Doon, to be followed by an excursion to Gangootree, the source of the Ganges, and to Jumnautri, the source of the Jumna, after which we were to cross the Nilung, pass into the valley of the Sutlej, and finish off with an expedition to Kashmere.

Dehra, being so central, is the best head-quarters for Doon shooting, and during our sojourn there we made several expeditions to different parts of the valley, enjoying first-rate sport, and rarely meeting with blank days. Elephant, however, were not so numerous as might have been expected from the likely appearance of the forest, having been driven into the more remote parts by the periodical burning of the Doon grass, which takes place in January and February. Notwithstanding we explored all the most favourable haunts, we only twice came across them; once near Jobrawallah, on the banks of the Sooswa river, and again in the Sankote Forest, when on both occasions we killed. We also had some excellent tiger-shooting in different parts of the Doon and amongst the Sewalic Hills, but as these hunts afforded no incidents out of the common, I shall not enter into any description of them, but describe a trip we made to the Ghuriali Hills, where we had excellent sport.

Some time before dawn, we were apprised that it was time to be stirring, from the noise made by the Lascars loosening the pegs preparatory to striking the tent; and donning our hunting gear, we partook of an early breakfast, reclining on carpets placed near the embers of a huge log-fire, whilst our people packed up our goods and chattels, it having been determined to move our camp to a valley in the Ghuriali Hills, which was considered by Fred's shekarries to be a certain find for large game; moreover, a herd of elephants had been seen in the vicinity a couple of days before. As soon as it was sufficiently light to discern the track, our tattoos (ponies) and coolies being laden, we commenced our march, ourselves and shekarries forming the advanced guard, whilst the baggage followed up in the rear.

Elk had already commenced bellowing, and their loud cries of defiance resounding from every side of the forest might by unaccustomed ears have been mistaken for the roaring of much more dangerous animals, so hoarse and hollow did they sound. At daybreak, pea-fowl, jungle-fowl, and partridge began calling in all directions; and as we did not expect to meet with any large game *en route,* some of our people having been over the ground the day before, it was determined to make a general bag, and, advancing in skirmishing order, we had excellent sport, killing several silver pheasants— besides black and gray partridge, chickore and hares.

After a tramp of about four hours, during which time our people were laden with small game, we arrived at the Ghuriali Hills, and, skirting their base, made our way for a couple of miles up a densely-wooded ravine, at the bottom of which flowed a turbulent mountain torrent; and as Fred informed us that this was to be our temporary head-quarters, we halted the coolies, and prepared the ground for our camp.

In a short time the tents were pitched, the dinner under weigh, and everything comfortably arranged for passing the night, so we adjourned to a pool at the foot of a small murmuring cascade, and refreshed ourselves with a most delightful bath before sitting down to table; after which we assembled our people round the log-fire, and held a solemn consultation as to the morrow's proceedings. It was determined that Fred and two of his people should go along the Tiri road and meet a Ghoorka chief, who had been invited to join our party; whilst the doctor and I, dividing our people into two parties, reconnoitred each side of the valley in search of game. A brew of Glenlivet was made, tobacco served out, and, after two or three hours' agreeable conversation, in which our people freely joined, the night watch was set, and we retired to rest.

The next morning, refreshed and invigorated by wholesome sleep, we breakfasted at early dawn, and shortly afterwards each set out on his way. Googooloo and most of the other shekarries went with the doctor along the course of the river, to look for elephant spoor; whilst Chineah and two of the Phaidee coolies, with the dogs, accompanied me in a clamber up the hills, where I hoped to get some venison for camp consumption.

We were obliged to follow the right bank of the stream for some distance, as the forest was too dense for us to penetrate; but at last, by creeping up the dry bed of a tributary torrent, and groping our way, often almost in darkness, under overhanging boughs covered with heavy foliage, we got into a deep cleft or narrow gorge in the side of the mountain. Here were some noble teak-trees, and a few clumps of bamboos of enormous proportions, besides patches of fern and luxuriant grasses. From a crack in the solid rock, about fifteen feet from the base, issued two small streams, evidently having the same source, which fell into a beautiful natural basin, bordered with short green turf. The dogs immediately made their way down to this spot to drink, and were engaged in chasing and diving after a couple of saucy-looking little dab chicks or lesser grebe, when suddenly I heard Ponto give tongue, followed by an unmistakable whine, which told me that we were not alone in the glen, separated even as it appeared to be from the rest of the world. From his attitude, as he stood snuffing the air with his fore paw raised, his head lifted, his lips apart, showing his teeth, and now and then giving a low growl, I knew by experience that some of the feline race were in close proximity, and made my preparations accordingly; bidding Chineah fasten up the Poligars in their slips, and give them in charge of one of

the Phaidee coolies, whilst he kept near me with the second
gun, for I only happened to have two out with me that day.
A small hill-dog, belonging to one of my people, kept running
backwards and forwards about twenty paces in front, in spite of
our endeavours to keep him back, to Ponto's great annoyance,
as he and I were making casts about the place in search of the
trail. A very few turns served to satisfy us both on this
point, for we almost immediately came upon the pugs of what
appeared to be a family of either panthers or leopards, which
we were steadily following up, when suddenly a female panther,
with a short low growl, pounced upon the poor Puarhee dog,
breaking his back with a blow from her muscular paw, and
carrying him off as a cat would a mouse. At this moment my
view of the transaction was partially obstructed by an inter-
vening bush; but getting a momentary glimpse, as she bounded
along, I gave her the contents of both barrels, which tumbled
her over, and made her relinquish her prey, but did not prove
mortal, for in the twinkling of an eye she recovered her feet,
and sprung towards us, uttering a savage roar, when the
Poligars, who, on seeing the game, had forcibly broken away
from the man who held them, dashed forward, and, scared by
their sudden appearance, she swerved, raised her head, and
looked round for a line of retreat; which action gave Ponto a
chance, and the gallant dog rushed in and pinned her by the
back sinew of the hind leg, whilst at the same time Hassan and
Ali fastened on each side of her, one by the ear, and the other
on the throat. I had received my second gun from Chineah
the moment my first was discharged, but I was afraid to fire
lest I should injure my dogs, and was waiting for a fairer
chance, when suddenly, with a scream of rage, the male panther
appeared, and made a leap which would have very summarily
disposed of poor Ponto, if I had not luckily stopped him in
mid-career by almost simultaneously giving him the contents

of. both barrels, killing him at once. The game was now becoming hot, for a violent struggle was still going on between my dogs and the wounded female, whose strength was so great, notwithstanding one of her fore arms was shattered and useless, that she twice managed to shake off the Poligars, although Ponto still kept his hold; and fearing lest my favourite might get a mauling before I should have time to reload, I drew my hunting-knife, and, watching my opportunity, plunged it up to the hilt behind her shoulder-blade, when she reared up, gave a hollow groan, and dropped dead on her side. The Poligars, when they saw their antagonist was dead, lay quietly down, and began to lick the scratches and bruises they had received in the conflict; but old matter-of-fact Ponto, in a most cautious manner, went up to each of the carcasses, examined them all round, as if to satisfy himself that there was no life remaining; after which he came trotting up to me as I was reloading, looked up in my face in a peculiarly knowing manner, wagged his apology for a tail, and lay down at my feet grunting with intense satisfaction.

Having rubbed the blood and dirt off the dogs, and examined their limbs carefully, so as to make sure that they had received no serious injury, we again took up the panther's trail, which led us to a shelving rock, where, in a small cave, we found two young panther cubs, one of which the dogs killed, and the other, a young male, we caught alive. He was not larger than a Clumber spaniel, but already very ferocious, scratching and biting at every one who approached; and as he would not walk, I had him slung to a bamboo so as to be more easily carried, having first taken the precaution of fastening up his mouth. I then sent Chineah to despoil the dead panthers, bidding the rest of the people go to the water and there wait, whilst I, accompanied by Ponto, continued my survey of the glen. I had not gone far when I came upon the slots of a

sounder of hog, and whilst I was following them up, I perceived
the fresh pugs of a panther, to which I did not give much
attention, supposing it to have been made by one of those I
had killed.　Ponto, however, was not so mistaken, but gave a
peculiar whine, as if apprehensive of danger, which I not understanding, and fearing lest the noise might alarm the game,
ordered him to fall back and lie down.　Hardly had he done
so, than I heard the grunting and shrill squeaking of a young
hog, and, guided by the sounds, I crept quietly forward on my
hands and knees through some high grass, until I got near
enough to see a fine sow, surrounded by a numerous litter,
turning up the soil and feeding upon the young roots of the
grass.　I watched her proceedings for a moment, and was considering whether to fire or not, being rather unwilling to kill
the mother of such a numerous small family, when I heard a
slight rustling noise within a few paces to my left, which at
first I imagined to have been caused by the dog, but on turning
round, to my surprise I saw a fine full-grown panther gathering
himself up as if to make a spring.　His attention was evidently
entirely centred in the prospect of a pork dinner, for he licked
his slavering lips repeatedly, and his green eyes were fixed
intently upon the sow, who, strangely enough, had not yet
caught the taint in the air.　I quickly raised my rifle, and
aiming behind the massive shoulder, which was fully exposed
as he couched, pulled trigger, and the panther sprang into the
air stone dead.　The sow, alarmed, dashed forward most
courageously to protect her young, and in self-defence I was
obliged to give her my remaining barrel as she charged close
by me.　The bullet passing through the body, " grassed " her
at once, and with the aid of Ponto, who came up immediately
on hearing the report, I managed to dispatch her with my
knife.　We now turned our attention to the squeakers, and
Ponto and I soon managed to catch five of them alive, which I

secured by fastening their legs together. This done, I made my way to the spring, where I waited until Chineah came up with the skins of the animals first killed, when I sent him and the coolies, under Ponto's guidance, to bring in the rest of the game. In the meantime I refreshed myself with a bath in the pool until their return, when we set out on our route towards camp, where I found Fred and his Ghoorka friend awaiting our arrival.

CHAPTER XII.

HAVING spent the best part of a month shooting in different parts of the Doon, where we had first-rate sport, a couple of days were devoted to preparations for our expedition among the mountains; stores, groceries, and supplies of all kinds were provided and packed securely, iron-shod alpenstocks were made, and a light portable bridge and ladder of my own invention constructed; which latter arrangement I shall describe, as it proved on many occasions very useful to our trip, for with it we could in a moment either bridge a nullah eighteen feet wide, or climb a scarp of twenty. It somewhat resembled the arm of a fire-escape, having a canvas back and strong male bamboo sides, bound with iron, strong hooks being fastened at one end and spikes at the other. The rings, however, were all of rope, except those at the top and bottom, which were of stout iron, and movable, so that the whole could be taken to pieces for carriage, or put together in a moment. We also, each of us, ordered three waterproof "kiltas" to be made, to save our supplies from damage. These are long, pottle-shaped baskets, lined with painted canvas within and leather without, having one side made flat to fit the back, against which it is fastened by straps, this being the ordinary mode the Puharrees or hill coolies carry supplies.

As the roads, or rather tracks, were impassable, even for mountain ponies, all our baggage had to be carried by coolies, which considerably swelled the number of our camp followers. The

Puharrees, a caste of Hindoos, are divided into two classes, the Gungarees or low-country men (from gunga, "a valley"), and the Purbutees, or hill men (from purbut, "a peak"). The latter are stout, robust, and hardy mountaineers, generally short

PUHARREES, OR HILL COOLIES.

in stature, but capable of undergoing much exertion and fatigue on very simple fare, their ordinary food being chapaties, or girdle cakes made of coarse flour mixed into a paste with water, seasoned with a little salt, and baked upon an iron plate. The men wear loosely-fitting tunics, gathered in and fastened at the

waist with a cotton belt, and wide peg-top trousers, tight at the
ankle, both garments being made of a coarse blanket-like
material, round cap of the same, or sometimes a white turban
and network sandals of curious construction. The coolies we
engaged were all of the latter class, and had been carefully
selected as good men some days before by Surmoor, their chief,
who had been with Fred on several former occasions. They all
received a month's pay in advance, with a thick, coarse, country
blanket, and as they mustered in front of the bungalow, I
thought I had never seen a more likely-looking set of fellows
for the work. The engraving represents two Puharrees with a
kilta as described.

Our baggage consisted of a good-sized routee, or hill tent,
which, slung on the portable bridge, was easily carried by four
men, two small scouting tents, somewhat resembling the *tentes
d'abri* of the French chasseurs, but larger and more commodious, although each was a light load for one coolie ; three
painted canvas packages, containing bedding, blankets, etc. ;
and twenty-six kiltas, sixteen of which were filled with clothes,
ammunition stores, and supplies of every kind that we calculated would last us for two months ; four contained " atar," or
coarse flour, rice, curry stuff, and salt for our people ; two held
our cooking utensils, two cheelpine torches and firewood ; and
two contained a complete breakfast kit, which, with one of the
scouting tents, was sent on the day before, so that our breakfast was always ready by the time we arrived on the new ground,
or half-way, when the march was very long. Thus, although
we eschewed beer, and curtailed all extraneous baggage, we had
thirty-two coolie loads, each man carrying about fifty pounds'
weight.

All our preparations and arrangements being completed,
sending on our people we drove to Rajpoor, at the foot of the
Mussoorie hills, the first range of the Himalaya, that rise about

four thousand feet above the Doon. The eastern part, on which is Landour, the military cantonment, rises about a thousand feet higher. After a first-rate breakfast at a comfortable hotel kept by a *ci-devant* trooper, we commenced the ascent, one of the most delightful walks that I ever met with in any part of the globe. The road winds in zig-zags cut along the face of the hill, but we frequently availed ourselves of native paths, which, although much steeper, cut off corners, and shortened the route considerably. As we ascended, a great change was observable in the nature of the forests, although the vegetation was everywhere most luxuriant. At the base the prevalent trees were sal and send, varied with banyans, patches of bamboo, wild banana, or acacia. Here and there gigantic festoons of leguminosæ, or the Pothos creeper, stretched high overhead, whilst wild vines, peppers, and convolvuli of every colour, formed natural bowers of living verdure that courted repose on every side. At an elevation of three thousand feet, the alteration of the appearance of the forest became strikingly apparent. The tropical trees gradually disappeared, and were replaced by evergreen oaks of magnificent foliage, noble rhododendrons with enormous lemon-scented blossoms, pines, magnolias, camellias and tree-ferns; whilst the underwood consisted chiefly of yellow raspberries, ivy, honeysuckle, and other plants of the temperate regions. The banks on the roadside, also, now began to be clothed with wild strawberry, geranium, violets, and different kinds of mosses and lichens never seen in the plains. It is difficult to conceive more beautiful forest scenery than the Mussoorie Pass exhibits. At every turn a varied view presents itself, either of magnificent vistas in the wood, or glorious landscapes of the park-like Doon below. We fully enjoyed it, and although the ascent was a stiff seven miles' tramp, we were not the least fatigued on our arrival at Mussoorie, where we put up at Wolf's Crag, a comfortable and elegant little bungalow

belonging to a friend of Fred's, that was beautifully situated on
a rising ground facing the valley of the Doon. So much has
been written about this far-famed sanitarium, that I shall not
enter into any detailed account of it; suffice it to say that the
most glowing descriptions I had read did not come up to the
reality.

The first view of the Himalayas from the north side of the
Landour ridge is, I believe, scarcely to be equalled for grandeur.
Wave upon wave of snowy ranges, surmounted by majestic
peaks of every conceivable shape, rise from the dark dense
forest below, clearly and sharply defined against the deep blue
firmament. This panorama is sublime beyond conception, and
offers a striking contrast to the southern view, where the valley
of the Doon, the Sewalic hills, and the reeking plains of India,
with the windings of the Ganges and the Jumna, lay stretched
before the eye as in a map. Even the genius of a Turner could
not do justice to such scenery. How faintly, then, would words
portray it!

The best day's thaar shooting I ever had was at Bengallee, a
small village at the foot of the Kanoolee hill, which is a spur of
the high ridge of mountains that divides the valleys of the
Ganges and the Jumna. Our party, which consisted of Graham,
Singleton, and myself, halted here for some days, and leaving
our heavy baggage at the village, we engaged a guide who knew
the ground, and clambered up the south face of the hill, carrying
only our small tent, bedding, a change of clothing, and provisions.
The slope was clothed with beautiful forests of chestnut, walnut,
and oak, varied with green patches and rocky ground; and as
we went along the dogs put up a brace of woodcocks and several
moonals; but they were allowed to go unscathed, lest the report
of our guns might disturb more valued game. We pitched our
tents under the shelter of some noble oaks, by a beautiful
purling stream, rather more than half way up the hill, which

rises about seven thousand feet above the valley; and then Fred and I, leaving the doctor to superintend the culinary arrangements, set out with the villager and Chineah to reconnoitre the ground.

It being so early in the season, the haunts of the thaar had not been disturbed for some time, so we had every reason to expect good sport. After passing through a belt of moura oak, we came to some rocky ground, where we found numerous fresh slots and traces, but no thaar; so we crept along some very awkward-looking places to the east face, and gained a grassy slope, where we found several gooral feeding. Desiring our people to lay down and remain quiet, Fred and I made a circuit, and gained the cover of a rock within a hundred yards of the game, from whence we should have had an easy pot shot right and left, when, just as we were about to fire, a brace of cheer pheasants got up, with a whirr, from almost under our feet, and gave the alarm. With a snort somewhat between a hiss and a whistle, they all made a sudden rush, and we had only time for a couple of snap shots each as they bounded up the slope at speed: one, a young male, rolled over paralyzed, with his spine broken, and a female, which went off with the rest, was observed to lag behind, and then lie down; having reloaded, we crept towards her as noiselessly as possible, but on our approach she regained her legs, and would most likely have got away had not Fred again fired, and dropped her with a bullet through the neck. Having gralloched the game, we were returning to camp, when we saw a couple of large yellow bears bowling along a piece of rugged ground a couple of hundred yards below us. As they were coming up-hill in our direction, we got behind a clump of rhododendron bushes, which afforded excellent cover, and awaited their approach. They travelled slowly, being engaged in turning over stones as they went along to look for insects, which search could not have proved very satisfactory, for they came up grunting and groaning, as if in very bad humour with each other, offering splendid shots. We let drive

THE GOORAL, OR HIMALAYAN CHAMOIS.

almost simultaneously, and both shots were effective, for the male dropped without a movement, whilst the female, rearing up on her hind legs, with a grunt betokening surprise, fell sprawling on her back in the last agony. We rushed up to give the *coup de grâce,* but it was not required—both were dead. Having reloaded our rifles, we continued our route towards the camp, leaving the operation of skinning until the morrow, as we did not care to lose our dinners and pass the night in the bush—the natural consequence of being overtaken by darkness in these regions.

The next morning, at daybreak, we all started in different directions to look for thaar, taking our breakfasts with us. I was accompanied by Chineah, carrying a spare gun, and a couple of coolies to carry back any game I might kill. After several hours' fag, during which I traversed several likely-looking patches of oak forest without seeing anything but an occasional moonal pheasant, which I would not fire at for fear of disturbing other game, just as I was thinking of making my way back to the tent empty-handed, a herd of five thaar was discovered browsing on the grassy slope of a little ravine some distance below us. With the aid of my glass, I made them out to be all males, with long shaggy hair streaming in the wind. Having carefully marked the spot, which appeared extremely favourable for stalking, I made my people lie down, and slinging my second gun over my shoulder, commenced the descent, taking care to keep well to leeward. Creeping noiselessly down I succeeded in gaining a long, low ridge, which ran parallel to the hollow in which I had marked them, and, looking cautiously over, there they were still, unsuspectingly feeding not more than sixty paces distant. Selecting the one that appeared to have the finest horns, I took a steady aim just behind the shoulder, and he dropped to the shot; my second barrel brought another fine fellow floundering on the ground, with a bullet through his loins, that passed out of the opposite shoulder. The three survivors, startled at the report of my rifle, rushed forward a few paces, and then turned and stood, as if bewildered, giving me another fair double shot with my second gun. I rolled over a third dead with a bullet through the neck, and broke the leg of the fourth, which, however, went off at a good pace. Elated with my success, I reloaded, and, leaving the game to be collected by the coolies, set off in pursuit of the wounded animal. I was soon on the trail, which, being plentifully sprinkled with blood, showed that the quarry was hard hit, and I had no difficulty in following it up. After a quarter of an hour's tracking, I came upon the wounded thaar lying down in some low bush. He was so weak from loss of blood that he could hardly stand, much more get away, for the bullet, besides breaking his hind leg, had entered into his body ; and I despatched him with my hunting-knife.

Leaving one coolie in charge of the game, and despatching the other to the camp for assistance to carry it, I was strolling leisurely along in the direction of our bivouac, when a fine male musk deer started up from almost under our feet. I let drive right and left, but missed with both barrels, when Chineah giving me my second gun, I managed to roll him over with my third shot as he was bounding away through the long grass. Musk deer-hunting is very pretty sport, and the best practice the sportsman can have to test his shooting, as the game offers a very small mark and bounds along with incredible swiftness. After taking out the pod, which must have contained nearly an ounce weight of musk, Chineah slung the deer over his shoulders, and we made the best of our way to the tents, where we found the doctor busily engaged in skinning and preserving a beautiful specimen of the argus, or horned pheasant, which he had killed high up on the mountain. This was the only shot he had fired, for although he had seen a flock of several gooral, they were so wild that he could not get near them. Towards sunset Fred returned, having killed a fine old male thaar, and two musk deer, besides wounding a bear, which escaped by taking refuge in a cave. After dinner we all assembled round the camp-fire to discuss the events of the day and our hopes for the morrow. Since that evening long years have rolled, yet it is not forgotten. Four head of thaar bagged in four consecutive shots made it a red-letter day in my calendar.

The next day we changed our camp, moving about three miles towards the east face, which was said to be the best ground for thaar, and here we remained four days enjoying fair sport, killing between us three snow bears, eight thaar, five gooral, two burrul, seven musk deer, and a surrow. After this, we descended the hill and returned to Bengalee, where we halted a day to rest and prepare some of the specimens, which we sent by a coolie to Fred's quarters at Dehra.

One of the best day's sport we had amongst the burrul, was a few miles below the great glacier in which the Ganges takes its source. Here the Triumvirate greatly distinguished themselves, and made a remarkable bag, so I shall give an account of their doings. Our camp was at Gangoutrie, the holiest shrine of Hindoo worship, and having seen all that the Brahmins had to show, which amounted to very little, we started for the Cow's mouth, the reputed source of the sacred river. An hour before day-break I opened the door of the tent without disturbing my sleeping companions, and looked out into the night. The gorge was still in darkness, for although the moon was shining brightly, the high lateral mountains intercepted her rays, and cast a deep shadow below. The air felt cool and bracing, but not a leaf stirred, which was most favourable for effective stalking, as the taint in the air caused by man's presence is carried on the wind to almost incredible distances, and is immediately detected by the denizens of the mountains, whose organs of scent are most keenly developed. All was still save the rushing of the waters, and not a sound denoted the existence of animal life save that indescribable low hum, or soft murmur of the invisible insect world, which ever greets the hunter's ears in the early morning.

Having satisfied myself that we had every prospect of fine weather for our expedition, I bid the man who was on the look-out to rouse the people, and in a few moments we were all assembled round a blazing fire. Having partaken of a substantial breakfast, and superintended the packing of our baggage, we lighted our cheroots, and waited until there was sufficient light to distinguish our way, when we shouldered our rifles, and set out for the glacier, distant eighteen miles. We kept an extended line whenever the nature of the ground permitted, and beat the most likely-looking patches of forest for musk-deer, of which there were numerous fresh traces. Fred got a couple of shots, and managed to bag a fine old buck with a pod that weighed over an ounce. I might have had a fair shot had I been prepared, for one started up from behind a bush within easy gunshot whilst I was fastening up my gaiter, but before I could raise my rifle it bounded away out of sight.

Notwithstanding the numerous obstacles *en route,* we had excellent sport as we advanced, twice falling in with burrul on the grass-covered slopes of the hill-sides ; and here I was very successful, for I killed two, right and left, and broke the leg of a third, which, however, got away, whilst two others were bagged by my companions. I also succeeded in stalking a snow-leopard, which had evidently been following the burrul, and knocked him over by a lucky shot through the head as he was stealing away over some craggy ground some two hundred yards distant. It proved a beautiful specimen, the fur being very soft and close, having a whitish ground with dark spots. These animals are very cunning, and, notwithstanding their traces are often seen on the snowy ranges, comparatively few are bagged.

Whilst I was performing the operation of skinning the

leopard, and my companions were breaking up the other game, Chineah espied something moving on a grassy patch in a ravine high up among the rocks on the left bank, and with the aid of my glass I made out a large flock of burrul, some of which were lying down, and the others quietly grazing. It was of no use I knew, approaching them from below, as the ground was unfavourable for stalking, and we should have no chance of getting within range without being perceived; so we arranged that Fred should creep along through the birch forest and clamber up the hill on the further side, whilst the doctor and I should try and get above on the near side, so as to take them on both flanks.

After a careful reconnaissance of their position, we crept noise-lessly upwards, keeping our bodies bent as low as possible, so as not to attract their attention; and by dint of hard climbing, often on all-fours, in rather less than two hours we emerged from out of the birch forest, and traversing a belt of stunted juniper bushes half covered with snow, reached the rocky crest of the hill, breathless and faint from continued exertion. Throwing ourselves down on a smooth slab of rock, to rest and regain our steadiness, previous to approaching the burrul, our attention was drawn to the magnificence of the panorama then before us, and for a time we gazed spell-bound. Before us lay the glacier world, with its interminable barriers of eternal snow, peak upon peak, rising one behind another in endless succession. From the valley, on account of the steepness and close proximity of its boundaries, little was to be seen except a narrow strip of sky above; but from the elevation we had now attained, which the doctor made out to be nearly 15,000 feet above the level of the sea, and about 4,000 above the bed of the river, the scene was grand beyond conception. Rising above an unbroken girdle of perpetual snow, seventeen peaks seemed to pierce the heavens, the lowest of which exceeded 20,000 feet in elevation. Most conspicuous, from its colossal proportions, was the mighty Soomeroo Purbut, or Rudru Himaleh, with its five majestic peaks towering high against the deep cerulean firmament. They rise in a semicircle facing the south-west, and from where we stood appeared to form an immense amphitheatre filled with eternal snow, in which the Ganges has its primary source.

Although the distance to some of these peaks from where we stood must have exceeded forty miles as the crow flies, yet the air was so transparent that their outlines were most clearly and sharply defined. From this point we had a very extensive view of the valley of the Ganges, now and then getting a glimpse of the river itself, as, like a silver thread, at a vast depth below us, it wound along from the east, and then took a southerly direction towards the plains. The general character of the valley is that of a grand ravine bounded by two precipices of almost vertical rocks, sometimes with only sufficient space between for the windings of the river, and at others opening out to a mile in breadth.

But it was time to look after the burrul. Having regained our breath, we examined our rifles, and stole quietly forward along the crest of the hill. We had not gone many yards, our footsteps scarcely making any noise over the crisp snow, when Chineah, who was a couple of paces in front, stopped short, and made a sign to attract our attention; a slight rustling was heard, and in an instant there was a rushing sound on the opposite side of a ridge of rocks like that of an animal bounding away at full speed.

"There goes our game. Is it not provoking?—after such a fag, too!" exclaimed the doctor, in a subdued voice: and he was pressing forward, when I thought I heard a second movement, and made a gesture for him to keep still; another moment, and I perceived the horns, head, and black breast of an old ram peering inquisitively over a narrow ridge of rock,

THE HIMALAYAN IBEX.

not fifty yards from where we were standing. To fling up my
rifle and press the trigger was the work of a second, but when
the smoke cleared away nothing was to be seen, but a shrill
snort, followed by a trampling of feet, was distinctly heard on
the other side of the crest, and for a moment I thought I
had made a mess of it. Not so Chineah: he insisted the
animal was hit; and so it proved, for, on running up to the
spot, there was a fine full-grown ram stone dead, the bullet
having entered the skull right between the eyes. The rest of
the herd galloped away in the direction of the ravine where we
had marked burrul in the first instance, and on the other side
of which Fred had gone to take post. As they had not seen us,
I did not think they would go very far, so we pressed on after
them, and at last arrived at the edge of the slope, when by
craning over, we saw a herd of at least forty burrul grazing
undisturbed on the grassy flats below us. Where now was
Fred ? Ensconcing ourselves behind some rocks, which served
as a screen, we waited impatiently his approach. At last I saw
three moving figures in clear relief against the sky on the
opposite hill—it was Fred and his two shekarries. I watched
him with my telescope, cautiously creeping along the broken
ground, rifle in hand, prepared for anything, and halting every
now and then to sweep the ground with his glass. Perceiving
from his movements that he could not see the flock from where
he was, I stepped back a few paces, and fastening a handker-
chief to my ramrod, made a signal that "game was afoot,"
which was instantly understood and answered. Fred, with the
precaution of an old sportsman, now sent one of his people
along the hill at the entrance of the gorge, so as to drive back
the herd in case they should break in that direction, whilst I
did the same on my side, and then leaving the doctor, I posted
myself at the head of the ravine. Hardly had I reached it,
than I heard a couple of shots from Fred, and the reports were

still reverberating among the rocks when the doctor also let drive right and left, and I saw the flock scatter in all directions, as if puzzled to know from what point the danger threatened. Again Fred's rifle cracked, and a magnificent old ram, leading half-a-dozen females, plunged suddenly forward, regained his legs a moment, and then dropped. Again there was a confused hurrying to and fro, a gathering as if for consultation; then the whole herd burst into a gallop, and disappeared over the crest some distance below the spot where the doctor was posted, and in a few moments I saw them dashing across a distant hill miles away with undiminished speed. As matters turned out, I did not get a shot, for I did not care to fire at random among the herd, which was my only chance; but my companions had no reason to complain, for Fred killed one outright, and wounded a second, which was bagged after a long chase, and several more shots; whilst the doctor killed one, and wounded another, which got away. Our game being collected, and gralloched, was much heavier than we could carry, so we had to leave two men in charge whilst we made the best of our way to the rest of the people, whom we left in the valley, and sent coolies to fetch it.

As it was now too late to think of continuing our march, we determined to bivouac under the cover of a patch of pine forest which offered some shelter. Our scouting tents were soon pitched, a shanty constructed, and a huge fire lighted, round which we assembled, for as the sun declined the evening became chilly. We were very well contented with our day's sport, having killed a musk-deer, a snow-leopard, three male burrul and four females—a bag which has rarely been equalled in one day by any three guns.

SPORT IN THIBET.

Gratifying as the magnificent scenery of these regions is to the traveller, any very detailed description of daily marching can scarcely be otherwise than monotonous to the reader. I shall therefore simply confine my relation of this expedition to pointing out that which will be most useful to any brother sportsman taking the same route.

Crossing the Ganges, we made our way along the banks of the Goomtee Gadh, and for three days directed our course up the Neila Valley, a delightful spot called by the Puharrees Pool-ke-daree—the Road of Flowers ; and *en route* we had some very fair burrul shooting. Crossing the Neila Pass, an altitude of 16,000 feet, which somewhat tried our powers as mountaineers, we entered the head of the Buspa Valley, and following the down-stream course of the river of that name, in three days arrived at Chetkoul, the first village on the Koonawaur side, where we halted a day, as our people and the coolies were somewhat knocked up with seven days' continuous marching and the difficulties of the way. Our next stages were to Raugchum, and Sangla, and from thence, over the Barung Pass, an elevation of 16,300 feet above the sea, into the Valley of the Sutlej. Crossing this wide, rapid, and muddy-looking river by a very precarious rope suspension-bridge, at Poaree, a few miles from Chinee, three more marches brought us to the Askrung Valley, where we halted for five days, and had some capital ibex hunting, Fred greatly distinguishing himself by his excellent shooting at long ranges. The ibex, although plentiful, were very wild and difficult to approach, having been recently disturbed ; consequently, all the game killed was by long shots, Twice Fred killed running ibex at distances considerably over four hundred yards, which is the *ne plus ultra* of brilliant marksmanship.

THE NEILGHERRY IBEX.

From Askrung we marched through Libi over the Mannerung Pass (18,600 feet) to Mana, the first village in Spittee, and from thence along the Spittee River and over the Parung Pass (18,800 feet) into Rupsha, halting for three days at Kiang-dam, on the Choomarera lake, a magnificent sheet of fresh water, about twenty miles long by five broad, situated at an elevation of 15,000 feet above the sea. In the country round about the lake we first came across the kiang, or wild horse, of which we shot a few as specimens. The kiang is about fourteen hands at the shoulders, and resembles the ass much more than the nobler quadruped. They are generally of a reddish-grey, with a dark stripe down the back, and almost white under the belly and inside the legs. The head is large and ugly, the mane hogged, and they are usually cat hammed. There is a great similarity between the South African quagga and the kiang in general appearance. We saw great numbers of these animals during our wanderings in this part of the country, but, our curiosity satisfied, we did not care to pull trigger at them.

Leaving the Choomarera lake, we crossed the Nakpokonding Pass to Latok, near the Cheumo salt lake, and here, whilst hunting over a bleak and desolate-looking region, we fell in with a wandering tribe of Tartars who were returning to their summer camp near the Pang-kung lake. Their chief, a very intelligent man in his way, gave us such excellent accounts of the game in that part of the country, more especially as regarded the naheen, or ovis ammon (the largest species known of wild sheep), that we determined to explore it. We sent off the yaks with the heavier portion of the baggage under charge of some of our people to Ladak, by the Tungrung Pass (18,100 feet), whilst we accompanied the Tartars, who carried about a month's supplies for us on their spare yaks. Branching off to the east-ward, we struck and followed up a small stream to its junction with the Indus at Mahe, and continued our way along the banks of the latter river until we came to Nioma, when our route lay in a northerly direction. We now crossed the Sakala Pass (16,000 feet), and halted at Chushul, which we made a temporary head-quarters.

We hunted in this neighbourhood five days, and, under the guidance of the Tartar chief, had excellent sport, falling in with numerous flocks of burrul and ovis ammon. The finest specimen of the latter animal, which was as large as an ordinary bullock of the plains, Fred killed after a three hours' stalk. His horns were sixteen inches in circumference at the base, and forty-six inches round the curve. I killed three fine rams and a female, but none of them equalled in size that killed by my companion. The female is an insignificant looking creature in comparison with the male, and the horns are not more than fourteen inches in length, and but slightly curved. We all contributed clothes, knicknacks, and sundry articles that we could spare, as a present to the chief, and put him in such a good humour that he volunteered to accompany us to a range of mountains to the eastward of the Pang-kung lake (which I believed to be part of the Kailas range), where we should find bunchowr or wild yaks. We closed at once with the desirable offer, and started off to the eastward early the next morning.

After seven days' continuous marching through a most deso-late-looking country, where the only human beings met with were a few wandering Hunnias, we passed round the north end of the lake, and struck a range of lofty mountains, which our Tartar guide informed us was the haunt of bunchowr. Burrul and ovis ammon were frequently seen *en route ;* but we only killed sufficient game to maintain ourselves and our people in food; and now that there was a prospect of nobler game we did not dare to fire a shot, lest the report of our rifles might scare it away. For the first two days we explored these mountains without success; no bunchowr were to be seen, although we found numerous traces of their existence. The third morning, soon after daylight, we saw five dark objects moving slowly over the snow, about a mile distant. Our field-glasses were put in requisition, and to our great delight we made out five gigantic, shaggy bulls, quietly browsing, perfectly unconscious of our presence. The ground was tolerably favourable for stalking, and, as we had taken the precaution of wearing white shirts over our ordinary hunting-gear, with linen cap-covers, we were scarcely distinguishable from the snow. Fortunately a strong breeze was blowing at the time, of which advantage we did not fail to avail ourselves, by keeping well to leeward, and after an exciting quarter of an hour's work, we managed to get within easy range (150 yards) of the herd, who were chewing the cud quite unconscious of their fate. A moment more, and two shaggy monsters were on their backs on the snow, struggling in their last agonies, whilst the other three, more or less wounded, were galloping about in wild but grand confusion. Having hastily reloaded, we gave chase; but this was scarcely required, for no sooner were we perceived, than two of the three wheeled suddenly round, and with heads down, and tails on end, made a most vicious charge towards us, evidently meaning mischief. Again our rifles cracked, and two more huge bodies were floundering in the snow, which was discoloured with their gore. The fifth bull, who was slowly following the other two, being more severely wounded, now came up, and was easily despatched. Thus died five stately bulls of undaunted pluck, and great was the joy of our Tartar followers at the prospect of such an immense supply of food. We carefully skinned the two finest specimens, and preserved the horns and tails of the others as trophies, but the hides were a great deal too heavy for our people to carry, so we were obliged to leave them on the ground and send the yaks for them.

The next morning we saw a solitary bull of immense dimensions, but he proved a very wary beast, and, notwithstanding all our precautions, the taint in the air betrayed our whereabouts, and he took himself off without giving us the chance of a shot. The day following we separated, Fred and the doctor taking one side of a hill, whilst I explored the other. I met with several fresh traces, although I saw no game worth pulling trigger at, but my companions were more fortunate, as they fell in with a herd of seven bulls, and managed to kill three of the number. Two days after this, I again caught sight of the same old solitary bull who had baffled us on a previous occasion, and this time I was more fortunate, although I was fully three hours in circumventing him before I dared venture within range. Even then I was afraid of attempting to get within four hundred yards of him, as he was standing like an outlying sentinel on a small eminence, so I managed to take up a position on an adjacent height, from which I could observe all his movements. I watched him for at least twenty minutes before commencing offensive operations, for the distance was too great for me to make certain of killing, or even mortally wounding him; and there was a deep cud or valley where the drifted snow appeared to lie deep, which I could not hope to cross without being seen. At last I fancied he was about to move away, and as his position seemed to offer a fair shot, I put up the back-sight of my heavy two-ounce rifle at the four hundred yards' range, and deliberately aimed at his brawny shoulder. The grooved bore carried truly; for, when the smoke cleared away, I saw the huge beast was brought to his knees, and in a moment more he careened on his side, and rolled over on his back with his four feet in the air. I gave him the contents of my second barrel, which did not seem to affect him, for his position remained unchanged; so, having carefully reloaded, I approached him, keeping myself in readiness to receive his charge, which would be the more impetuous as it would be made down-hill. As I drew near, I heard him making a peculiar moaning noise, accompanied by a succession of loud grunts, which I knew betokened extreme distress; and when I mounted the crest of the hill, I saw at a glance that the game was nearly over. The poor beast was in his last agony, and too far gone to notice me; so, stepping up, I put him out of pain by shooting him between the eyes, when a convulsive quiver passed over the body, and all was still. I found my first shot had proved fatal, having entered just behind the shoulder and penetrated the lungs; whilst the second had passed through the neck. The dimensions of this bull far exceeded any we had hitherto killed, and his mane, forelock, and the hair on his flanks was much longer. His horns were nearly eighteen inches in circumference at the base, and short in comparison. The bunchowr, although not so high at the shoulder as the bison of the low country, is a larger and more formidable animal than the American species. He is very short in the legs, and massively built, yet very active, and capable of getting over the most difficult ground in a surprisingly short time. Their general colour is black, with dark ash under the belly and inside the legs; but they vary. I have seen some skins that were altogether black. We hunted over this part of the country for ten days, having famous sport; when, finding our supplies getting short, we retraced our steps, and made the best of our way back to our former camp in the Chushul valley.

After hunting for some days in the mountains between the Pang-kung lake and the Indus, we proceeded in a northerly direction up the Chushul valley, and crossed the range by the Changla Pass (16,500 feet), striking the Sakety river, the downward course of which stream we followed until its junction with the Indus, near the village of Marsilla. Two-days' marching along the banks of this river brought us to Leh or Ladak, the capital of Little Thibet, where we found our people rather uneasy at our prolonged absence. Halting here for three days, we visited the Rajah's palace and the Buddhist monastery of Hemes, being shown through the place by the lamas.

Having seen all that was worthy of notice in Ladak, we started for Cashmere, keeping along the banks of the Indus for three marches; and passing through Nurila, Lamieroo, and Drass, halted at Pandrass, where we had three days' hunting amongst the hills adjacent to the glaciers, and killed several shalmar, a species of wild sheep different to any we had hitherto fallen in with. From Pandrass four marches, *viâ* Soonamurg and Kungur, brought us to the celebrated Lake of Cashmere, where, finding boats, we entered the capital on the twentieth day after leaving Ladak.

CHAPTER XIII.

UNLOOKED-FOR RENCONTRES.

WHEN a hunter is in the forest he should always keep on the alert, with his arms ready for service, in case of an unexpected rencontre with some of the feline animals that may be prowling about. The following example will show the necessity of being ever prepared against eventualities. Whilst hunting in the Andior jungle, I was clambering down the dry sandy bed of a nullah, and peering between the trees in the expectation of getting a shot at a brood of pea-fowl that I could hear chirping and scratching up the ground in the underwood close at hand, when, turning stealthily round a large jummon bush, (a kind of willow,) I suddenly came face to face upon an immense tiger, who had evidently been taking his "*siesta*" under the cool shade of the shelving bank, for when I first caught sight of him he was stretching himself and yawning as if only just awake. Doubtless it was a mutual surprise, but I was the first to recover self-possession, for without a moment's hesitation I swung round, and notwithstanding we were barely six feet apart, and my gun (a double eight-guage by Westley Richards) was only loaded with No. 4 shot, I let drive right and left full into his face. Before the smoke cleared away, the tiger, uttering an appalling shriek of rage, sprang clear over my head, and fell with a crash against the opposite bank; whilst I, without waiting to watch his further movements, gave "leg bail," and ran in a contrary direction down the nullah. Finding that I was not pursued, I reloaded with ball, when "Richard was himself again," for I must

AN UNLOOKED-FOR RENCONTRE.

own my serenity of mind was somewhat disturbed at such an
unlooked-for rencontre. Chineah, attracted by the double
report, now came up, and, having taken my pet rifle from him,
I slung the smooth bore over my shoulder, directed him to
remain quiet in a tree, and again made my way to the scene of
action. I soon came across the tiger's pugs, and followed them
up to a pool of water where there were marks of his having
quenched his thirst a few moments before.

The double charge of shot I administered at such close
quarters had evidently taken effect, for the trail was marked
with large crimson drops, and I knew that his sight was partially if not entirely destroyed, as from time to time he had
struck his head against the steep banks on each side of the
nullah, leaving large gouts of blood behind him. In a few
minutes I heard sundry strange noises in a patch of reeds and
corinda-bushes by the side of the nullah, and from the "swear-
ing" of a troop of monkeys in the trees overhead on each bank, I
knew what to expect. I clambered up a boulder of rock, from
whence I could see the tiger going round and round evidently
quite blind, for every now and then he knocked his head against
stones and bushes, when he would give a short angry roar, tear
up the ground, and bite at everything within his reach. I saw
at a glance how matters were, so stealing gently up I aimed
just behind the shoulder, and the ball passing through the
heart, immediately put him out of his misery, for he sprang
high into the air and dropped stone dead. On examination I
found the whole of the upper part of the face was blown to
pieces, and both eyes destroyed with the effect of my first shots;
indeed, the head was a mass of congealed blood, none of the
features being distinguishable; however, such is the tenacity of
life in the feline race, that he managed even in this condition
to make his way for upwards of half a mile, although totally
blind. . ...

This is only one case out of some scores, in which I have met with a startling surprise whilst wandering through the forest, and it shows the absolute necessity of always being on the alert, prepared for any danger that may present itself.

A VOYAGE IN A CORACLE DOWN THE BHOWANI AND CAUVERY RIVERS.

I HAD been shooting for some months in the Coimbatore jungle, when I was compelled to return to Madras, and there being no railways in those days, instead of marching the three hundred miles by tedious daily stages, I determined to embark with my servants, two favourite horses, my dogs, and all my gear at Metrapolliam, on the Bhowani River, close to the Neilgherry Hills, and make my way down stream to the east coast. For this purpose I had three famously strong bamboo saucer-shaped basket-boats constructed, each about sixteen feet in diameter and thirty inches in depth. These were strongly covered with bison and raw bullock hides sewn together, and one of them was carefully fitted with a plank flooring to prevent the horses' hoofs from breaking through. All being prepared, a fair stock of provisions and liquor was stowed away, our baggage, horses, dogs, and people, embarked in two of the boats, whilst Kenny, of H.M. 84th, Chineab, my head boy, a boatman, and myself occupied the third. Bidding good-bye to several friends from Ootacamund, who had come to see us off in our primitive craft, the boatmen pushed off and our voyage began. No rowing was required, as we were carried down the stream by the force of the current at the rate of nearly five miles an hour, the boatmen keeping our craft in deep water by means of a broad paddle, which not only acted as a rudder, but also prevented the boat from turning round and

round, as it would have done if left to itself. There is no possibility of capsizing these strange-looking craft, and the only
accident that can happen is, that the leather covering may be
torn by sharp ledges of rock or trees half buried in the
bed of the river, a mishap of rare occurrence, as, although the
coracles can carry an immense weight (two or three tons),
they rarely draw more than from four to six inches of water.
Besides, this accident is easily remedied, as the boatmen
always carry the necessary materials for repairing damages;
the boat is drawn ashore, and a leather patch makes it as
water-tight as ever. As we glided down the stream, which in
many parts was fringed with dense forest jungle, the howling
of my dogs repeatedly attracted my attention to the numerous
alligators that were swimming with only just their noses
above water, and Kenny and I had some very pretty rifle
practice, turning several of them over with a conical ball
between the eyes, when they would show their dark yellow
throats, lash the water with their tails for a moment, and sink
to the bottom.

The river was very full, and rapidly and smoothly we glided
over its dark surface, now and then startling from the overhanging trees swarms of pelican, blue and white herons, ibis,
and kingfishers of various kinds; whilst at times we would
drive out from their places of concealment in the reed, gigantic
cranes of the adjutant species, or troops of scarlet winged
flamingoes. As the moon was nearly at the full, the nights
were as light as day; so we continued our voyage throughout
the night, and rested for six or seven hours in some shady place
during the intense heat of the day. Sometimes, in the evening
or the early morning, we got shots at deer or other forest
animals, as the stream carried us noiselessly past the place
where they were drinking; and on one occasion we surprised
a tiger, and hit him hard just as he had struck down a fine

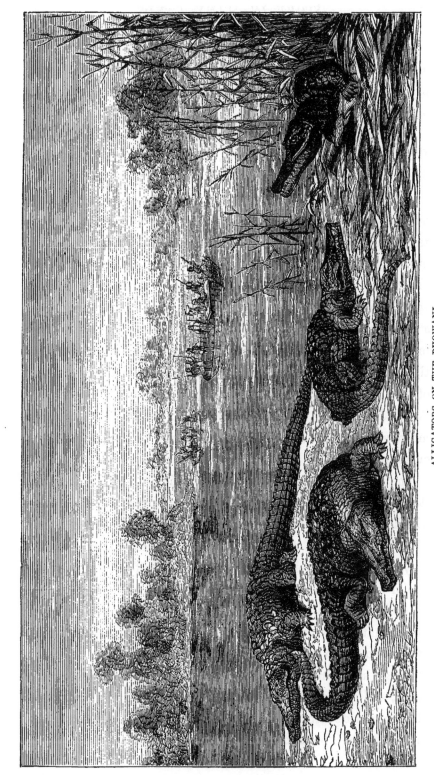

ALLIGATORS ON THE BHOWANI.

fat doe chitel; but he managed to escape into the thick bush, leaving a bloody trail; so we contented ourselves with appropriating the venison, which was still warm when we put it in our boat.

On the third morning we arrived at the confluence of the Bhowani and the Cauvery rivers, and here we made a couple of days' halt, so as to stretch our horses' legs with a gallop after nilghau, which are plentiful in the neighbourhood, and to give our boatmen a good rest. As soon as our arrival at the traveller's bungalow was made known in the village, several of our old acquaintance came to see us, for on several occasions I had made Bhowani my head-quarters, as supplies of all kinds were plentiful, and in those days the surrounding jungle was a sure find for large game. The village shekarries wanted me to halt for a week, as they said they could show me several tigers at no great distance, but I told them that I was afraid of the river falling shallow, and could not spare the time, so it was determined to have a grand hunt after nilghau on the morrow, and renew our voyage towards Trichinopoly in the evening.

The nilghau is the largest of our Indian antelope, the bull standing nearly fourteen hands at the shoulder. The male, which is often called "the blue bull," is of a slatish-grey colour, whilst the female, which is a much smaller animal, is of a greyish fawn. These animals are generally found in herds of five or six together, in the neighbourhood of low jungle-covered hills adjoining cultivation, or on the sites of deserted villages, unfortunately too common all over India, which are usually overgrown with long rank grass and low bush. Nilghau, although awkward animals to look at, have a very fair turn of speed, and it is capital sport to drive a good bull out into the plain and ride him down with the spear. In districts where they have not been much harrassed they are not difficult to approach, and they are easily stalked. Their flesh is coarse and poor eating, but the marrow-bones are considered a *bonne bouche*.

As evening drew on, after we had dined, Mother Garrow and her train of dusky nymphs from the pagoda of the dread goddess Kali, "the destroyer," made their appearance, and we were entertained with an admirable nautch. Several of the younger dancing-girls were very fair, and had soft, oval faces; large brilliant, almond-shaped eyes, fringed with long lashes, and set off with beautifully arched, black eyebrows; noses finely cut; tempting-looking lips, which disclosed pearl-like teeth; rounded arms and well-proportioned figures, which were admirably set off but not concealed by richly coloured silks and flowing drapery. Singing and dancing continued to a late hour, when, having distributed our largess to the fair votaries of Bhowani, we turned in. Early the next morning we started under the guidance of a couple of village shekarries, who posted us in the dry bed of a dry watercourse, and as soon as we had taken up our position the beat began. Although we had ridden all the way to the spot where we were placed in ambuscade, the jungle was too dense for us to attempt to ride down our game, so we gave up all thoughts of doing so, and waited patiently to see what might turn up. At last an old female bear and her cub emerged from the cover and made their way into the open, when Kenny (who had won the toss) fired first, hitting the old one hard with one barrel, and finishing her with the second. The young one, frightened by the reports of the gun, ran to the dead mother for protection, and was easily secured by Chineah in his turban-cloth. Shortly afterwards a herd of spotted deer, followed by a troop of seven nilghau, broke out, and we discharged all our guns into the brown of them as they crossed the open ground. One spotted deer and two nilghau dropped in their tracks; and two other spotted deer that were hard hit, were followed up by our people and the dogs, and brought to bay. In a second beat we killed another spotted deer, with fine branching antlers, and two jungle sheep, and then returned to the bungalow to dinner.

About an hour before sunset we re-embarked, and early in the morning of the next day but one, we landed at the ghaut of the sacred island of Siringam, on which stands the famous temple of the god Vishnu. The temple of the god, where Vishnu is said to repose in eternal sleep, is surrounded by seven concentric enclosures, 25 feet high and 4 feet thick. In the first, Hindoos of all castes reside ; in the second, Brahmins only may dwell ; in the third, the families of the priests of the temple and the dancing-girls reside ; the fourth contains several temples, or *mandapams*, one of which contains a thousand columns, in sixteen rows of sixty-five columns in a row ; and in others may be seen colossal monsters and mounted figures carved out of the solid stone, and columns ornamented with gigantic sculptures in relief. The central enclosure, or "the holy of holies," is not shown to ordinary visitors, but some officers of the Civil Service, who insisted upon seeing all over the place when there was reason to suppose that arms were secreted there, said there was nothing remarkable in the place except a black granite throne, on which stood several rudely carved gods and goddesses, and some stone lingums and bulls. In Trichinopoly several hundred dancing girls are attached to the pagodas, whose services are hired for weddings and gala days, by wealthy natives fond of display. Six miles south-west of Trichinopoly, in the middle of the jungle, is a large deserted pagoda, full of beautiful carvings, which bears the name of " Shitan Rowil," or the " Palace of the Devil," and all round about the district are similar stupendous Hindoo monuments, none of which, however, are believed to be of any great antiquity.

SNIPE.

The district round about Trichinopoly is famous for small
game-shooting, more especially snipe and wild-fowl.   Perhaps
there is no part of the world where snipe abound as they do in
this part of India.   The alluvial soil, which at certain seasons of
the year is covered with water, operated upon at the same time
by the influence of a fierce sun, generates and swarms with
vermicular and insect life, which constitutes the chief food of
the grallæ tribe.

Sportsmen who are fond of snipe-shooting may satisfy themselves to their hearts' content, should they ever wade through
the rice-fields of Trichinopoly during the months of October,
November, and December.   At this season the rains have
ceased, and the stagnant waters left behind, covering a vast extent
of country, filling all the tanks and inundating the low lands,
having to a great extent evaporated, thousands upon thousands
of grallæ swarm over the land.   At this time snipe rise by the
score, from almost under the sportsman's feet, and often, when
literally gorged to repletion, alight again a few paces distant.
The birds at this season are in famous condition, and would
weigh down the generality of our English birds.

Snipe and different varieties of water-fowl begin to arrive in
India from the steppes of Central Asia in October; and before
the end of November every lake, tank, and swamp, swarm with
wild-fowl.   The common grey teal, the whistling teal, and the
blue winged teal, are the first to make their appearance; then
come flights of widgeon, the red-headed pochard, the pintail,
the gadwall, the mallard, the Brahminee duck, the shovel-
billed duck, the grey goose, the black-backed goose, and a host
of different kinds of herons, cranes, storks, ibis, and wading
birds, which are found in clouds in the pools and marshes not
much frequented by man.

Partridges and quail of one kind or another are extremely
plentiful all over this district.   The common grey partridge,

COMMON OR GREY PARTRIDGE.

which in appearance closely resembles the English bird, feeds foully, and is found on the outskirts of every village surrounded by cultivation. In some parts of the country red-legged partridges are very numerous; in Upper India is found

THE PAINTED PARTRIDGE.

the black partridge; and in various other parts the painted partridge, a game-looking bird, excellent for the table and affording admirable sport, is found round the outskirts of the jungle.

Besides these, there are several other varieties peculiar to different districts, the appearance and habits of no two being exactly alike. Of the other winged game, the grey quail—one of the best of Indian game birds both for sport and the table—is found at certain seasons in great numbers in most grain districts, and in some places a hundred brace have been killed by a single gun in a day. There are besides, the three-toed or florakin quail, the rain-quail, the button-quail, and the brown quail, which are more or less common all over the country.

The ordinary way of shooting all kinds of small game in India, is by beating it out with a line of men; but for sport I much prefer shooting in the early morning, when the scent is good, with a team of well-broken Sussex spaniels. The grey quail (*Tetrao coturnix*) is a pretty, bright-eyed little bird, not much larger than a lark, but resembling a partridge both in shape, plumage, and in the build of the legs. A "bevy" of quail generally consists of about a dozen birds, and, as a rule, they lie very close, and may easily be passed over if the sportsman has no dog with him. When they rise, they do so with a whir, and, instead of soaring, sweep along in a straight line with great velocity.

The shrill whistling of a quail, which is generally repeated three times in rapid succession, is so seldom heard when the breeding season is over, that the males are then said to have lost their voice. The nest is generally found among clover or long grass, and consists of a mere hollow in the ground lined with dry grass and moss. The eggs, from seven to twelve in number, are white, tinged with yellowish red, speckled with brown. The female sits upon them three weeks, and the young follow her as soon as they leave the shell, commencing at once to feed upon seeds, grain, insects, and green leaves.

I halted a couple of days at Trichinopoly to beat up some old friends, and here I parted with my friend Kenny, who had to rejoin his regiment, the 84th Foot, then forming part of the

QUAILS AND YOUNG.

garrison of that station, and then continued my voyage. From Trichinopoly the Cauvery river takes the name of the Coleroon, after one of its principal tributaries, which it retains until it reaches the sea. Leaving Trichinopoly, in the evening of the third day afterwards we arrived at the *embouchure*, a few miles from Tranquebar, where I put up with my old friend Campbell, then in command of the military detachment stationed in the fort. Here I heard that a steamer was expected in a few days at Karical, a French settlement a few miles distant, on its way to Pondicherry and Madras; so, sending on my horses and servants by road, I proceeded to that place, and put up at the Hôtel de l'Orient, a very comfortable establishment, until its arrival, when I took my passage and embarked for the Presidency. My voyage of over three hundred miles down the river was a very agreeable one ; and, considering that it was accomplished under a fortnight, including halts and stoppages, it certainly was an expeditious mode of travelling in those days, although at the present time the journey can be made by rail in about twenty-four hours.

THE SAMBUR.

THE Sambur or Rusa deer (*Rusa Aristotelis*) which is found in most of the large jungles surrounding the hill ranges throughout India, is considerably larger than the Scotch red deer, and more powerfully built. A full-grown stag averages from 14 to 15 hands at the shoulder, and his hind-quarters are as well shaped as those of a high-caste Arab, whereas the Scotch red deer generally falls off low behind, and is more or less cat-hammed. The head is beautifully formed, the forehead being broad and massive, whilst the line of the face is straight, and the muzzle very fine. The eyes are very large and beautiful, being fringed with long, black eyelashes, and the suborbital sinus—which is very conspicuous—expands greatly when the animal is excited. The horns of the sambur vary very much in their development, according to the district in which they are found, some being long and slender, whilst others are massive and short. The horns are rather upright, having two short *brow* antlers only, and at three years old two points at the extremities of each beam, as shown in the engravings. Sometimes the inner and sometimes the outer tine of the terminal fork will be found the longer ; and occasionally, but rarely, three tines are seen at the summit of the beam. The horns of a mature stag average 35 inches in length from base to tip, having a circumference of 11 inches round the burr at the base, and 8 inches at the thinnest part of the beam ; but I have seen antlers which greatly exceeded these dimensions. The colour varies slightly, but is usually a very dark slate mingled with grey, nearly black about the face and points, and a light buff between the haunches and underneath. The hair immediately next to the jaw is longer than on any other part of the neck, and when the animal is alarmed or excited, it stands on end and forms a kind of ruff, sometimes called the mane. The hinds are smaller than the stags and of a lighter colour ; and both sexes have canine teeth in the upper jaw.

The horns vary in size, according to the age of the animal, and, until the stag gets in the " sere and yellow leaf," are cast annually ; not, however, always at the same time, for one generally drops a day or two after the other. The new horns attain their full growth in about three months, appearing about a week after the old ones are shed, and are covered with a thick leaden-coloured skin or velvet, which after a time peels off. At this period the horns are very sensitive, and the stags avoid bringing them into collision with any substance. Old stags shed their horns very irregularly. Captain Forsyth says :—" I have taken much pains to assure myself of a fact of

SAMBUR HUNTING.

which I am now perfectly convinced—namely, that neither in the case of the sambur nor the spotted deer (both belonging to the Asiatic group of Rusinæ, as distinguished from the Cervidæ, or true stags) are the antlers regularly shed every year in these Central Indian forests, as is the case with the cervidæ in cold climates. No native shekarry who is engaged all his life in the pursuit of these animals will allow such to be the case, and all sportsmen out at that season must have seen stags with full-grown horns during the hot weather and rains, when they are supposed to have shed them. Hornless-headed stags are seen at that season ; but the great majority have perfect heads. I have also known certain stags for successive years always about the same locality, which I have repeatedly stalked at intervals during this time along with natives who constantly saw them, so that I could not be mistaken as to the individual, and all the time they never once dropped their horns."

Old stags remain solitary, except during the rutting season, in October and November, the younger harts only remaining with the herd. During this period they are extremely vicious, and may be heard roaring all over the forest, calling and answering each other. When they meet they engage in savage conflicts, rearing themselves on their hind legs, sparring with their fore-feet, and butting each other with their antlers, until one feels himself worsted and leaves the herd, the hinds, who generally watch the engagement with the utmost nonchalance, bestowing their favours on the conqueror.

Sambur move from place to place according as food becomes scarce. They feed on a variety of jungle products, more especially the flower of the mohra, wild figs, the fruits of the chironji, the bher, and many other trees, the roots of young trees, and herbage of different kinds. When the villagers' crops are green, they issue forth at night and commit great devastation, nibbling close off all the tender young shoots ; but at break of day they retire into the forest, or high up the hills where they make forms in the long grass, and lay down for the day. Each animal makes its form under the shade of a tree, and they have the discrimination to select a spot where the deepest shade falls during the hottest hours of the day. In some secluded places hundreds of forms may be found on a hill-side, each of which will be shaded during the intense heat of the day by the foliage of a sheltering tree. The form of an old stag is generally apart from those of the hinds, from which it may be readily distinguished by its superior size. When lying down for the day in their forms, sambur will frequently allow the sportsman to approach quite close without getting up, trusting to the high grass concealing their presence. A some-what curious incident, exemplifying this occurred on the Anna-mullai Hills, where Burton and I had three months' glorious sport. We were crossing a grassy plateau, some five or six thousand feet above the plains, when we came to the crest of the hill, and a fine old stag suddenly appeared to rise from the ground right in front of me. He had evidently only just awoke from deep slumber, and was unsuspicious of danger in his mountain fastness ; for instead of bounding away in an instant, as he would have done if alarmed, he began to stretch himself, and I rolled him over with a bullet in the back of the head. Hardly had I fired than the clattering of hoofs was heard all along the hill-side, and I think quite a hundred sambur started from their forms in the high grass. Burton killed a fine hart, as well as a young hind, as they tore over the crest of the hill past him, but I refrained from firing, as I saw no other good heads pass within shot. I never, either before or since, saw so large a herd together.

Sambur, like every other kind of deer, are exceedingly fond of salt, and a herd will frequently travel a score of miles during the night to get to a salt-lick, as a jheel in which saline in-

A SAMBUR AT BAY.

crustations are found is called in India. The native shekarries, who are aware of this fact, secrete themselves near such places, and often kill bison and various kinds of deer during the night with their matchlocks. This, however, is rank poaching, and should be discouraged as much as possible, as for one animal that is killed and bagged, half a dozen go away wounded and die a lingering death. There is scarcely a sport I know of that affords a true sportsman more pleasure than sambur-stalking, when the hunter, accompanied by a couple of native scouts who know their haunts, and his dog, gets on trail soon after daybreak, whilst the herbage still glistens with dewdrops, and when every footprint made the previous night is clear and sharp, and follows up his game by the slots until he steals upon his quarry in his day retreat, and kills him fairly in his own domain. This is real sport; and a stag killed in this manner gives infinitely more satisfaction than half a score slaughtered in a drive or from an ambuscade.

A thoroughly-broken dog is extremely useful in tracking up and bringing to bay a wounded deer; but, unless they are perfectly well trained and know their business, the hunter had better leave them at home. Whilst in Southern India I had a large nondescript kind of dog—a cross between an English fox hound and a Bhinjarry greyhound—that was perfectly *au fait* at every kind of sport, and in the jungle he rarely left my heel, except when trailing up a wounded animal. When he was with me I rarely lost a wounded deer, as he generally managed to keep them at bay until I came up and dispatched them. His instinct was perfectly wonderful; for whilst on trail he would remain as silent as the grave, but when the stag was at bay his deep, hoarse bark resounded through the forest, and guided me to the quarry. In some districts sambur are driven by a long line of beaters past the sportsman posted in ambuscade; but, although by this arrangement a good bag is often

THE GREAT BUSTARD (*Otis tarda*).

made, if it is often repeated the country becomes disturbed and
the game gets very wild.

THE GREAT BUSTARD (*Otis tarda*), although, unhappily, extinct in England, is at certain seasons common enough on
the plains of Asia Minor.

Unquestionably, the great bustard is the finest game bird
we have for the table, as the flesh is more tender and delicate
in flavour than either the pheasant or the turkey, consequently
it is much sought after by pot-hunters. The bustard is essentially a bird of the plains, as it is never found in densely
wooded country, and it makes its nest amongst high rank grass,
where the hen lays three or four olive-coloured eggs, splashed
with brown. Bustards are very slow and heavy in their flight,
but they can run very fast, and when alarmed they generally
run for some distance before they take wing. The best way
of killing bustard is with a stalking-horse, and circling quietly
round them until within shot. Another mode is to load a
big-bore gun with Eley's green cartridge, containing No. 1
shot, and to ride carelessly to leeward of them until they show
signs of alarm, and then to make a sudden rush upon them
at full speed, and pull up and fire as they take wing. In some
districts, where the birds were wild, I tried a native dodge,
and found it answer exceedingly well. This was to construct
a kind of screen with green branches of trees, which a man
carried in front of me until I got well within range, and quietly
picked them off with a small-bore rifle. Without some such
arrangement it was quite impossible to get within a couple of
hundred yards of them.

THE FLORAKIN, or lesser bustard (*Otis tetrax*), is found on
the plains, and it is also esteemed a most delicious bird for the
table. The male bird when in full plumage is a very hand-

some bird, being most beautifully marked ; but the hen . is much plainer looking. They are usually found in pairs, and are very shy and wary, hardly ever taking to the wing if they can avoid doing so.

THE FLORAKIN.

Wherever florakin are found, sand-grouse (*pterocles bicinctus*) may be seen. These birds, although always associating in pairs, are often to be met with in large flocks. They are very beautifully marked, but their flesh is coarse and tasteless. The hen makes no nest, but merely scratches a small hole in the sand, in which she lays three or four eggs. Soon after the young birds leave the shell they become strong enough to run about and hide if alarmed.

SAND GROUSE.

END OF VOL. I.

LONDON: BRADBURY, AGNEW, & CO., PRINTERS, WHITEFRIARS.

Lightning Source UK Ltd.
Milton Keynes UK
UKHW022210280119
336364UK00008B/1282/P